SIMON & SCHUSTER

NEW YORK   LONDON   TORONTO   SYDNEY   TOKYO   SINGAPORE

A

WILLIAM J. BRENNAN, JR.,

JUSTICE

AND THE DECISIONS

FOR ALL

THAT TRANSFORMED AMERICA

KIM ISAAC
EISLER

SIMON & SCHUSTER
Rockefeller Center
1230 Avenue of the Americas
New York, New York 10020

SIMON & SCHUSTER and colophon are registered trademarks
of Simon & Schuster Inc.

Designed by Nina D'Amario/Levavi & Levavi
Manufactured in the United States of America

1 3 5 7 9 10 8 6 4 2

Library of Congress Cataloging-in-Publication Data
Eisler, Kim Isaac.
A justice for all : William J. Brennan, Jr., and the decisions that transformed
America / Kim Isaac Eisler
p.   cm.
Includes bibliographical references and index.
1. Brennan, William J. (William Joseph), 1906–   . 2. Judges—United States—
Biography. 3. United States. Supreme Court—Biography. I. Title
KF8745.B68E37   1993
347.73'2634—dc20
[B]
[347.3073534]
[B]   93-5610
CIP

ISBN 0-671-76787-9

Photo credits:
Collection of the Supreme Court of the United States: 1, 3, 4, 5, 6, 7, 8, 9, 10, 12,
13; University of Pennsylvania: 2; Ray Lustig,
The Washington Post: 11

For Judy

CONTENTS

INTRODUCTION

THE JUSTICE AT THE
END OF THE BENCH

IT WAS JUST AFTER 10 A.M. ON AN unseasonably chilly Monday in March when the velvet red curtain parted and one of the most remarkable assemblages of jurists in history took their seats on the bench of the United States Supreme Court.

For two centuries the Marble Palace and its predecessor buildings had been anything but a haven for excellence. With the exception of a few spirited, great justices like Marshall, Holmes, and Brandeis, its bench had just as often been filled with political hacks, cronies, and even bigots. Although Justice John Marshall had given the court the power of judicial review, the ability to assess the constitutionality of legislative action, the Court had mostly remained a stubborn bastion of the status quo.

But on March 26, 1962, history had conspired against mediocrity. The eight men were led by Chief Justice Earl Warren, a man of moral rectitude and fairness, who, denied the presidency, would become more influential than any chief executive of his time. Seating himself next to Warren was the Court's next most senior member, Justice Hugo Black. A resolute Alabamian, Hugo Black had grown to embody the belief that the Bill of Rights should apply to every American regardless of color or position. His unflinching, absolutist faith in the Constitution had made him a hero to liberal America and ensured him a position as one of nation's most heroic judges.

Flanking Warren on the other side was Justice Felix Frankfurter. A diminutive man of not more than five feet, three inches tall, Frankfurter was the intellectual giant of his age. Arrogant and contemptuous of those less gifted, Frankfurter had thrown himself into the life of his times as perhaps no other American. From his seat on the Court, he advised presidents and affected politics. If nothing else, his feelings of superiority were totally sincere. In his tiny scrawl this Austrian-born Jew maintained legendary correspondences with hundreds of individuals from kings and princes and presidents to average citizens who frequently wrote him commenting on his opinions.

The perfect counterpoint to Frankfurter was William O. Douglas. Equally enmeshed in the political and social movements of the age, the Supreme Court was as little an isolated "temple" for Douglas as it was for Frankfurter. A rude, blunt man of impetuous brilliance, but hardly as cunning or calculating as Frankfurter, Douglas was the leading force behind a movement for a more activist Court. Like Warren he had desired the presidency and saw his life on the Court as his opportunity to change society. Justice Black, no small intellect himself, believed Douglas to be the most brilliant man he had ever met.

To Frankfurter's right sat John Marshall Harlan. The name alone spoke volumes. He was the grandson of one of the country's most illustrious justices, John Marshall Harlan of Kentucky. The second John Marshall Harlan had been a distinguished and highly honorable Wall Street lawyer, then a federal judge. He had, it could be said, been bred to the high position he now held.

Three of the remaining four justices would be treated more quietly by history. Justice Tom Clark would generally be considered one of the least capable ever to serve on the Court. The same could be said for Justice Charles Whittaker, who was not at the Court this day but in the hospital. The junior justice on the Court in 1962, Potter Stewart, would have a solid but unspectacular career.

But on this busy twenty-sixth of March in Washington, the eighty-eighth birthday of Robert Frost, who at that exact moment was at the White House presenting a book of poems to President Kennedy, it was none of the above who shuffled his papers, cleared his throat, and prepared to announce one of the most revolutionary decisions in the history of the Court.

The name of the case was *Baker* v. *Carr* and for sixteen years, Black and Frankfurter had been feuding over the issue it raised. Did the federal courts have the right to tell sovereign state governments how to apportion their legislatures? Frankfurter, the model of judicial restraint, had long said no. It was not for the Supreme Court of the United States to get involved in political questions and certainly not in the politics of Nashville, Tennessee, or Springfield, Illinois. Black had held the opposite view.

In a 1946 case involving the state legislature of Illinois, called *Colegrove* v. *Green*, Frankfurter had won the day. The federal courts, he had declared in a 4 to 3 decision, with two justices abstaining, had no right to become involved in state politics. It didn't matter that in Illinois, a county of 1,000 could have as much representation as a city of 100,000. It simply wasn't the Court's business to correct that situation. It had to be done by the people of the state through constitutional revision or through the election process. It was that limiting view of the Court's role that had been the vehicle by which rural, conservative interests continued to control the country's politics.

But a series of events beginning in 1959 had led the Court to a reconsideration of its decision in *Colegrove* v. *Green*. That was when a group of Tennessee residents from Knoxville, Nashville, and Memphis had filed a class-action lawsuit against Tennessee's secretary of state, Joseph Cordell Carr, alleging that city voters in their state were underrepresented in the state legislature. Following the lead of *Colegrove* v. *Green*, the federal courts dismissed their claims at every turn. But in an appeal to the Supreme Court, where it took the vote of only four members to hear a case, Black was successful in having the Tennessee case reargued.

On April 19 and 20, 1961, the Supreme Court had heard three hours of arguments on the case, even though important cases ordinarily only got an hour.

For more than a year the justices of the Supreme Court had discussed the case over and over again. Unknown to the general public, because their deliberations were totally secret, the justices had continually rehashed the case. In a desperate effort to save his decision in *Colegrove*, Frankfurter had repeatedly lectured his colleagues about the prerogatives of the Court, the pitfalls of becoming involved in politics, and the dangers of overruling precedents. Douglas was equally adamant, but on the other side. The right to vote was as basic as it gets; it could not be abridged by any state. The lobbying between the two sides on the Court took place at lunches, dinners, and in the conference room itself.

Now, on March 26, the Court was ready to announce its decision publicly. Inside the Court's ivory-veined Italian marble walls, the chamber filled with expectation, then surprise, as Chief Justice Warren looked past Frankfurter, then looked past Black to recognize a gravelly voiced New Jerseyite, Justice William Joseph Brennan, Jr., seated next to Potter Stewart at Warren's right. Rarely did such landmark rulings come from the end benches where the junior justices resided.

Brennan nodded to the chief justice and slipped on his reading glasses. As was the custom, Brennan began to read and summarize the lengthy ruling. The voice was deep, workmanlike, betraying with each heavy syllable its Newark origins. With Black, Warren, and Douglas looking on approvingly, Brennan declared that the drawing of state legislative districts was within the purview of federal judges and that the Court should show no reluctance to enter what Frankfurter derisively referred to in 1946 as "the political thicket."

In the gallery there was the silence that accompanies a truly momentous event. A few were confused as to which justice was speaking. How could it be Brennan? wondered one spectator. Hadn't he been a student of Frankfurter's at Harvard? For most of the visitors the three newest justices—Brennan, Stewart, and Whittaker—were faceless, seeming to blend into one another.

But with each word, Brennan changed the very essence of American politics. He repeated that courts did indeed have the power, even the duty, to become involved in politics. Coming just three years before the passage of the Voting Rights Act, Brennan set the stage for a peaceful transition of power from rural to urban America. What would the vote have meant to black America if legislatures could ignore their population in drawing legislative districts?

For Court watchers, the ruling was momentous. Who was this Brennan, who had managed to attract five other justices to his opinion and accomplish in an easy 6 to 2 majority, something Black had failed to do in sixteen years? Who was this man, this virtual unknown, appointed by the conservative President Eisenhower, who seemed to be stepping past even the most tepid predictions of his influence? And how could he issue such an opinion having studied at Harvard Law School under the tutelage of Frankfurter himself?

Even on that early spring day in 1962, no one could have predicted that fifty-six-year-old Bill Brennan—not Frankfurter, not Black, not Douglas—would become the most influential justice of the twentieth century. He would never be the most brilliant, the most committed, nor the most absolute. But more than any justice in United States history, Brennan would change the way Americans live: writing laws on obscenity and pornography; defining free speech by his landmark rulings in libel cases; making many of the important rulings in criminal cases; working behind the scenes as the shadow author of the 1971 abortion ruling; and finally moving the country forward by aggressively promoting affirmative action and equal rights for women.

The secret of his success on the Court, however, is not a profile in courage. That's not William Brennan. Nor was he a Great Dissenter. Quite the contrary.

His accommodationist, political attitude to Court rulings was in sharp contrast to the methods of Douglas and Black, who had little interest in voting against their deeply held principles merely to end up on the winning side. They were resolute, stubborn men who would rather lose than compromise. On the issue of reapportionment of state legislatures, decided in *Colegrove v. Green*, Black went down in flames in 1946. Douglas was a loner rarely able or interested in attempting to influence his Court colleagues. *Independent Journey* is the apt name of a Douglas biography written by James Simon.

But Brennan had figured out a strategy to bring about landmark change in the nature of American government. He was able to fashion an opinion that affirmed the principle of one man, one vote, and thus changed the entire structure of political power in America. In doing so, he persuaded the more conservative Justice Potter Stewart that his was a narrow ruling that dealt only with the power of the plaintiffs to challenge the statute. He convinced Black and Douglas, the liberals, that change could come slowly, that building law was a little like building a house—one had to lay the foundation first. Sure enough, *Baker*

v. *Carr* would give way to more radical rulings in future years, decisions that would even more forcefully compel once mighty counties to
give up power to city folk.

This refinement of democracy was Brennan's greatest accomplish-
ment. He realized, largely through the philosophical influence of
Black, that a democracy without the guarantees of the Bill of Rights
could be as tyrannical as any other form of government.

Those who wish to diminish his achievements might say that the
liberal Court of the mid-1960s was simply ripe for the string of rulings
that brought the Bill of Rights to all Americans. But this was not so.
To create precedents it was necessary to fuse the opinions of a Douglas
on one side with a more conservative Stewart or Harlan on the right.
Convincing the liberal Douglas to relent on an opinion, as Brennan
did in the landmark privacy case of *Griswold* v. *Connecticut*, would ultimately be just as important as convincing the then-conservative Justice Blackmun about the validity of a right to privacy, as Brennan did
in the abortion case *Roe* v. *Wade*.

With the departure of Chief Justice Earl Warren in 1969, it seemed
the Supreme Court would follow a conservative path under his successor, Warren E. Burger. But it did not. Egged on by Brennan, the Court
tackled social issues such as abortion, job discrimination, and capital
punishment. Ultimately it came to respond to equal employment and
affirmative action. On virtually every issue, well into the 1980s, Brennan, and not the chief justice, whether it be Burger or later Rehnquist,
defined the direction and ideology of the Court.

Many observers argue that Brennan "changed" while on the court.
President Eisenhower, who appointed Brennan while wrongly believing
that he was the protégé of conservative Republican jurist Arthur Vanderbilt, was reported to have said just that. The truth is not that Brennan changed, but that he grew. Arriving on the Court as a virtual
novice in constitutional law—he hadn't even studied it in law
school—Brennan spent thousands of hours reading and pondering
such humanistic thinkers as Plato and Thomas Aquinas.

Even as late as his final term, when the Court had been heavily
laden with Reagan appointees, Brennan could still win a majority to
defend free speech in flag-burning cases; or minority preference programs in FCC license applications.

His performance confounded his philosophical opponents and mystified even his friends. How could it have been that a man from an ob-scure position on a state supreme court, not even the chief justice or the most influential member of that court; a man who had spent his career in private law practice harassing labor unions; a man who had never demonstrated any discernible political philosophy or party iden-tification during his entire young adulthood; how could it be that this man, appointed almost serendipitously to the U. S. Supreme Court, would emerge as the seminal justice of our time?

Judge David Bazelon, for years the senior judge on the U.S. Court of Appeals in the District of Columbia, was a close associate of Bren-nan's. They had shared lunch hundreds of times. But even Bazelon spent nights trying to figure from where Brennan's success emanated. Asked to explain in 1980 the riddle of "what makes Brennan run," Bazelon pleaded the impossibility of the task. He called Brennan "too rich to be encompassed by categories . . . even the best description will be incomplete before it is printed." He added: "One can only speculate in what fires those convictions—and this man—were forged."

He was neither the greatest thinker on the Court nor its best writer. His opinions were often boring and clunky. There was little flash. His own favorite self-description was of a mule at the Kentucky Derby. But his achievements at the end had surpassed them all. No one doubted when Holmes or Brandeis arrived on the Court that those famous men would be important and historic justices. But no one, not even his for-mer classmates at Harvard who ridiculed the fact that his grades weren't even good enough to make *Law Review*, expected such great-ness from Brennan. No one, that is, except his proud Irish parents, who had come to America by boat and changed their new land forever.

NEWARK

I T WAS LATE APRIL, THE SPRING OF 1906, and along the streets of Newark's sprawling Irish-Catholic neighborhoods knots of parishioners were answering Cardinal Gibbons's call to seek relief contributions door to door. Only a week earlier, on April 17, 1906, the greatest natural disaster in American history, the San Francisco earthquake, had laid waste to that great city. But on narrow New Street in Newark, New Jersey, Irish immigrant William Joseph Brennan wasn't receiving callers.

On the night of April 24, his twenty-four-year-old wife, Agnes, had gone into labor with their second child. Hardly calm, William ran into the street and called out in his thick Irish brogue, "I need a doctor."

Riding by in a carriage was Dr. Haggarty, a physician from New Brunswick, New Jersey, passing through Newark on his way to a wedding. He postponed his wedding journey and in the early-morning hours of the following day, April 25, 1906, William Joseph Brennan, Jr., was ushered into this world by a gentleman in striped pants and morning coat.

The family's first son, he was named William after his father. "Big Bill" Brennan had high expectations for his new son. And even though he was thirty-one, he still had high expectations for himself. He could not know it at the time, but his dreams for both of them would be realized more profoundly than he could have possibly imagined.

William Joseph Brennan, Sr., had been born in French Park, a village in County Roscommon, Ireland. As a teenager he was driven by economic deprivation and famine to London, where he worked on the docks and practiced his English. In 1892, after just turning twenty, he boarded a ship for the United States. At first Brennan found work as a coal stoker in Trenton. He later moved to Newark, where he took a job as a coal heaver at Ballantine Brewery's monster furnace near the Passaic River at the foot of Fulton Street.

Searching for a place to live in the summer of 1896, Brennan, then twenty-three, had been directed to a boardinghouse on Plane Street. He had been told that the woman who owned the house was from Roscommon and might be willing to provide a room. What followed was reminiscent of a scene from an early Broadway musical. As Brennan approached the house he spied Agnes McDermott, the niece of the owner, sitting on the porch batting her eyes. In his heavy brogue, Irish Bill asked for a place to stay. It was only a matter of time before they would marry. They moved to the little house on New Street, where they had their first daughter, Katherine, and then little Billy. The second baby's arrival cramped their quarters and it wasn't long before the Brennans moved to a boxy three-story house at 119 North Munn, two blocks north of South Orange Avenue in a German-Irish section known as Vailsburg.

The Munn Street neighborhood reverberated with the sound of Irish tenors and sweet ballads from home rendered by player pianos. At night on the stoops, the new Americans gathered to tell stories about their ancestors and the old country. Frequently when a neighborhood storyteller looked down from his rocker, he saw a serious little boy with big ears sitting spellbound under the runners, soaking up every word but asking few questions.

By the time Bill was two, Bill senior had stopped heaving coal and become active as an officer in the International Brotherhood of Stationary Firemen, the union that represented the men who poured coal into Newark's large factory boilers.

A true labor reformer, Brennan got into union work out of a sense of disgust at how his brotherhood was being operated. Brennan had no

objection to paying his union dues, but he expected something in return. He had begun to suspect that the union leaders were enriching
themselves but doing little for the working people they were supposed
to represent. So in 1908, he led a revolt that pitched out the entrenched union officials.

Feared for his wild temper but respected for his incorruptible, honest
nature, Brennan won the election as president of his stationary fireman's local. It was a position that automatically gave him a slot on the
board of the New Jersey Federation of Labor. In 1909, and for each of
the next five years, Brennan was chosen as president of the Essex
County Trades Council, the umbrella organization for all the trade
unions in the county.

Brennan's success in union politics whetted his appetite for elected
office. In May 1913, he addressed a meeting of trolleymen who had
gone on strike in pursuit of better wages. The basic problem with
Newark's city government paralleled the situation that had existed in
his union.

In repeated speeches to the labor unions in the Essex Trades Council, Brennan denounced the city's corrupt government and called for
reform. Often with his seven-year-old son clutching Mom's hand behind him, he cried passionately for "unity and unionism." But the city
government, dominated by old-line politicians, was not inclined to co-
operate with the trolleymen, or with any of the other union leaders.
William Brennan's activism in a time of turbulent union organizing frequently brought him into conflict with the police and the authorities.

A turning point in the life of the Brennan family came in 1916 when
ten-year-old Bill junior witnessed his father being carried into the
house by union brothers, bloodied and beaten by city police after a
particularly bitter union battle over the trolley-car drivers. Few events
in his childhood affected him more. Police beatings would never be
anything abstract to the Brennans. When city government is changed,
the elder Brennan would say, "there will be no more police beatings."
William senior called the family together and declared that things
would change in Newark. When the union leadership had failed to
serve its members, he had masterminded its overthrow. Perhaps the
same approach would work with city government.

Brennan became chief sponsor and spokesman for the abolition of
the mayor-alderman form of government in Newark. Brennan was so

troublesome that Thomas Raymond, Newark's Republican mayor, appointed him commissioner of police. The mayor reasoned it might be safer to have Brennan inside the tent than agitating from outside. Brennan accepted the post but did not curtail his efforts to abolish the city council and replace it with five commissioners.

By 1917, within a year of his beating, Brennan and his allies had succeeded in winning enough votes to change the city charter. He threw out the corrupt, cumbersome thirty-two-member city council and instituted a new five-member city commission. Of the five new commissioners, three were Irish, new mayor Charles P. Gillen, John F. Monahan, and William J. Brennan, Sr. Each of the commissioners chose an area of the city government to administer. Brennan took over the police and fire departments as Newark's director of public safety.

Just as he had with the union, Brennan had almost single-handedly taken the first steps to clean up city government. And in a career that would span thirteen years of public service, Brennan personally wrestled with such First and Fifth Amendment issues as pornography, free speech, and flag burning, as well as compulsory confessions and police beatings. Watching Bill senior operate gave young Billy a civics education unavailable in any school curriculum.

Shortly after his election, Brennan announced that all existing liquor and vice regulations would be enforced to the letter. Violations of the city's 1:00 A.M. closing law would not be tolerated, he announced. It was not just proprietors who would bear the brunt of what became known as "Brennan's law"; landlords were held equally guilty for violations of the law on their properties. Brennan thus eliminated a situation where saloonkeepers could get longer hours merely by bribing the police officers on the street.

Brennan was impetuous and often angry. One morning walking to work, he was spattered with wet snow and water from a car driven by a judge. By the time he reached city hall, Brennan's face had turned a fiery crimson, and he stormed into the city engineer's office and ordered every sidewalk and gutter in Newark cleared of snow. Those who failed to heed his warning, Brennan railed, "will be served with formal complaints." Brennan's order was read to every squad of departing policemen; and every mounted officer and those on motorcycles were sent to tell homeowners to "clear their gutters."

A saint he was not. Although Brennan never took a bribe or emolument from any city worker or vendor, the police commissioner was not above taking advantage of certain perks of his office, such as a city-owned cabin at the city reservoir or a city car. In fact all the commissioners had the city buy them cars.

On the night of March 2, 1918, Brennan was learning to drive his city car on Lincoln Highway in Kearny when the black coupe struck and killed a pedestrian who had reportedly stumbled drunkenly out of a saloon. Brennan later testified that the car was traveling about thirty-five miles per hour when the victim, Oscar Santholm, "seemed to dive off the sidewalk. He seemed to be running for a trolley car and his head was drooping." What was more difficult to explain was why the car left the scene of the accident.

Maria Santholm, the widow of the unfortunate Oscar, filed suit for $50,000 against Brennan and Whiting Motor Car Company, the maker of the machine. Judge William Speer granted a defense motion for a "nonsuit," stating that Brennan was "merely a guest" in the demonstration automobile. Although some believed that Brennan himself was at the wheel, he left the driving instructor and the Whiting Motor Car Company to split $8,000 in assigned damages.

But such embarrassing moments were outweighed by the mass of good publicity Brennan received for his efforts to clean up and police Newark without dampening its spirit. As the years passed, Brennan, as public safety director, became Newark's dominant politician. *The Newark Evening News* described him as stubborn, gruff voiced, and witty and observed that "Brennan doesn't give a tinker's damn what people think, when he thinks he is right."

As tough as Brennan was on his police and firemen, he exacted the same level of hard work and devotion from his children. For a teenage boy, Brennan senior was not an easy parent. He directed all of the decisions that his son would make, including beginning school at a Catholic elementary school before switching to a public high school, mostly for the sake of political appearances. Brennan felt city officials should send their children to the public high school.

When sixteen-year-old Bill asked his father what kind of curriculum he should take at Barringer High School, Bill senior ordered liberal arts. He had already chosen his son's career. "I'd like to see you become a good lawyer, lad. A good lawyer." When young Bill asked what that meant for a career in politics, Brennan senior replied, "Y'argue well here around the house lad and I think you'd make a good lawyer. But as for politics, I think you'd be happier out than in." A lawyer in the family could do a lot for the workingman, Bill senior told his son.

Agnes couldn't have agreed more. Bill junior was more than her pride and joy; he was in many respects a momma's boy. Bill junior was also the protector of the family against his father's irrational periods and wild mood swings. As the oldest son, Bill considered it his duty to side with his mother against his overbearing dad. That was almost a full-time job.

Agnes was the good Irish wife, but if there was one part she would have liked to leave out of her life, it was the fishbowl of public life, the parades, the rallies, the endless speeches. "Whatever you do," she said in one candid moment of exasperation, "stay out of the headlines." That was a piece of advice Brennan would follow until well after her death some fifty years later.

The Brennan clan, which totaled eleven, including Grandmother Elizabeth Kane, lived well in the Roaring Twenties. Despite the family's material comfort, Bill junior had a succession of odd jobs. He left high school in the afternoons and made change for passengers waiting for trolley cars and later worked in a filling station at South Orange Avenue and Munn Street. Pete Walsh, who ran the station, remembered Brennan as a kid "with a quick comeback and a quick way with the fifty-gallon cans he yanked forward for curb service." Those who had seen him among the trolleys shared the description of Brennan as "quick and nimble," doling out nickels on the old cement safety isles.

Brennan spent summer vacations working. He sold suits and worked as a street-repair inspector. Across the street from his home was a dairy farm, and often at 5:00 A.M. Bill and his younger brother Charlie would milk cows. Then after the milk had cooled they would deliver it to the houses in the neighborhood. In the afternoon the boys distributed newspapers. Brennan would later explain to *Life* magazine that, contrary to popular image, his was no Horatio Alger story. His childhood jobs weren't to survive; his family wasn't impoverished. They were to collect extra money and to satisfy his father's concept of the work ethic.

He admitted to no hobbies or athletic achievements. He didn't particularly enjoy fishing with his dad. Nor was he interested in collections. He worked hard during the day and studied hard at night. Expectations of his success were high, but his studies didn't come easily to him. He got A's, but had to work for them. Ultimately it paid off. As one classmate recalled, "Bill took home so many academic prizes from school, none were left for the rest of us." To his teachers, Bill was the perfect young man, thoughtful and polite, never a cutup. Every Sunday he held his mother's hand as they walked to Mass.

In the evenings, Bill and his five brothers and two sisters gathered around the family's player piano or listened to the phonograph records of the great Irish tenor John McCormack. On the end table lay a stack of the magazine *Irish World*. Every aspect of his life, from church until bedtime, was absorbed with Irish feeling and the tales of Irish rebellion and courage against their occupiers.

In February 1921, Brennan senior came face to face with the issue of desecration of the American flag. A Newark patrolman, Thomas Durkin, publicly complained that a night watchman at a garage had vilified the flag, spat on it, and declared that he wished to burn it. When told of the remarks, Brennan excoriated the officer, telling him his failure to arrest the offender made him unfit to "wear the uniform."

Brennan's hardball tactics with the police and firefighters over whom he had responsibility did not make him universally loved. Despite his roots in the labor movement, he frequently fought pay raises for policemen when he felt they weren't putting out enough effort.

Brennan drew even more resentment when he openly opposed a liberal pension plan approved by the policemen's union. The bill drafted by the police would have provided half salary to policemen with twenty years of service when they reached the age of fifty. Despite his union background, Brennan said that was just too much, "The only thing I have asked from the police and firemen is honest work for a decent wage. No man or woman in either department can say he has ever had to give a five-cent cigar for anything he or she was justly entitled to." To drive home the point that graft was unnecessary, Brennan saw to it that firemen's pay was increased from $800 a year to $1,400.

Under a withering assault from the policemen, Brennan defended his actions in a speech on March 20, 1921. "If in asking that every policeman or fireman, regardless of how he voted or what districts or wards he holds in the hollow of his hand, give the taxpayer 100 cents worth of service for every cold American dollar paid him by the tax-payers is being 'too strict' I must plead guilty and throw myself on the mercy of the people," Brennan declared.

He added: "If being a friend of the police or firemen means helping them put something over on the rest of the citizens, you can put me down as no friend of theirs.

"When you hear these grumblers talk about me and call me the Taskmaster, Simon Legree and the Czar, ask any one of them if I ever asked him to do any more than his duty," he said. "Ask whether they have had to pay for promotions. Ask whether they have had to fear politicians. Ask whether they have had to go truckling to some political boss to get what they deserved and whether the man without political influence hasn't been treated on the same basis as the so-called influential policeman or fireman."

His stand in opposing the police union surprised both political supporters and opponents who assumed Brennan would be an easy target for the unions. With his first term nearly over, the long knives of the police were out for Brennan. Ironically it was old foes like the anti-union *Newark Daily News* who were left to laud him. Said the paper, "Originally elected as a labor man, Brennan has shown honest independence for the city's interests and unusual courage in public service. To turn him out would be construed as reestablishing in their interference the organizations of the policemen and the firemen and is an invitation to the outside influences in the Building Department. He is inexperienced, but strong in honesty and grit."

Not many of Brennan's old friends deserted him. Brennan's popularity with the workingmen—the carpenters, brewery workers, machinists, and molders—mellowed his initial instincts about taking a hard line against vice. Over time he developed a much more selective sense of what was lawful and what wasn't. He flatly refused to condemn gambling. Pressed by the city's Protestant-based Anti-Saloon League, Brennan claimed to have conducted his own investigation of gambling at one particularly notorious establishment. His conclusion: "I had a personal inquiry made. There was no evidence of bookmaking or gambling . . . and I don't think anything could be pulled off without our patrolmen knowing about it."

Brennan paid mere lip service to the idea of enforcing Prohibition. After an investigation into liquor selling at the Berwick Hotel, officers reported that they had been able to purchase bottles of White Rock in which liquor had been inserted before the tops were resealed. Brennan, however, refused to order arrests, claiming a public case would reveal the identities of his undercover men. "It is impossible to make people good by the use of the nightstick, some magic wand," Brennan told the church leaders. "Despite all the slander to which our city has been subjected, the fact remains that the people of Newark are as law abiding, as moral, as immune from human follies and mistakes as the citizens of any other municipality in New Jersey, aye, in America.

"I am the elected representative of a metropolitan American city, elected not to govern but to represent them and to carry their will into effect."

Despite the enmity of many police officials and Protestant church leaders, who continued to clamor for his impeachment, Brennan was a hero to the masses of immigrants and certainly the swelling Irish-Catholic community. As the second biggest vote-getter in the city, Brennan's third election was no contest. Four years later, on May 13, 1925, his electoral power was proven supreme: After eight years in office, he was the top vote-getter in the city and could have demanded the mayor's chair if he desired it. But Brennan did not.

"I know how to handle the police," he said. "But in the mayor's job, I would be out of my element."

Long before his son would help make sure that it became the law of the country, Brennan worked hard to guarantee that those arrested for crimes in Newark would be treated humanely. In 1925, Brennan announced that forced interrogation would be eliminated from his police department.

"The use of unnecessary force in making arrests, and violence in any form towards the citizens, has been done away with," he told a campaign crowd. "Nightsticks should last a long time. The police have been made the servants of the people and not their masters."

Brennan also gained a reputation among Newark's impoverished black community as a man of fairness. When he took office the police department employed only one black officer, whose job was exclusively to look out over Negro dances, church conferences, and lodge conventions. William Ashby, the first director of Newark's Urban League, had tried to change that but without success. Time after time, young black men would take the police examination, but none had ever gotten a job offer. That changed when Ashby confronted Brennan with the problem.

As Ashby later recalled the exchange:

"You know what the Negroes of Newark are saying about you?"

"What?" Brennan snarled.

"They are saying that if some of the Negro boys pass you won't appoint them."

"That's a lie," Brennan said sucking on a pipe, one leg stuck up on his oak desk.

"I know it's a lie," said Ashby. "But the Negroes don't know it's a lie."

"I'll appoint them if they pass," he pledged. Brennan kept his word, and on the next list, three blacks were appointed to the department.

Shortly after his 1925 election, Brennan became embroiled in what would become his best-known controversy. In marked contrast to a son who would later be criticized for permissiveness, Brennan became infamous for trying to stop the showing of a sex education film at the downtown Capitol Theater.

Earlier Brennan had been criticized for being too permissive with the movies, just as he was thought to be too lenient on drinking and gambling. He had once again stirred the enmity of the Protestant Anti-Saloon League by refusing to ban either Sunday movies in general or the films of a sultry actress of the period named Mabel Normand in particular.

But Brennan did agree to censorship with regard to a movie entitled *The Naked Truth*, which had been distributed as an aid to sexual hygiene by the U.S. Public Health Service. Although the film had been playing in nearby Kearny for three weeks, when its distributor attempted to show it at Newark's Capitol Theater, Brennan was unequivocal. "I will revoke the operating license of the Capitol Theater and order the arrest of everybody who had anything to do with it," Brennan declared. The distributor of the film begged Brennan to look at it himself, but he adamantly refused. Fortunately Brennan's decision was overturned by the city's vice chancellor.

Despite the controversies, Brennan received 59,000 votes in the 1929 elections, 17,000 more than his nearest competitor. Said one national union leader of Brennan, "He has contributed more to industrial peace in Newark than all the talk heard on the one side by employees and the employers on the other. He has been more responsible for peaceful conferences in industrial disputes than all the business representatives we have on the street."

Of his own career, Brennan summarized: "I have never belonged to any political organization since I have been in politics. I am a Democrat. I have never cast a vote that I have to apologize for. If I had to cast the same vote over again I would do just as I did.

"I have been accused of everything but dishonesty. I have never been dishonest. I have received many tempting offers. But I have spurned them. Men have tried to affiliate me with schemes that would not have reflected well upon me and upon you who helped to make me."

The strains of his battles had begun to take their toll on old Bill Brennan. By 1930 his once-red hair had turned ghostly white. His kidneys were giving him trouble, and he suddenly appeared much older than his fifty-seven years.

Bill junior had left home in 1924 to attend the University of Pennsylvania. Like his dad, he seemed to gravitate not to be the leader of school organizations but to find jobs that would put him in the middle of things. Brennan served not as president of his fraternity but as secretary. He was not a star or even a player on the Penn football team; he signed on as the manager in charge of uniforms and balls. He became known to the student body only after a cameraman for the school paper caught Brennan tumbling over on the field with the team's water bucket. He continued his habit of earning his own keep, tutoring other students at night. His own course load was heavily laden with business courses, and he graduated in 1928 with a degree in economics. But it was always presumed he would go to law school.

Having steered his son in the direction of law, Brennan senior next decided which law school his son should attend. The school of choice in the late 1920s was Columbia. Its dean, Harlan Fiske Stone, had quietly edged the New York City school past both Harvard and Yale in prestige. But Bill Brennan did not like the idea of his son going to school in New York. Too wild and too much partying, he believed. Brennan took it upon himself to conclude that the night spots in New York might impede his son's scholarship, and so it was decided that Bill junior would attend Harvard Law School.

On May 5, 1928, four months before leaving for law school, Bill junior married Marjorie Leonard, a woman he had met at a tea dance in

Newark's Washington Hotel. She had come with another date, but Brennan had managed to engage her in conversation, and several months later he asked her to marry him.

She was an orphan who had grown up with an older sister in Belfast, New York. Bill told friends that he found Marjorie "fascinating and bright." She promised to be, and ultimately became the same kind of shy but loyal Irish wife Agnes had always been. Brennan's marriage assuaged some of big Bill's concerns, but he still didn't want his boy living in New York City. Thus, in September 1928, Bill junior packed up and moved to Cambridge.

The Harvard Law School class of 1931 produced two great scholars, Milton Katz and Paul Freund, both of whom would return to Harvard as teachers. Neither, however, paid Brennan any attention or even knew who he was. Those who did recall him from law school described Brennan as a "workaholic" and a "prodigious notetaker."

The one member of the class who would later be honored with an appointment to the U.S. Supreme Court was not its outstanding student. Hard working and friendly, he was of remarkably average intelligence. Despite intensive study and few distractions, Brennan's grades were neither good enough to get him on the *Law Review*, of which Freund was editor, nor to get him a position as student adviser, the tier for the second-level academics. Brennan later claimed that not making *Law Review* didn't mean he wasn't bright, just that he had more trouble than others putting his thoughts down on paper.

By his third year, Brennan's academic standing had improved enough that he was able—barely—to make the third rank of honor groupings, the Harvard Legal Aid Society, a distinction that classmates say would have meant he was among the top sixty members of his class. The Legal Aid Society did what its name implies. A student organization, its lawyers were permitted to practice in the Massachusetts court system. For the most part, the legal-aid lawyers helped people with landlord-tenant problems or divorces and wills. Frequently Brennan went to the courthouse to represent indigents in civil cases. In his short tenure with the society, Brennan did little that was memorable to his colleagues.

Nonetheless, when he was appointed to the U.S. Supreme Court twenty-five years later, scores of classmates scratched their heads in frustration, trying to remember who he had been. His obscurity was not something with which Brennan was comfortable. He told one audience that the position of editor of the *Harvard Law Review* "eluded me." That's true, but Brennan was never even close to being selected for *Law Review*, much less editor. He also told groups in a joking fashion that Justice Felix Frankfurter, who had taught Brennan in public utilities while a Harvard professor, "has no memory of any signs in me of being his prize pupil." Brennan was hardly Frankfurter's prize pupil.

Harvard's curriculum was loaded with legal philosophy and analysis but very little of what was needed to practice in the profession. The law was simpler in 1930 than it is today. The arrival of Franklin Roosevelt and the Democratic control of the Congress was still two years away. There was no Securities and Exchange Commission or even a National Labor Relations Board. Most of the federal agencies and rules and regulations with which members of Brennan's class would wrestle their entire professional lives had not yet been created. Unlike the curriculum at such law schools as New York University, where a student learned how to practice law, Harvard prided itself on teaching lawyers how to think. Electives were rare and specialized courses were few. It was a curriculum that easily bred more teachers and scholars. The faculty was the stuff of legends with such professors as Samuel Williston, Zechariah Chafee and Felix Frankfurter.

It was Professor Chafee who, during a course on obscenity law, used *Public Welfare Pictures* v. *Brennan* as his case study. It was the then-recent tale of how William Brennan, Sr., had tried to stop the showing of *The Naked Truth*. Brennan said nothing during class, but was inwardly amused. He couldn't wait for the term to end so he could go home and tell his father of his fame in law school circles. The elder Brennan found nothing funny in his notoriety and began railing against Chafee and the Harvard Law School. Bill junior decided not to mention it again.

One of Brennan's colleagues, Frederick Hall, would later sum up their experience: "Most of us learned very little about how to be a lawyer and practice law. We did acquire some experience in brief writing and appellate argument so that when we graduated we perhaps could argue an appeal but could not safely advise a client or try a case in a lower tribunal. Bill Brennan, however, did get some taste of the real world and a chance to deal with people's problems firsthand through his membership in the Legal Aid Society."

Student life was an existence that he found almost serene compared to the whirlwind in which he had grown up and which continued in his absence. Early in 1930 Brennan's father set off what would be his final political tiff when he announced restrictions on the holding of outside jobs by city employees under his control. Even the issue of taxi-cab licensing nearly brought the increasingly volatile commissioner to blows with the city's director of licensing. In an apparent dispute over turf, Brennan ripped off his glasses and lunged at the younger man with fists clenched. After the incident, one city employee told *The Newark Evening News* that Brennan was now "100 percent Simon Legree."

Seeing that Brennan's temper was foul and his health failing, the family doctor suggested that a weekend visit to the Pequannock watershed might do the commissioner some good. The visit had the opposite effect. On May 12, 1930, shortly after returning from what was supposed to have been a restful period, Brennan contracted pneumonia. Told of the illness, Brennan pledged not to give an inch. "I'm going to fight this until I get better," he said.

But when his temperature soared to 105 degrees, a priest was called in to administer last rites. At his bedside was Police Sergeant Philip Davenport, who had been Brennan's chauffeur for the past ten years. Also present, in addition to Agnes, were Brennan's eighty-year-old mother Bridgett, his twenty-five-year-old daughter Katherine and his son Charles, twenty-one, who came up from Penn. William junior stayed at Harvard Law to finish his exams.

At 4:00 P.M. on the thirteenth, Father Dugan arrived from St. Rose of Lima's Catholic Church. Brennan took communion, settled back on his pillow, and smiled weakly. He was taken to the hospital and the following morning, at 10:23 A.M., he was dead.

For the city of Newark the death of the senior Brennan set off a wave of mourning. The body lay in state and the mile-long funeral procession stopped all city business. *The Newark Star-Eagle*'s headline read "Whole City Mourns at Brennan Funeral." He was a person, the newspaper summed up, "who, once he believed he had taken the right course, nothing could change him."

The death was swift and stunning. If Bill Brennan had ruled the city with an iron fist, it had been even more so at home. Finally Bill junior would no longer have to live under the demanding requirements of his father. With Bill senior, Brennan told a friend: "You had to be doing something all the time."

But the loss of his giant personality was only half the story. When Bill and his brothers, Charles and Thomas, went to the bank to find out what the commissioner had left them, the answer was not pleasant. Basically an honest politician, Brennan had spent every penny he earned. There was nothing that could even begin to take care of his eight children, four of whom were still of high-school age or younger. There was Betty, seventeen; Margaret, fourteen; Helen, twelve; and Frank, ten.

With one year left in law school, Brennan had no money with which to finish. At first he was sure he would have to leave Harvard, but after consultation with the family, and the generous help of the law school administration, he changed his mind. His early years of odd-jobbing came in handy. Brennan made it through the last year by waiting on tables at a Cambridge fraternity house.

He graduated in May 1931 and returned home as the head of an extended family. With his sister Katherine working for Newark's Prudential Life Insurance Company, and brother Charles laboring away at United Color and Pigment Company, Bill began to think less about legal aid and more about how he was going to support such a large family in the midst of the depression.

A YOUNG LAWYER ON
BROAD STREET

THE NATION WAS IN THE THROES OF a depression when Bill Brennan finally got his diploma from Harvard Law School. For a young Irish lawyer, even exiting Harvard did not bring offers of big money from famous Wall Street firms. Big monied law was still the province of the Protestant establishment. The Irish, like the Jews, were largely excluded from corporate practice. For Brennan, it was no great loss. His obligations to his new wife and family almost called out for him to return home to Newark. Normally a lawyer of Brennan's ancestry and education might have tried to hang out his shingle. But in New Jersey admission to the bar came only at the recommendation of another practicing lawyer. The tradition in the state was that all young lawyers would serve apprenticeships for other practicing attorneys. After two years, they could be recommended for full admission to the bar themselves.

Although no New York or Boston firms came calling for Brennan, one hometown law firm was interested. And it so happened that it was the premier corporate firm in Newark, anxious to break its religious barrier and finally hire its first Catholic.

The Newark law firm of Pitney, Hardin & Ward symbolized both the best and the worst in American law. Like so many corporate law firms, Pitney Hardin attracted the best and the brightest, then unleashed them, often to protect the most exploitative practices of the mid-twentieth century: business against the worker and consumer.

Founded just after the turn of the century, Pitney Hardin was the creation of John Oliver Halstead Pitney, founder of Mutual Benefit Life Insurance Company and the younger brother of Supreme Court justice Mahlon Pitney. The Pitney brothers were bluebloods by any standard. A great-grandfather, Henry Cooper Pitney, had served in the Revolutionary War. Their father had been a wealthy and successful Newark attorney, and there had never been any doubt John and Mahlon would become lawyers. Mahlon once wrote: "I could hardly have escaped it, for my father lived in his work . . . he was a walking encyclopedia of the law."

Both Pitneys pursued political careers, but Mahlon's was by far the more successful. He was elected to two terms in the New Jersey house, then moved over to the state senate, and in 1901 was named a justice on the New Jersey Supreme Court. On February 12, 1912, President William Howard Taft met Mahlon Pitney at a political fund-raising dinner in Newark. The president was so impressed by Pitney's conversation that just one week later on February 19, he offered Pitney the appointment to the U.S. Supreme Court to succeed the just-deceased Justice John Marshall Harlan.

Scared that a wild-eyed Theodore Roosevelt might soon win back the presidency, Taft wanted the most conservative, mainstream justice possible. That was certainly Pitney. He was approved by a 50 to 26 vote and became a staunch opponent of civil liberties. Pitney's most lasting legacy on the Court was writing the opinion upholding the murder conviction of railroaded childkiller Leo Frank in *Frank v. Mangum* 237 U.S. 309. Despite blatant constitutional violations by the judge, including the defendant's exclusion from the courtroom when the verdict was read, it was Pitney's view that a mere violation of certain rights of due process was no reason to throw out the decision of the jury or even to require a new trial.

It is often reported that Pitney, Hardin & Ward, now located in Morristown, New Jersey, was founded by one Supreme Court justice and produced another. But it is not true. Mahlon Pitney had little to do with the firm. It was Mahlon's brother, John, who built up the law firm that later became best known as Pitney, Hardin, Ward & Brennan. And it was Mahlon's son Shelton who had the more lasting impact on the firm. Along with John Ralph Hardin, he developed Pitney, Hardin & Ward into one of the most sophisticated and wealthy corporate law offices in the East. The firm's banking clientele included the powerful Howard State Bank, United New Jersey Railroad, New Jersey Bell, and the Duke Power Company. Their specialty was strikebreaking, which earned them the nickname "Pluck-em, Hook-em, and Skin-em."

Until the arrival of Brennan, all the lawyers in the firm were Protestants and every partner was a Princeton graduate. If there was diversity in the various law schools that Pitney Hardin lawyers attended it was easily explainable: Princeton has no law school.

In 1928, after John O. H. Pitney dropped dead at his desk, Shelton Pitney realized that age was overtaking the law firm and new blood was needed. He packed his bag and announced to his partners that he was taking the train to Boston to find some good, youthful Harvard lawyers to hire. On his arrival he placed a notice on the bulletin board at the law school placement office. The note indicated that Pitney Hardin was particularly interested in any prospects from New Jersey.

Pitney met with several young lawyers but was especially impressed with Donald Kipp and William Brennan. The two law students had been friends since their first year at Harvard when the two New Jerseyans realized they were both frustrated athletes. Kipp had been manager of the Princeton crew team, and Brennan, the manager of the Penn football squad. Together they had written a paper entitled "Law of Future Interests of New Jersey." Pitney read the legal tome and was very impressed. He returned home to Newark with pledges from both Kipp and Brennan that they would begin work the following September of 1931.

Pitney Hardin was the last place in Newark anyone would have expected to find the son of a devoted labor man like Bill Brennan senior. It wasn't just politics, either. Pitney Hardin had never offered a partnership to a Catholic, and furthermore, it had never offered a job, let alone a partnership, to anyone from an undergraduate college other than Princeton. Moreover, Pitney Hardin represented some of the most notoriously antilabor corporations in the state of New Jersey—Phelps Dodge, Western Electric, and General Electric. Brennan would quickly be put to work doing their bidding, working to figure out legal ways to fire striking workers and to stop picketing and union organizing.

The son of such a solid labor man, Bill Brennan had never figured to enter corporate law on this level. His father had always imagined young Bill as a wonderful litigator, using his debate skills for the benefit of the underprivileged and the oppressed immigrants. "You argue well," his father had often said proudly. But faced with the financial pressure generated by the depression, the death of his father, the need to support his wife and seven brothers and sisters, plus the cost of repaying his law school loans, Bill junior put his father's philosophy second and a steady income first. He had become, in the truest sense of the expression, a victim of the depression.

If there was any place in Newark that seemed logical for Bill Brennan, it would have been across the street at the law offices of Arthur T. Vanderbilt. Then a liberal Republican—although he grew increasingly conservative as he got older—Vanderbilt had been practicing in his native Newark since 1915. He was best known for his representation of socialist leader Norman Thomas. He also shared the Brennan family's incorruptibility and self-righteousness. His fights against corrupt Jersey City Mayor Frank Hague were legendary. But instead of working for Vanderbilt, Brennan became a competitor.

During his first few years at the firm, Brennan arrived by 8 A.M. and often stayed until 2 A.M. Even to Shelton Pitney, known for the hard-driving example he set for his associates, Brennan seemed tireless. When told to research a brief, Brennan invariably produced too much—sometimes as much as 300 to 400 pages of scholarly research. Yet when Brennan was confronted with real-life situations, as opposed to research and writing, his results were mixed. Once when sent down to the city jail to help a client who had been involved in a knifing, Brennan himself was confused with an escaped prisoner and briefly jailed until another lawyer could come down and straighten things out.

Another time, fellow lawyer Worrall Mountain walked into a downtown Newark restaurant and saw Brennan sitting alone and in a daze. A full plate of roast beef rested untouched on the plate.

"What's the matter," Mountain asked. "You look terrible."

Brennan was distraught and didn't immediately answer. Finally Brennan mumbled morosely that his law career was over. He began to explain how he had been helping a senior partner in a steel company merger. Brennan's job had been simple: All he had to do was file one stack of papers with the county court and another stack with the secretary of state.

"Well, Brennan had delivered the wrong sets to the wrong offices. It didn't exactly ruin Brennan's career," Mountain recalled later. "And the merger was hardly even affected."

Another misadventure occurred when Brennan was defending a young man accused of automobile manslaughter. Uncharacteristically, Brennan hadn't adequately prepared because he thought the case would be a snap. As he later admitted, "I didn't talk beforehand, as I should have, to a retired policeman who testified as a character witness." When he got to trial, Brennan asked the officer three separate times about his client's reputation for "veracity." Three times came the same reply. "He's a good automobile driver." The witness didn't want to admit that he didn't know the meaning of the word "veracity." But Brennan wasn't sharp enough on his feet to figure that out.

Brennan's face had turned red with irritation at the third repetitive response when the judge interrupted.

"Is this boy in the habit of telling the truth?" the judge snapped impatiently.

"Oh yes, your honor," the retired cop said. "I've never known him to tell a lie."

Said the judge, "That's what Mr. Brennan was asking, but he's a Harvard graduate and doesn't speak English."

Like many after him, Mountain found that Brennan was slightly prone to hyperbole. The two associates played poker every Friday or Saturday night. "He was good as well as lucky," Mountain says. On other occasions, Mountain recalled, a game of golf would precede the gambling. On the first occasion that they ever played, one of the foursome told Mountain that Brennan had mentioned being a star on the University of Pennsylvania's golf team. When Brennan looked at the ground in ersatz modesty, and said nothing, Mountain felt duly intimidated but later he recalled, "This feeling faded after the first few shots. It was apparent that Bill had been no nearer a college golf team than I had." Actually as a golfer, Brennan rarely broke 100.

His small rectangled office on the twenty-first floor of the National Newark Building was spartanly decorated, and Brennan shared space with an associate and another partner, William Considine. On the wall above his desk he kept a cartoon portrait of his father, showing Big Bill combing the hair of an unruly child—the Newark Police Department. There were other reminders of his father. Brennan had inherited his dad's sizable collection of pipes and pipe racks. Bill often smoked while he worked late into the night. Then he walked onto the streets his father had helped keep safe and rode home to South Orange on the Decamp Bus Line.

Despite the family reminders, Brennan went to great lengths to point out the differences between himself and his father. Unlike his father, who was an avid collector, Brennan would remind people that he had no hobbies. While his father had liked to fish, Brennan didn't. He pointedly told a newspaper interviewer that while his father had liked fast cars, "I take the bus."

Pace was certainly the biggest difference between father and son. Big Bill had been a whirlwind. Just as he had been at law school, the future justice was a hard-working, diligent grinder. The lights in his office rarely went out before 1 A.M. Getting home early meant arriving at his Wyoming Avenue home in South Orange between 7 P.M. and 7:30 P.M. When he did get home, Brennan's activities were of the sedentary variety. He lit a pipe and read his cases, occasionally taking a diversion to read a biography or to pull out a copy of *Plutarch's Lives* or some Irish poetry. Marjorie would sit quietly with her husband, preferring detective stories.

His memory for law was said to be remarkable. He could remember not only the names of cases but the volume number and even the page on which a particular case could be found. The clients for whom he performed much of his work, Johnson & Johnson and the Duke family, demanded toughness as well as scholarship. Says one former colleague, "He didn't come into court with a fiery red face, but he wasn't namby, if he had a position he would hold to it."

Shelton Pitney could hardly believe that someone who hadn't gone to Princeton could make such a fine attorney. He adopted Brennan as his personal associate for complicated tax and labor work. With the passage of the Wagner Act in 1935, Brennan spent an increasing percentage of his hours on labor matters. The act, named for its chief sponsor, New York senator Robert Ferdinand Wagner, Sr., gave workers the right to organize unions and bargain collectively. When the

Supreme Court ruled in 1937 that a state had the power to establish a minimum wage, there was no denying that a new era had dawned for the American laborer. In addition to allowing workers to unionize factories without interference from management, the legislation set up the National Labor Relations Board, which was empowered to certify the proper bargaining representatives and to prevent unfair labor practices.

The practical effect of the Wagner Act was to set off a torrent of litigation over employer-employee relationships. Brennan found himself in the middle of all the controversy and was designated as Pitney Hardin's up-and-coming expert in the area of labor law. The selection of Brennan was natural. He understood, perhaps better than any big firm management attorney, the concerns of labor leaders. He could talk to and negotiate with both sides. Everyone in labor had known his father, who had served on the executive board of the AFL-CIO and had rarely missed a national convention of the union, even during his tenure in public office. The recognition gave him an instant advantage, and on numerous occasions Brennan approached the unions on behalf of Johnson & Johnson president, Robert Wood Johnson. Brennan had a pleasant, winning demeanor that attracted people to him. Johnson noted his skill at dealing with people of all economic backgrounds. Brennan seemed as at home walking the floor of a factory, bantering with the workers, as he was advising the board of directors about potential labor pitfalls. While other companies fought with their unions, Johnson & Johnson's workers organized quietly and peacefully. That suited the Johnson family just fine and comported with their basic concept of a humanitarian company.

On January 1, 1938, Brennan had so pleased Robert Wood Johnson that the firm had no choice but to make him the first Catholic invited to become a partner. Ultimately, eleven years later, the name of the firm itself would be changed to advertise Brennan's presence, so great had his draw as a labor expert become.

In the seven years that Brennan had toiled as a young lawyer, a series of events occurred in Washington that no one would have ever predicted would have anything to do with him. But step by step, as chance created them, each occurrence would ultimately affect Brennan's life in a most profound way.

The sequence began on March 8, 1930, two months before the death of William Brennan, Sr., when the world was stunned to find that not one, but two justices had died on the same day. William Howard Taft, the former president and later chief justice, had actually resigned from the court two months earlier. And he was joined in death that day by a sitting judge, Edward Terry Sanford. Sanford's death was felt particularly at Harvard. He was, after all, a Harvard Law School alumnus, and a former editor of the *Harvard Law Review*. It was Sanford who, in 1923, had been chosen by President Harding to replace Mahlon Pitney.

President Hoover had already decided that Taft's successor would be former justice Charles Evans Hughes. Hughes had already served on the court from 1910 to 1916, when he resigned to run for president. Endorsed by both the Republican and Progressive parties, Hughes lost his challenge to Woodrow Wilson by 23 electoral votes. After his defeat he returned to the private practice of law. When the Republicans regained the White House in 1920 Hughes was chosen as Harding's secretary of state, where he stood out as virtually the only honest man in an administration soaked by scandal.

Despite a glowing record, his appointment met with considerable opposition. Senator George Norris of Nebraska said of Hughes, "No man in public life so exemplifies the influence of powerful combinations in the political and financial worlds as does Mr. Hughes." He was finally confirmed by the Senate on February 13, 1930.

For his second appointment, Hoover settled on the North Carolina federal judge John J. Parker. But Parker drew more heat than Hughes, although for a completely different reason. While on the bench, Parker had upheld the legality of "yellow-dog contracts," labor contracts that allowed employers to break strikes. The opposition proved too great for Parker to overcome.

When the Senate failed to confirm Parker's appointment, Hoover finally turned to Owen J. Roberts, a graduate of Brennan's alma mater, the University of Pennsylvania and in later life the dean of the University of Pennslvania Law School. Roberts, a onetime prosecutor from Pennsylvania, had been appointed by President Coolidge as a special investigator into the Harding administration corruption. Through his work, Roberts had uncovered a labyrinthian network of bribes to administration figures. He then returned to private law practice.

Hoover got yet another appointment just before leaving office in 1932 when Justice Oliver Wendell Holmes finally resigned at the age of ninety, after serving thirty years on the Court. Although there were already two New Yorkers on the court, and a Jewish justice, Louis Brandeis, Hoover named Benjamin Nathan Cardozo, a Jewish judge from New York. As one Harvard professor observed, "Hoover ignored geography and made history."

In a letter written in 1958, Republican Hoover explained his decision to appoint the Democrat Cardozo. "The facts were that I was one of the ancient believers that the Supreme Court should have a strong minority of the opposition's party and that all appointments should be made from experienced jurists. When the vacancy came, with the aid of Attorney General William D. Mitchell, I canvassed all the possible Democratic jurists and immediately concluded that Justice Cardozo was the right man and appointed him. As I recollect my only conversation with him prior to his appointment was a telephone call in which he agreed to serve."

Cardozo, however, did not have enough time to make history. After just six years on the Court, he passed away at the age of sixty-eight, in Port Chester, New York; Franklin Delano Roosevelt had no doubts about who would replace Cardozo. FDR had been close friends with Brennan's old Harvard Law professor, Felix Frankfurter, for nearly twenty years. Frankfurter was named to the Court on January 5, and twelve days later was confirmed by the Senate on a voice vote.

While these changes were taking place in Washington, Bill Brennan labored in the obscurity of Newark. For what seemed like his entire career at the firm, Brennan had worked on a complicated and cumbersome tax assessment matter for Duke Power Company. The Somerset County tax board had assessed Duke $17 million in personal property taxes. Brennan's defense was to contend that the municipality lacked jurisdiction and had failed to specifically state in its complaint what the property was. It was typical of the mundane legal practice into which he had fallen. Although doing well financially, Brennan seemed mired in a life that was far from the expectations of his high school friends and teachers. In 1937, Brennan accompanied his friend Kipp to the World Series between the Giants and the Yankees at the Polo Grounds. Brennan told him that he felt trapped by financial necessity.

In addition to caring for his extended family, Brennan now had two sons of his own. Ironically, while it seemed that the one thing Brennan had going for him was financial security, that was not his own perception. The nervous thing about private practice was not knowing where the next client was going to come from. Brennan frequently fretted to Kipp: "What if one day no one walks in the door?" It was every young lawyer's worry.

Even as far back as 1937, Kipp suspected Brennan might one day be more comfortable doing something where the work would be on his desk each morning, something, he suspected, like being a judge. But for the moment, it appeared Brennan's destiny was as a corporate man— even if it was hardly the combative law practice envisioned by Bill senior when he had first pushed law school on his eldest boy.

COLONEL BRENNAN
AND THE WAR

In THE SUMMER OF 1942, DESPITE
the war, Bill Brennan was enjoying all the creature comforts that his
ten profitable years in private practice could provide. Sitting on the
porch of his rented Cape Cod summer home, he watched a ferry approaching from a distance.

The moment of calm was broken by the ring of the telephone. Major General Levin Campbell of the Army Ordnance Department was
on the line. He was curt. Would Mr. Brennan come to Washington the
following day to discuss the possibility of joining the ordnance department as a legal aide? With two younger brothers, Frank and Charles,
already in uniform, Brennan was in no position to decline an invitation to help his country. Nor could he risk offending one of his favorite
clients, the wealthy, powerful president of Johnson & Johnson, Robert
Wood Johnson.

Johnson, twelve years Brennan's senior, was the son of the founder
of Johnson & Johnson. He had been born in New Brunswick, New Jersey, where at the time Johnson & Johnson maintained its headquarters. His father, also named Robert Wood Johnson, had been a New
England druggist. It was the elder Johnson who invented adhesive tape

and created Johnson & Johnson in 1896 with his brother, E. Mead Johnson. The young Robert Wood Johnson attended Lawrenceville School and Rutgers Prep, but when the time came, he refused to enter college, opting instead to go to work for the family business. At the age of twenty-five he became a vice president of the company as well as mayor of Highland Park, New Jersey.

By 1938, he was chairman of the Johnson & Johnson board of directors. When Johnson assumed his position of leadership, Johnson & Johnson was not the billion-dollar company with ninety factories it was destined to become. Johnson & Johnson of the 1930s rarely exported products overseas and annual sales were only $11 million. Under the guidance of Robert Wood Johnson, his family firm's product line grew to include pharmaceuticals, hygiene products, and textiles. He was rare among industrialists of the period as an advocate of worker benefits. A Republican, Johnson paid more than minimum wage and pioneered employee programs in job training. "To ignore the conditions of the many underpaid people in the United States is as foolish as it would be to ignore public health, crime and the need for education," Johnson said in a speech at Catholic University. To structure his innovative programs, Johnson often turned to Bill Brennan for legal advice.

A fierce self-proclaimed patriot, Johnson was one of a number of high-paid industrialists who volunteered after Pearl Harbor to help the war effort. He was commissioned a colonel in the army's $36 billion Ordnance Division. On May 4, 1942, Johnson was assigned to a small desk with five other officers and six stenographers "in a room that measured about twenty by twenty with loops of telephone and light wires dangling in spiral festoons from the ceiling." From this place, Johnson observed, "We undertook to spend some $36 billion for army ordnance. We placed orders wherever there was most likelihood of immediate and substantial deliveries and we sought justification in the old army motto: 'You never get court-martialed for ordering too much.' "

After just two months on the job, Johnson had called General Campbell and recruited his favorite attorney to pitch in. Thus, in July 1942, at the age of thirty-six, Brennan was commissioned a major in the army. "I hadn't thought particularly about going into the army, but the first thing I knew, I was in uniform," Brennan later recalled.

His Pentagon interview was brief. Brennan, who confessed that he couldn't even spell "ordnance," was met by an impressive array of army brass. The military's problem was simple. They needed someone familiar with labor problems to deal with the complexities of wartime industry. Brennan took the job, stopping after the interview at an army and navy store and asking the clerk to provide him with the uniforms and bars appropriate for his rank. He didn't need the major's uniform very long. Within a year, Brennan had been promoted to lieutenant colonel and made chief of the Labor Resources Section, Office of the Chief of Ordnance.

Johnson chafed under the bureaucracy of the army and by January had moved out of Washington to New York. Brennan began working more closely with Under Secretary of the War Robert Patterson, the head of army procurement, and a man with whom Brennan felt an immediate kinship. Patterson's paternal grandfather had come from County Sligo, Ireland. After receiving his law degree from Harvard, Patterson, a native of Glen Falls, New York, had taken a high salaried corporate position at Wall Street's Root Clark Buckner & Howland. Like Brennan, Patterson did not appraise himself as a scholar. Once offered the job as Harvard Law School dean, Patterson turned it down, saying the position called for "a genuine scholar."

After World War I, in which he won the Distinguished Service Cross, the Silver Star, and the Purple Heart, Patterson formed his own law firm, Webb Patterson & Hadley. In 1930, he left his law partners to accept an appointment from President Hoover as a U.S. district judge, the federal equivalent of a trial judge. Nine years later, President Roosevelt named Patterson to the Second Circuit Court of Appeals.

Even before World War II broke out, Patterson had enrolled in a reserve officer's "refresher's course" in Plattsburgh, New York. There, while on KP duty, he received the telegram from FDR requesting his service as assistant secretary of war. "They could get a better man," Patterson said after reading the telegram. "But if they want me, I'll accept."

Patterson adopted Brennan as his primary aide-de-camp. Along with General Motors president Lieutenant General Bill Knudson, Patterson and Brennan feverishly tackled the problems of the warplane industry. In late 1943 they staged a monumental rally at the Los Angeles Coliseum to instill pride and patriotism in the weapons-production industry. From there, Brennan and Patterson shot up and down the West

Coast from Seattle to San Diego, speaking day and night and arranging such employee conveniences as staggered shifts to ease transport jams, night banking hours, and better lights and working conditions.

Brennan threw himself into the work with his usual inexhaustible supply of energy. For one who craved order, he found the work extremely hectic. He was also nervous about all the flying. "Patterson would go up whenever the need came and he'd fly in all kinds of weather. Sometimes I prayed hard when it was touch and go, whether we'd get up and down," Brennan recalled. (Patterson was killed in a plane crash after the war.)

In 1943, Brennan's work with Patterson earned him a position as chief of the Southern California special management project team. Then he was made chief of the civilian personnel division of the Ordnance Department. Brennan was about to be named head of personnel for the Pacific region but scotched the offer. It would have meant moving permanently to the West Coast, away from his family. On July 12, 1944, Brennan was instead named chief of the army's Industrial Personnel Division, Labor Branch, a job that kept him at the Pentagon for the last few months of his duty.

Brennan found himself in the thick of decisions not only involving civilian labor but in determining the order of troops being brought home from Europe or being redetailed from the European to the Pacific theaters. One of Brennan's most controversial decisions involved requests that front-line soldiers of certain occupations be given priority in being shipped back to the United States. It was Brennan's determination that any such favoritism would wreck military morale. He insisted that all soldiers be treated alike.

On July 27, 1945, the special war committee of the U.S. Senate called Brennan to testify and demanded an explanation for his stubbornness. The concern of the senators was the seemingly slow pace of moving men and matériel from the Atlantic theater to the Pacific. As equipment and supplies began to roll west, the railroads had begun to complain that many of their best railroadmen were still stuck in Europe. Hugh Mitchell, a Democratic senator from Washington State, complained that four million tons of coal were stuck on the rails, with no railroadmen to move them. He was one of many western congressmen who urged that soldiers be furloughed and shifted to civilian employment to ease the railroad logjam. Four thousand troops had been authorized for release, but Brennan, as the officer in charge of man-power, had refused to issue any furloughs based on occupational pref-erence. He had inherited his father's legendary stubbornness.

The Senate committee demanded to know of Brennan why the army had failed to supply no more than 2,500 soldiers to the railroads, even though 4,000 had been authorized. Senator James Mead of New York began the inquiry with a pointed question. "On June nineteenth, the War Manpower-Labor Policy Committee concurred in a recom-mendation that the 719th Transportation Battalion, now located in Italy, and composed primarily of railroadmen intended to handle the railroads during the war in Europe, be released immediately."

Looking sternly at Brennan, he bellowed:

"Why was this not done?"

"I can't answer in terms of that particular unit," Brennan replied: "We still have the Japanese war to fight."

Brennan reminded the committee that after the last war, GIs had complained because some received discharges to work in factories while others were stuck on the battlefield.

"You may recall," Brennan said. "We had them in ammunition plants, rubber plants, and cotton duck plants. And the GIs who were still fighting in the foxholes of Europe made a very real issue of the fact that some of their buddies, no better qualified than they, were per-mitted the soft spots in industrial employment, while they had to con-tinue fighting in Europe."

"Couldn't we confine it to those not in the foxholes?" Mead asked.

"The point I am trying to make," Brennan said, "is that the guys who still have the war to fight in the Pacific are the fellows to whom that is not fair, and who will resent any deviation from the system of dis-charge." Every time you make an exception for one soldier, Brennan said, "there is somebody else whose discharge is delayed or perhaps doesn't come out for a long time. . . . Let me try to answer it this way," Brennan said. "We cannot explain to the soldier why this kind of prob-lem cannot be solved with civilian labor."

By the following September, Brennan was released from his Penta-gon duties. But his explaining before the Mead Committee was far from over. In July 1946, Brennan was subpoenaed to come back to Washington to defend himself and Patterson against charges that the War Department had given in to influence and conspired with a Kentucky congressman named Andrew May, the chairman of the House Armed Services Committee, to give army contracts to nonexistent companies.

One of the chief villains of the scandal was Henry Garsson, a Chicago businessman whose web of companies included Batavia Metal Works, a major manufacturer of much-needed eight-inch artillery shells. Garsson had paid bribes to important political figures in exchange for government contracts. Many of the companies that won contracts were merely paper entities, without employees, a plant, or even incorporation at the time the contract was offered. In addition, Garsson repeatedly received special permissions from the War Department to increase production at his plants.

Although the congressman denied it to his death, investigators established that May had received $48,000 in cash payments from various contractors. In exchange for the cash many of these war profiteers had received special favors from May. The specter of a congressman conspiring with war profiteers was made worse by the disturbing implication that May was actually successful in his pressure tactics. In other words, Secretary of War Patterson, who could have stopped May, apparently played along with him, in detriment to the national interest. As *The Washington Post* wrote on July 7, 1946: "His [May's] interference, it is plain, was considered an adequate excuse for according special favors to the Garsson companies. . . . This facile yielding to Congressman May's appeals should be thoroughly probed. For if Mr. May had been dealing with government officials impervious to the voice of influence, he certainly could have done very little for his contractor friends."

Brennan's liability in the scandal was more than just theoretical. Brennan was the *Post's* mystery bureaucrat, unwittingly responding to Garsson's pressure. He had been dragged into the middle of the scandal by Patterson, who himself was aware that Congressman May's interest in Garsson was not routine.

In October 1944, five months after D day, Patterson had received an urgent cable from General Eisenhower complaining about a shortage of artillery ammunition. "If there is anything you can possibly do to step up shipments over the next ninety days, it will have a definite effect upon the campaign," Eisenhower said.

A day later, Ike sent another urgent cable to the Pentagon. "I must urge that every expedient be applied to step up production. Tactical plans for the immediate future are now awaiting assurance of an adequate and continuous flow of ammunition. I cannot overemphasize the inescapable effect upon future operations of an adequate ammunition supply."

Patterson discussed the problem with Secretary of War Henry Stimson. "Go out and visit all the plants and present to them the urgency of this program and dramatize it all you can," Stimson advised.

Patterson grabbed Brennan and together they went to Buffalo, western Pennsylvania, West Virginia, and finally to Chicago to pay a visit to Garsson's Batavia Metal Works. Patterson and Brennan were shown around the plant by Garsson, who complained to Brennan that anti-Semitism was affecting the award of manpower ceilings by the army. He currently had authority to employ only seven hundred civilians. If he could have a thousand-employee ceiling, Garsson claimed, he could produce the eight-inch shells Eisenhower needed.

On the way out of the plant, John Slezak, the locally based chief of ordnance in Chicago, told Patterson that the problem was not anti-Semitism but rather that Garsson had in the past been found to be pirating employees from other war-contract plants, without getting clearance from the War Manpower Commission.

Patterson responded by telling Slezak to forget about problems and to get on the with the business of shell production. There was a war to be won. He ordered that Garsson's requests be fulfilled. The only problem was that Garsson didn't use the additional men to speed up his artillery shell production. He had received a new contract to manufacture a much less needed M74 bomb, and shifted the new workers to the lower-priority project.

Patterson was determined to get the shells to Eisenhower no matter what. It fell on Brennan to be the middleman. He then met with Colonel F. R. Denton and told him that Garsson was alleging anti-Jewish discrimination on the part of the War Manpower Commission. Although uncomfortable with the order, Brennan urged that Garsson's ceiling be raised. Denton and Slezak replied that the Chicago committee overseeing War Manpower in the region would resign if Garsson's ceiling were increased. Brennan then talked to army officials in Washington and requested that a directive be put out by War Manpower Commission headquarters raising Garsson's ceiling.

This was done on November 14, 1944. Slezak and the Chicago-region people then complied.

But Patterson was not done leaning on Brennan.

On February 28, 1945, Patterson wrote Brennan again telling him: "He [Garsson] states that he now has 900 people in his plant. He needs 75 more at once. Mr. Garsson also states that production will be reduced 25 percent in March if the ceiling of 739 stands. The proper ceiling, in his opinion, is 1,000 to fully man and to take care of absenteeism."

Continued Patterson: "The eight-inch shell program, as you know, is of the most critical importance. It seems silly to me for the War Manpower Commission to split hairs in a case of this kind, where a plant is devoted wholly to urgent war programs and where the production output is excellent."

Patterson told Brennan to cut through the red tape and offered himself as "available for any assistance that may be needed." Brennan was a good soldier and followed Patterson's orders. But from recorded telephone conversations, it was clear that he wasn't happy about what he was asked to do.

On March 5, 1945, in a taped telephone conversation with Slezak, Brennan documented his frustration with the process. "You know that man Garsson. He makes me so angry sometimes. He called over our head . . . he's got Patterson all exercised and got us in the position that we are now. We must accomplish that ceiling of a thousand and we are supposed to accomplish it by this week."

"Patterson put the rest of us in the soup," Slezak responded.

The taped phone conversation made it clear that Brennan had been following Patterson's orders. And when the Garsson hearings ended, Mead was more charitable than at Brennan's earlier appearance. "The afternoon session," said Mead, "has brought forcibly to my mind the evil effects of meddling in the proper routine of army procedure. I can see where you were suffering from a mental hazard as a result of unnecessary interference.

"The higher and more powerful the meddler may happen to be, the more widespread is the chaos and confusion. I think you should be commended for standing up to the pressure and serving as well as you did," the senator concluded.

The war-production scandal was not completely closed for Brennan. Ironically it was not so much that he had responded to pressure for

Patterson but rather the revelation that Brennan was taping his phone calls. For a man who would later play an important role in condemning President Nixon for taping conversations, Brennan, then thirty-nine, was considerably more cavalier about recordings when he was the one with the wire.

Reports in *The Washington Post* about Brennan's taping habits had received comment from politicians as exalted as the Speaker of the House. Texas congressman Sam Rayburn voiced great displeasure at the transcriptions and he was joined by Republican House leader Joe Martin, who called Brennan's habit, "a mean practice."

Brennan insisted it was not wiretapping but transcription, a routine method of speeding work by having calls on record. "I know that when I arrived at the War Department in January of 1942, there was made available to me a recording device. I used it for a short time.

"It had a button on the telephone for that purpose. Some of them had little levers. I know that every phone made available to me was wired. I used it only for a short time personally."

"Would you call it wiretapping?" asked the committee's counsel.

"No, it was just recording a telephone conversation served many useful purposes."

"What are those purposes?"

"Depending on how busy we were—it was helpful to have a record of a telephone conversation as a memorandum to remind one of things to be done," Brennan replied.

It was clear that a right to privacy, which Brennan would later make a basic part of his constitutional jurisprudence, hadn't yet occurred to him.

RETURNING TO
PRIVATE PRACTICE

W O R L D   W A R   I I   H A D   G I V E N   B R E N N A N
much to think about. His dearest brother Charles, with whom as a
child he had arisen early in the morning to milk cows and deliver milk,
had been killed in the landing at Leyte Gulf with the army's Seventy-
seventh Division. His younger brother Frank was shot down and bailed
out over Germany in December 1944 and was soon to return home as
an ex-prisoner of war. In September 1945, Brennan left his Pentagon
office, put on a business suit, and, with Marjorie in hand, boarded a
train crowded with servicemen to his home at 2 Brookwood Lane in
South Orange.

Visitors to Brennan's Pentagon office in early 1945 recall his enthusiasm about returning to private practice. He was especially excited
about what were called the "portal-to-portal" cases, a string of suits by
unions and workers organizations demanding that hourly minimum-
wage rates kick in the moment an employee walked into a factory, not
from the time they sat down at their machine.

But no sooner had Brennan returned to his downtown Newark office than he was rattled by another death. Pitney Hardin's senior attorney, John Ralph Hardin, collapsed and died at his desk on December 7,

1945. Hardin had been the firm's rainmaker, the key partner who goes out and gets the business on which all the other lawyers work.

Little more than a month after Hardin's death, Shelton Pitney dropped dead of a heart attack at home. Of all the senior partners, he was the one who had worked closest to Brennan. The death of the two men who had built the firm's modern-day reputation might well have ended the venerable partnership right then and there. A bow-tied Bill Brennan and Donald Kipp called a meeting of the partners and pledged to go forward. Brennan had become more than Pitney Hardin's token non-Princetonian and first Catholic. In its most trying hour, he had become not only its chief rainmaker but also its leader.

Just as his arrival as a seasoned lawyer in the mid-1930s had coincided with the activity generated by the Wagner Act; he was now returning at a time when labor unrest would reach an all-time high. For the four years of the war, workers and unions had promised not to strike. In exchange they had agreed to the "little steel formula," which set pay raises at not more than 15 percent of the level on January 1, 1941. In addition, Executive Order 9017, enacted in 1942, required compulsory arbitration of any labor agreements.

Brennan's labor law expertise, sharpened by his experience in the military, was once again the most needed legal speciality in the land. Hardly had Brennan settled back in his office than the phone began ringing with queries from corporate clients full of labor troubles. One of the big questions was whether workers could be fired to make room for returning servicemen. Another major problem was wages. Now, with the war over, the unions wanted a reward for their compensation sacrifices. New Jersey industries had made a fortune during the war. Companies like Johnson & Johnson had supplied virtually all of the bandages for the entire war effort. General Electric and Westinghouse had made the engines that drove the war. Much of the war production had been right in Newark's backyard.

One by one, corporations like Western Electric, Phelps-Dodge, American Hair & Felt, Celanese, Jersey Bell, and the Association of General Contractors of New Jersey came calling to welcome Brennan back and to pay hefty retainers for him to help them with their labor troubles. Many of the companies, such as American Insurance Corporation, asked Brennan to replace Hardin on their board of directors.

Labor had never been the main part of Pitney Hardin's corporate practice, it had always been a sideline. Brennan was the first partner to really develop the specialty. But it became such a profitable sideline that the other partners wanted to send a message to the industrial community that when you hired Pitney Hardin, you were getting a top partner in the firm. So, to advertise Brennan's labor practice more widely, the name of the firm, which once would never even hire a Catholic, was changed to Pitney, Hardin, Ward & Brennan.

By January of 1946, while many servicemen still waited in Europe for orders to come home, at least seventy-eight major plants were shut down by strikes. The steel industry was in chaos. In Newark, on January 2 and then again on the third, five thousand striking workers from Westinghouse, Phelps-Dodge, Western Electric, and General Electric jammed a rally on Broad Street's town green as labor leaders called for pay raises promised when the war was over.

The following day, at Western Electric's mammoth Kearny plant, where most of the nation's telephones were manufactured, twelve thousand members of the Western Electric Employees Association walked out on strike. At 11 A.M., groups of thirty to forty pickets had gathered at each entrance to the plant. As supervisors and management personnel approached the entrance at gate two, they were subjected to taunts and threats. The picketers refused to let them through. Police officers stood by and did nothing.

On the next day, the violence at the Kearny plant intensified. A crowd of a hundred supervisors appeared at gate two demanding that the police allow them through. A general melee broke out as the picketers attacked the management people with fists and signs. Eighteen were hospitalized.

In the face of this brutal union power, it was Brennan whom Western Electric chose to map out a strategy for containment of the picketers and to find a way to let the supervisors into the plant. Brennan rejected company officials' suggestions that an injunction be obtained halting the picketing completely. In a tense session, Brennan used his understanding of the laborer's mind to convince the business leaders that such a plan would be self-defeating and only lead to more violence. Instead he drew up papers asking the court merely to restrain the picketing. "How about no more than ten pickets at the two entrance gates, and five pickets at the other seven gates?" Brennan asked. Western Electric agreed. In addition, Brennan drew into his documents the requirement that the picketers remain at least ten feet apart.

While the violence and confusion reigned at the Kearny plant, Brennan strode confidently into Newark's Chancery Court for what would be a three-day hearing on the motion. Union lawyer Maurice Brigadier denounced Brennan's plan as antilabor. Unions, he said, had a right to picket with as many members as they desired. The violence, he added, had been initiated and provoked by the supervisors.

As always in his private law career, Brennan was the lawyer's lawyer, even in the midst of strike chaos. He was matter of fact in his presentation and always courteous to the union men and their attorneys. In a calm delivery, Brennan reminded the court that he understood picketing and he understood its point. When a union sets up pickets, Brennan said, it is attempting, first and foremost, to garner publicity for its cause. When a union builds a solid line in front of individuals wanting to do business at the plant, Brennan said, it is totally defeating the purpose of the picketing in the first place.

Tom Dunn, later to become the mayor of Elizabeth, was a union representative with the Western Electric Employees Association. During one moment in the hearings, Dunn, who knew the reputation of William Brennan, Sr., stopped to study Brennan. From the striped suit and briefcase, he seemed just another company lawyer, another arch-conservative, as Dunn like to put it. "Our lawyers looked like Bohemians," Dunn recalled. "They looked like the typical revolutionary union leaders. So you had to be impressed with Brennan. Here was the son of a labor leader who looked like one of the blue bloods from Essex County. He had the look of a guy who was really on his way up the ladder."

But at the same time, Dunn felt Brennan was just a little different. That feeling was born out when Brennan unexpectedly approached Dunn in court. Dunn, who had experienced a family tragedy the previous day, wondered what Western Electric's lawyer could possibly have to say to him.

"I just want you to know," Brennan said, "I've asked the judge to postpone our case. I just found out your father has passed away. We'll have the hearing another day."

Dunn was touched at the gesture and the genuine compassion. Brennan, he realized, was personally a gentle man. But professionally Brennan remained an unrelenting legal foe.

Recalled one lawyer who saw Brennan on many occasions: "He never lost his cool, he was never abrasive. But he was extremely competitive and he never forgot that he was there to win for his corporate clientele."

By February 11, 1946, Brennan had won his restrictions on the pickets. The court ruled that large numbers of pickets, "grouped together in a solid mass," presented an intimidating force in and of itself. That sort of picketing, said the judge, "is coercion; it readily leads to violence." The decision halting the mass picketing broke the back of the Western Electric strike. Following Brennan's victory, police were able to lead the supervisor's into the plant. Within four weeks the Kearny strike had ended.

That single victory made Brennan the most famous strikebreaking lawyer in New Jersey. Union officials charged that Brennan had engaged in "steamroller tactics" to break the strike. Said one union leader, "At no time has Western Electric made any peaceful attempt to settle or compromise." The company's only antistrike weapon had been Brennan.

When the strike finally ended on March 12, 1946, Brennan refused to drop contempt proceedings against the unions that had been brought before the settlement. "A contempt action does not automatically stop with a strike settlement," Brennan noted. When one of Brennan's associate's asked him point-blank how he could stomach such actions, which at the least seemed gratuitous, Brennan gave a evasive answer. "I can't let my personal sentiments interfere," he said in his Jersey brogue. "While I'm at this firm, I have a job to do." Ultimately the New Jersey court disagreed and dismissed the action as moot.

The answer reflected the conflict that Brennan felt within himself. Yet he continued to resolve it in favor of his job. He was first and foremost a lawyer. His job was to represent his clients and to provide a living for his family.

By mid-April of 1946, the worst of the labor unrest in Newark had subsided, but serious problems remained. Brennan had spent much of the month working on the aftermath of the Western Electric strike. The work stoppage had left deep scars in the community, and Brennan had exacerbated them by insisting that the prosecution of picketers continue. Personally, Brennan was not comfortable with the

notoriety. He took advantage of civic clubs addresses to explain his actions, although he did not back down in his criticism of the unions. In
one speech, at the Essex County Bar Association, Brennan acknowledged, "I do not believe all strikes are bad." The alternative, he said,
was coerced settlements that would be destructive of labor and management.

But Brennan argued that the almost free license to organize, strike,
and picket, granted by the "radical" Wagner Act in 1935, had to be
curtailed. Unions that were guilty of violence, Brennan said, should
not have the right to organize and strike. The failure of the Wagner
Act, he said, was that it had given unions many rights, but "nowhere
mentions union or worker responsibilities. . . . I ask labor, must it not
admit in 1946, that the legislative scales heavily weighted in its favor
ten years ago now need some adjustments? Won't labor see the reflection of public impatience with the present epidemic of strikes, but
more fundamentally with labor's insistence that everything is right
with the world and that any suggestion of the need for correction is
evidence of a labor-hating mentality?"

Brennan, who called himself a Democrat, increasingly took the Republican, probusiness stand on the passage of the Taft-Hartley Act, the
1947 measure that severely restricted the power of unions to organize.
Although Taft-Hartley was fiercely opposed by labor, Brennan termed
it "Labor's Bill of Rights." Brennan specifically endorsed the outlawing
of closed shops, which compelled many workers to join unions. Brennan told a Rotary Club, "The position of the individual worker is improved in that he can make his own decisions." He claimed to support
the right of the worker to be free of corrupt union domination.

Brennan also stressed the need and hope that trade unions would
purge themselves of Communists. In an address to the Newark College of Engineering, Brennan declared, "We can take great comfort in
the fact that American trade unions are unalterably the bitter enemies
of the Russian virus. I do not mean that that there are not Communists in the movement and that there will not have to be a ceaseless
vigilance to contain them. But Russia knows that its battle to commu-
nize America will be won or lost within our trade union movement,
and our unions, as they mature, are making it clear they will be barren
soil."

If labor wasn't the issue, Brennan worried excessively about such things as congestion in the courts and the reputation of the bar. He was active in professional committees to reform the courts and to improve the ethics of attorneys. He was at the pinnacle of success in the private bar. Although Pitney Hardin attorneys never talked about money, it was rumored that his yearly draw exceeded $50,000, among the highest at the firm. To be sure, Brennan was making more and more money. There was hardly a soul in the firm who imagined that Brennan would ever leave. Only his closest friend, Donald Kipp, sensed a worry that underlay his colleague's outer calm. To his associates and secretaries, Brennan seemed a man without a financial care in the world. One of his best-known idiosyncrasies was his inability to gossip. Brennan rarely talked about family matters and even more rarely socialized with his coworkers and partners. Only to Kipp did Brennan confide his innermost fears. "I'm a child of the depression," he told Kipp over a scotch one night after work. He persisted in fretting that one day the business would dry up. "Not a day goes by that I don't think about it."

But the business did keep coming in the door. There was no disputing the fact that the son of Newark's most famous labor partisan had become one of corporate America's most reliable counsels.

HIS TOUGHEST CHOICE

Brennan was on his way back to his 744 Broad Street offices from the chancery court, when *The Newark Evening News* of April 22, 1946, brought the unexpected front-page news that Chief Justice Harlan Fiske Stone had been stricken with illness while presiding over the Supreme Court. When he arrived on the twenty-first floor, it was the talk of the office.

Even though it was initially thought to be just indigestion, Stone's sudden discomfort was cause for news bulletins on the radio and banner headlines in *The Newark Evening News*. His departure from the Court could have major ramifications, especially in New Jersey. Arthur Vanderbilt had risen to the top of the list of potential Court nominees. Beyond that, Stone had become one of the nation's best-known and loved justices.

Born on a farm near Chesterfield, New Hampshire, in 1872, Stone originally intended to succeed his parents as a farmer. After high school he enrolled at Massachusetts Agricultural College to study scientific farming. Then Stone got in a fight with a teacher, a brawl that ended with his expulsion. So Stone moved across town to Amherst College and decided to study medicine. At Amherst, Stone was a star football player, Phi Beta Kappa, and elected by his classmates as most likely to succeed. Instead of practicing medicine, however, Stone decided to become a teacher and he moved to Newportbury, Massachusetts, to teach high school chemistry and physics. He then transferred to Columbia University Law School and after graduation remained there to teach.

In 1910 Stone became dean and a professor at the law school. His curriculum emphasized what he called "functional law." Unlike the system at Harvard, where students almost exclusively studied past cases, Stone and Columbia's approach featured an understanding of how corporations worked and what economic factors affected decisions. Thus Columbia lawyers, much more than Harvard graduates, were ready to face the real world of big-time corporate law. One of his students, a red-haired kid from Yakima, Washington, named William O. Douglas, called him, "the greatest teacher I ever knew."

In 1923, Stone left Columbia to accept a partnership at New York's establishment firm of Sullivan & Cromwell. So when Stone was appointed by President Coolidge to the Supreme Court on February 5, 1925, he was viewed as a probusiness conservative with close ties to Wall Street mogul J. P. Morgan.

But on the court, Stone underwent one of the most radical philosophical transformations in Court history. If scholars would later argue that Brennan had "changed" after he got on the Court, Stone's case foreshadowed Brennan's in what would be some remarkably similar ways. In the New Englander's case, it was mostly a matter of personalities. Justices Oliver Wendell Holmes, who would remain on the court until 1932, and Louis Brandeis, who had joined the Court in 1916, took Stone under their wings. Their opponent, the manipulative Chief Justice Taft, trying desperately to keep the Court on a conservative path, simply could not control Stone's growing hatred of Justice James Clark McReynolds, the reigning conservative on the Court.

McReynolds had been born in Kentucky in 1862 to a fundamentalist family that glorified the Confederacy, opposed the creation of public schools, and strictly forbade drinking, smoking, and even sports. McReynolds was valedictorian of his class at Vanderbilt University in 1882. He then went to law school at the University of Virginia, where he reveled in the law and Constitution as permanent and unchanging.

He returned to Tennessee to practice law and teach at Vanderbilt. His interest in politics was fed by his involvement in reform campaigns aimed at eliminating gambling, prostitution, and pornography. In 1903, through the intervention of a Republican Nashville lawyer, McReynolds was appointed assistant attorney general in the Roosevelt administration. McReynolds was put in charge of pursuing, through antitrust actions, James Buchanan Duke's American Tobacco Company. When he resigned in 1909, McReynolds was asked how a political conservative could justify the attack on Duke's property. McReynolds replied by calling Duke's company "commercial wolves and highwaymen." And he asked, "Since when has property illegally and criminally acquired come to have any rights?"

For all his political rigidity, when it came to politics, McReynolds displayed the traits of a chameleon. When the Democrats came back to power in 1912, McReynolds had backed the winning horse, campaigning among his right-wing brethren for Woodrow Wilson. The new president rewarded McReynolds by naming him attorney general. Once in office, however, McReynolds quickly began to offend congressmen, fellow cabinet members, and most anyone else who crossed his path. Wilson gracefully removed McReynolds from the cabinet by appointing him to the Supreme Court in 1914.

When Stone arrived on the Court in 1925, he couldn't decide what to hate about McReynolds the most. The man was an anti-Semite who refused even to talk to Justice Brandeis. When the rare female attorney appeared before the Court, McReynolds would invariably snarl, "The woman is here again." He hated blacks and distrusted men who wore wristwatches, feeling the bracelet made it a sign of homosexuality.

Stone and McReynolds could barely restrain their contempt for each other. When Stone once commented on the dullness of a particular brief, McReynolds replied: "The only duller thing I can think of is when you read one of your opinions." McReynolds became one of America's hardiest judges, continuing on the Court until 1941. He ultimately outlived Stone by four months and two days.

When McReynolds finally died of bronchial pneumonia in Washington on August 24, 1946, at the age of eighty-four, it was learned that this bitter man had bequeathed over $100,000 to the Children's Hospital of Washington. It was further revealed that after World War II, he had financially adopted thirty-three European children, orphaned in the Nazi invasion of France. McReynolds had been afraid if news of his activities had gotten out while he was alive, it would have ruined his reputation.

But McReynolds wasn't the only person driving Stone away from his innate conservatism. Despite Taft's support of Stone's nomination, the Phi Beta Kappa graduate of Amherst came to see the former president from Ohio as an intellectual lightweight. So while McReynolds and Taft attempted to maintain the Court's long-held view that cases should be decided as narrowly as possible, Stone came to the view of Brandeis that the Court could be an important instrument of social change.

In 1936, when Stone supported President Roosevelt in ruling the Agricultural Adjustment Act as unconstitutional, he was considered to be solidly in the Court's liberal bloc. Four years later his standing as a civil libertarian was boosted when he alone among Court members claimed that schoolchildren had a right not to salute the flag.

On June 12, 1941, Roosevelt named the Republican Stone as chief justice to replace Hughes. In 1945, on Stone's twentieth anniversary as justice, *The Washington Post* editorialized, "He has never sought to govern his fellow justices, but he has brought to their deliberations an atmosphere of tolerance and friendliness which has served to temper the vigor of their intellectual differences."

For six years Stone had presided as chief, but on April 22, at the age of seventy-three, he was stricken while reading an opinion from the bench. One moment Stone had been holding his paper in reading position, the next he began fumbling through the pages and muttering. Hugo Black reached for the gavel and banged the session closed. Justice Black and Stanley Reed grabbed Stone by the arms and carried him behind the curtain to a washroom, where he remained for some time incoherently mumbling legal talk. A Court doctor examined Stone and concluded it was "indigestion." He ordered that an ambulance take the chief to his home. There, at 6:45 P.M., a massive cerebral hemorrhage took his life.

The speculation that Stone's death set off seemed to be a million miles away from Newark. Had Thomas Dewey been elected president in 1944, there was little doubt who the choice as chief justice would be. Dewey was committed to naming his longtime friend from Newark,

Arthur T. Vanderbilt, to the Court. The former president of the American Bar Association and dean of New York University Law School, Vanderbilt had worked actively in the Dewey campaign. His regard as a jurist had risen so high that Vanderbilt haughtily scoffed at the possibility of being offered anything as low as an associate judgeship.

But Dewey was not president. From Vanderbilt's perspective the timing of Stone's death couldn't have been worse. If Stone had just held on for two more years, Vanderbilt would have had his judgeship. Indeed Stone's plan had been to resign after the expected victory in 1948. For while Dewey had lost to Roosevelt in 1944, there was little doubt that Republicans would take the White House in 1948. But Roosevelt died in office and changed all that.

Now the choice was all Truman's. It was widely assumed that his pick would be sitting justice Robert Jackson. Truman had already shown his partiality to Jackson by naming him chief prosecutor at the Nuremburg trials. Indeed, at the moment Stone died, Jackson was in Germany and very much in the headlines.

Jackson, who thirsted after the position, knew instinctively that his being in Germany wasn't going to help. His chief rival seemed to be another sitting justice, William O. Douglas. The youngest member of the court at forty-seven, Douglas had once been a student of Stone's at Columbia. But Jackson rejected the advice of friends who urged him to come back to Washington for the funeral. As Jackson later wrote one friend, "I've never gone seeking a job and I wasn't going to seek this."

When the choice came down on June 6, 1946, it was neither Jackson nor Douglas. Instead, Truman sidestepped the feud by selecting Frederick Moore Vinson, his secretary of the treasury. Although Vinson had served as a federal judge and an adviser to President Roosevelt, it was his personal friendship with Truman that was his outstanding qualification for appointment. To Truman's daughter, Margaret, Vinson was known as "Papa Vin." And each week Vinson played in Truman's weekly poker game. Truman had hoped to run with Vinson as his vice-presidential nominee in 1948 and thus set the Kentucky native up for the presidency itself in 1952. Vinson told Truman that he didn't want to be president. Taking over as chief justice at the age of fifty-six, Vinson figured to tie up the chief justice's post until the mid to late 1960s.

• • •

No one was more miserable than Jackson, except perhaps Vanderbilt, since the Vinson appointment meant he would never be chief justice. Vanderbilt's setback meant that he would be staying in New Jersey, where he would come to have a major impact on the development of Brennan's judicial career.

For many years, Vanderbilt had spearheaded an effort to bring court reform to the state of New Jersey; which was generally regarded to have the most antiquated and arcane state court system in the nation. He was rewriting the state constitution to set up a more traditional court system. In 1947, after many unsuccessful years of effort, Vanderbilt's court-reform package became a reality. And when it did, he would become the state's chief justice and be in a position to make recommendations about state court judges.

For Brennan, meanwhile, life had at least become financially sound. That was some consolation to the nagging guilt he had now felt for years about representing management against the unions. His self-rationalizations often took the construction that he was working for the betterment of workers, if not for the unions.

In 1946, Brennan joined seven other New Jersey lawyers to comprise the editorial board of the *New Jersey Law Journal*. The journal, then the semiofficial paper of the New Jersey bar, was foursquare behind Vanderbilt's reform efforts. Brennan was recruited to the editorial board panel by Nathan L. Jacobs, the top graduate of his Harvard Law class of 1929. Despite his highest ranking, Jacobs, because of his Judaism, was passed over as president of the *Harvard Law Review* in favor of a fellow classmate, Erwin Griswold. His religion also kept him from getting any top job offers with corporate firms.

In the fall of 1929, he came home to Newark to join Vanderbilt's law firm. In addition, he would teach for nineteen years at Rutgers University School of Law. Jacobs, much more so than Brennan, had become a major figure in the activities of the state bar. In 1938 he had written a treatise on the administration of law that he was able to put into practice as deputy commissioner of the New Jersey Alcoholic Beverage Control Board. Then during the war, while Brennan was in Washington, Jacobs stayed at home and took over the state branch of the Office of Price Administration.

In the years that followed these successes, no one, save Vanderbilt himself, devoted more effort to the plan for state constitutional revision. In 1941, Jacobs began service on a seven-member commission to revise the New Jersey court system. At the time the New Jersey courts were considered the worst in the country. As *The New York Times* had editorialized, "The courts come out of Dickens. There are Chancery courts as well as courts of law. The two systems overlap and interfere with each other. Jersey justice has a leaden heel. Its delays are notorious. Judges are numerous. There must be 20 different kinds of courts."

On January 21, 1947, after continuous prodding by the editorial board of the *New Jersey Law Journal*, Governor Alfred Driscoll called on the state legislature to submit the question of constitutional revision to a referendum. That was no coincidence. Driscoll and Jacobs were the closest of friends and had been classmates at Harvard Law. Furthermore, while Driscoll had served on the ABC Board, Jacobs had also been ABC commissioner.

After the referendum passed, Jacobs was asked to chair a special committee to implement the court system. It was continuously prodded by *New Jersey Law Journal* editorials, many of which became models for the structure the committee was forming. Brennan himself wrote one schematic on June 12, 1947, entitled "A Modern Court Structure for New Jersey."

Vanderbilt became the chief justice of this grand creation. To make sure that it all worked, Jacobs himself had decided to accept a lowly position as a state superior court judge. It would cost him considerably in salary; the new judgeships would only pay $20,000. As he was determined not to bear the sacrifice and the challenge alone, each of the seven members of the New Jersey law review panel were also asked to join him on the court. None was more unwilling than Bill Brennan.

The prospect was not particularly tantalizing. In private practice Brennan was the chief client-getter and earner in his firm. His income was now nearly $60,000 per year, a sum he considered astronomical for the time. He was, however, supporting a mother and several sisters who lived at home in addition to his own family of Marjorie and two sons, William III and Hugh, who had just turned fifteen and twelve. It was hardly a time to start thinking about that kind of salary cut.

Brennan resisted. It was too much to ask him to leave a position as top-name partner in New Jersey's wealthiest law firm to become merely a lowly state court judge. But Jacobs, who wanted Brennan at his side, browbeat him into accepting. Vanderbilt had expended tremendous political capital, indeed, his reputation, on the belief that he could start the best and most efficient court system in the country. This wasn't just any judgeship, Jacobs told Brennan. It was the chance to be a part of something important, to make the long-sought changes work—to make theirs the model for court improvement throughout the states.

In a meeting at Brennan's office, Jacobs revealed that Governor Driscoll had already offered the position to state senator Edward O'Mara. But O'Mara had absolutely refused. The news that he wasn't even the first choice made Brennan even more reluctant.

In a meeting with Jacobs at his office, Brennan said it wasn't just the money, it was his lack of experience in the trial courts. Brennan's practice had almost exclusively been in New Jersey's chancery court branch, where juries were rare. With all due respect, Brennan pointed out to Jacobs, he had far too much corporate experience to sit on the lowly trial courts. It was out of the question.

Jacobs left the meeting with Brennan and walked across the street to Vanderbilt's office. "Leave it to me," Vanderbilt said. That evening Donald Kipp was walking outside his office building when Vanderbilt's limo stopped and offered Kipp a ride to the railroad station. On the way, Vanderbilt told Kipp that he simply must persuade Brennan that it was all right to leave the firm and to become a judge. Kipp replied that Brennan just didn't feel that becoming a superior court judge was much of a career move. Vanderbilt understood. He told Kipp to tell Brennan that he would move him up to the appeals court and then the state supreme court just as quickly as he could. "If I last, he will be on the supreme court," Vanderbilt declared. Vanderbilt also pointed out to Kipp that the benefits to the firm of having a judge on the court, ultimately on the New Jersey Supreme Court, would outweigh the loss of the firm's biggest rainmaker. As Kipp left the car, Vanderbilt's final exhortation rang in his ears. "You've got to persuade Bill to take this appointment," he said.

The following morning, Kipp walked into Brennan's office and relayed Vanderbilt's promise. In his gray suit and always present bow tie, Brennan sucked thoughtfully on his pipe. "It might be worse for us if you don't go," Kipp said. "We wouldn't want to be on Vanderbilt's wrong side." With that combined threat and promise, Brennan relented, but only on a trial basis. He told Kipp to relay the message to Vanderbilt that he would accept. But if he didn't like it, or couldn't afford it, Kipp said, obviously Pitney Hardin would be more than happy to take him back.

Ironically it was not Brennan who initially got the credit for his giving up a lucrative private practice for public service. The congratulations were all going to Jacobs. Everywhere in Newark it was seen as a great coup for Jacobs that he had convinced a name partner in a firm to give so much up for the meager emolument and lowly prestige of a state court superior judge. No one knew that Jacobs had in fact failed in his mission and that it had been the intervention of Vanderbilt that had carried the day.

As one friend wrote years later: "It was surprising to outsiders when he turned to a judicial career in 1949. . . . While he had many friends in high places, he was never active in politics and his was a nonpolitical appointment."

There was, of course, no reason for his colleagues and associates to suspect that Brennan had any political agenda. Other than his speeches on Taft-Hartley, he had never done anything to indicate deeply held political feelings.

To his closest confidantes, Brennan had seemed overly obsessed with the little amount of money he would be making. The memory of his father's death, the realization that a family of nine had been left with nothing, lingered endlessly. If it weren't for the fact that Pitney Hardin would have taken him back on a moment's notice, he wouldn't have dared to take the chance. His life had been a cautious advance. The decision that he would go to Harvard over Columbia or New York University had been because Harvard was a more conservative school. His decision to choose a job at one of Newark's most establishment law firms had been with little risk. And once at the firm, he had taken few chances. While his brothers, Frank and Charles, had gone off to fight the war, Bill had settled for the safety of the Pentagon. He even felt the need to tape phone calls, just to be on the safe side. Philosophically, it was the same. Although a Democrat, Brennan was no flaming New Dealer. His role models more often than not seemed to be moderate Republicans, people like Robert Patterson, who had also made the transition from Irish immigrant to blueblood.

From his golf game to his poker nights, to his afternoons at the

Newark civic clubs, Brennan had become a pillar of the establishment. He even had managed to purchase a summer cottage in Buck Falls, Pennsylvania. He was very much the child of his mother. Even his choice of Marjorie, an Irish orphan devoted to family, was one that entailed little risk. She was much like Agnes, devoted to hearth and family. Her reading consisted mostly of detective novels, and she, too, had settled solidly into middle-class suburban life by taking up golf.

While his father would have been out all night with the boys, smoking his pipe and plotting political upheaval, Bill junior often worked quietly in his office until after dark. At home, he settled into his easy chair and quietly read a history or biography, or continued to work on a brief. In a sense, moving to the bench was a risk, but not a particularly large one. If he returned to the firm later, his service on the court might actually work to his advantage. At the least he would always be respectfully known as "Judge," just as Patterson had been despite only a few years on the bench.

By February 13, 1949, Brennan had made up his mind. He walked out of Pitney Hardin for the last time. And for the first time he was free to begin to become the kind of man his father had always envisioned he would be, if he wished.

A NEW JERSEY JUDGE

ARTHUR T. VANDERBILT HAD A special task in store for the man Jacobs had recommended to him so highly. Brennan's reputation was as a straight-arrow, a no-nonsense lawyer. And there was no more crooked or nonsensical court district in New Jersey than Hudson County, where the political machine of Mayor Frank Hague had ruled for decades. Vanderbilt had long looked on Hague and his entire Jersey City operation as a blight on the state. Under the old chancery court system in New Jersey, Hague had controlled the locally elected judges. Now, with good men being appointed by the governor, Hague had lost his control of the courts.

Vanderbilt's pledge had been to speed up the trial system, to make justice efficient. As American Bar Association president and later dean of New York University Law School, Vanderbilt had been able merely to expound upon his theories on the administration of justice. Now he was given the opportunity through the court reform bill of proving that they worked. With the exception of Jacobs, there was no more important judge in his stable than the diligent Brennan.

Hudson was the most litigious county in New Jersey, and Brennan set about working day and night to eliminate the backlog that clogged the county's court system. Colleagues thought Brennan had put in long hours while in private practice. Those unfamiliar with his work ethic whispered that he might have taken his new job to relieve the stress of his busy labor practice. Until 1947 being a judge in New Jersey had been a sleepy job. It was exactly that image of the judiciary, in by ten, out by five, that Brennan desired to erase.

His first year as superior court judge in Hudson County was extremely difficult. A fellow judge, Hayden Proctor, had to be called in from Camden County to assist. Brennan was hearing trials in the afternoon and then holding court sessions at night to assign trial dates. Proctor himself was awed that a lawyer of Brennan's stature and reputation worked so hard. But what most surprised Proctor was Brennan's age. Here was a man with a huge reputation in private law practice, the most productive partner at the state's toughest law firm, yet Brennan was just forty-three. Proctor was impressed by Brennan's youth and vigor. He could work late into the night, then attack several rounds of scotch, then attack a game of checkers at the Old Union House Pub. It was the classic University of Pennsylvania mentality— work hard, play hard.

Brennan's career as a state court judge passed meteorically. He took on the Hague machine in voter fraud cases, struck down bidding procedures that allowed favoritism to Hague's pals, and eliminated city policies allowing favoritism in the dispensing of bonuses to public employees. It could hardly be said that Brennan cleaned up Hudson County—it would take federal grand juries years of effort even to make a dent on the county's deeply engrained corruption—but by working days and nights, Brennan succeeded in getting control of the court dockets. Vanderbilt couldn't have been more pleased. He felt Brennan brought order to a situation that had been filled with chaos.

After just eighteen months on the superior court, Brennan was moved up to the New Jersey Court of Appeals, the second step on a three-rung ladder. There his cases tended to be more mundane, and Brennan found time to relax. A third child, Nancy, had been born in 1946. Every other Wednesday Brennan worked at home and took care of his daughter while Marjorie went to an afternoon movie.

His cases were rarely judicial landmarks. On November 27, 1950, in one of his first written opinions as an appellate-level judge, Brennan had to decide whether a butcher who strained his back lifting an eighty-pound hog was entitled to permanent disability benefits under New Jersey's workers' compensation laws. In *Dunofrio v. Haag Brothers*, Brennan found that he was.

In another case, *Palestroni v. Jacobs*, Brennan had to decide whether a trial judge in Bergen County had erred in allowing a juror to look up the definition of a term in the dictionary. In this case, Brennan ditched the dictionary. "The use by a jury of a dictionary has an obvious potential for harmful influence," Brennan concluded. "The danger is ever present it may be employed to ascertain meanings not just of one but of many words used in the court's charge or in papers in evidence. The juror's word alone that its use was limited is too weak a reed upon which to rest the difficult decision whether the verdict was subject to improper influence. Jurors should be required to advise the judge in open court of their doubt and desire for guidance and should be instructed by him in the presence of counsel if counsel care to attend."

The dictionary case illustrated how at an early stage in Brennan's judicial career he was willing to grant a defendant a new trial for what might be considered a fairly minor procedural point. "A new trial should be granted or refused," Brennan declared, "not so much to the attainment of exact justice in the particular case; as [rather] to the ultimate effect of the decision upon the administration of justice."

But his views could hardly be taken for granted, even when cases seemed to hit close to home. On March 19, 1951, Brennan heard a coal shoveler, George Wilford, argue that his long exposure to coal gas and dust had caused his lung problems. Wilford wanted workers' compensation to pay for his medical bills. One might have thought that the son of a coal shoveler would have been sympathetic to such a claim. Brennan was not. "Our careful examination of the transcripts leads us to conclude that is more than doubtful that he [Wilford] had a meritorious claim of any kind," Brennan wrote in *Wilford v. Sigmund Eisner Co.*

It wasn't merely a case of being permissive in criminal matters while being tough on labor cases. Brennan's views seemed unformed and inconsistent in cases involving criminal rights. In May of 1951, he was confronted with a request for the overturning of a conviction because the defendant, a man named David Tierson Graham, accused of a misdemeanor count of incest, was not allowed in the courtroom for the delivery of the verdict. The defendant's attorney, Robert E. Dietz, had not objected at the time, but now, three years later, had resurrected the issue as an avenue of appeal.

For weeks Brennan wrestled with his ruling in the Graham case. It was clear to him that in the case of a felony, the defendant had a right to be present. But Brennan refused to extend that privilege to non-felonies. Brennan was no expansionist. "So far as the diligence of counsel can discover or our own research reveals," Brennan said from the bench, "it has not been suggested that the requirement that the accused be present in person has been written into the Constitution of this state even as to offenses as to which at common law his presence was indispensable to a valid verdict.

"Graham's counsel argues that a privy verdict in the case of every offense violates the guarantee of a 'public trial.' Not so. The provision, like similar provisions in the federal Constitution and in the constitutions of the several states, was purposed to protect the accused from the abuses of the secret or star chamber trial so the public may see that the accused is fairly dealt with and not unjustly condemned and that the presence of spectators may keep his triers keenly alive to a sense of their responsibility and to the importance of their functions. That requirement was met in this case by keeping the court open to receive the verdicts."

These were the types of solid conservative rulings that pleased Vanderbilt. In March 1952, Republican governor Driscoll had decided to promote his friend Jacobs to fill one of two vacancies to the New Jersey Supreme Court. The other was to have been filled by state senator Edward O'Mara, the chairman of the state's Democratic party whom Driscoll had tried to appoint to the superior court four years earlier. State law required that the position be filled by a Democrat to maintain a bipartisan court. Four years earlier, O'Mara had refused the appointment, citing family obligations. He couldn't accept a salary of just $20,000 per year. So instead, Driscoll had named Brennan. Now the scenario was to repeat. O'Mara again declined the judgeship, this time to the state's highest court. Again Jacobs, with Chief Justice Vanderbilt's blessing, was successful in persuading Driscoll to make Brennan his alternate choice.

On March 13, Jacobs and Brennan were sworn in as the newest justices of the New Jersey Supreme Court. Jacobs was sworn in first and was therefore considered the senior justice to Brennan. Each took one of the end seats on the bench and thereafter were always referred to as the "Harvard ends."

While Driscoll had been considering the elevation of Brennan to the state's highest court, President Harry Truman faced his own decisions about court appointments, but with far less success than Driscoll. Reminiscent of 1930 when Taft and Sanford died, the nation was jolted in 1949 by the deaths of two U.S. Supreme Court justices, Wiley Rutledge and Frank Murphy.

Murphy had been a unique figure on the Supreme Court and his appointment itself was a paradox. Born on April 13, 1890, in Harbor Beach, Michigan, Murphy was an Irish Catholic who would have cut cards with William Brennan, Sr., any day of the week. He attended law school at Trinity College in Dublin and returned to Michigan in 1919 where he became an assistant U.S. attorney. Murphy's political career advanced rapidly. He served first as mayor of Detroit and then in 1937 was elected governor of Michigan. The following year, Roosevelt asked Murphy to come to Washington as attorney general.

In 1939 Murphy immediately became the leading contender for the Supreme Court seat of right-wing Justice Pierce Butler, who had died. There was a simple religious reason for the constant surfacing of Murphy's name in conjunction with replacing Butler. Since Brandeis had come on the Court in 1916 to establish what became for fifty-three years the "Jewish seat," Catholics had become possessive of an established seat as well. Their historic presence on the Court was a little better than that of the Jews, but not by much. Chief Justice Roger Taney had been the first Catholic to win a Supreme Court appointment in 1836. But it was only because Taney was married to a good Episcopalian that he was able to overcome religious opposition to his nomination by President Andrew Jackson. Although Taney felt strongly about his Catholicism, he cut a deal with his wife, Anne Key, the sister of Francis Scott Key of "Stars and Stripes" fame. All the daughters of their marriage would be brought up as Episcopalians and all the sons would be Catholic. Taney's bishop in Maryland was none too amused when the union produced six daughters in succession. So it seemed only appropriate that when Taney left the Court in 1864 he was replaced by an Episcopalian, Salmon P. Chase. For the next thirty years there were no Catholics at all on the court. Then in 1894, after considerable prodding from Catholic organizations and bishops, Edwin Douglas White, a Catholic Democrat from New Orleans, was appointed by President Cleveland. In 1910, White was named chief justice by Republican President William Howard Taft.

Taft's motives in choosing the elderly White were totally self-serving. Taft's ambition was to become chief justice himself after his second term ended in 1916, assuming that the Republicans kept the presidency. The good thing about White was that at the age of sixty-five he was the oldest of the possible contenders Taft considered. The plan went awry when Democrat Woodrow Wilson beat Taft in 1912 and then was reelected in 1916. But White did his job masterfully, remaining alive throughout the entire Democratic administration of Woodrow Wilson and then dying promptly after the election of Republican Warren Harding. The sixty-four-year-old Taft then got his long-delayed appointment.

From 1886 to 1925 there were two Catholics on the Court. White served with Irish-Catholic Joseph McKenna of Pennsylvania from 1896 to 1921, when White was replaced by Taft. Then in 1922 religion became a major factor in the appointment of Justice Pierce Butler. McKenna was still on the Court but was extremely ill and not expected to remain much longer. So when non-Catholic Justice William Rufus Day retired from the court on December 21, 1922, at the age of seventy-three, the Catholic archbishop of New York, Patrick Joseph Hayes, immediately began lobbying President Harding on behalf of Martin Manton, a federal judge of the Roman Catholic faith from New York. Archbishop, later Cardinal, Hayes emphasized to Harding that Catholics were now entitled to a seat and that the appointment of his friend would guarantee the Catholics their own seat regardless of what happened to the infirm McKenna.

The conservative Chief Justice Taft worried that Manton would fall under the liberal influence of Justice Brandeis. He counseled Harding against the Manton appointment and instead suggested his own candidate, Pierce Butler. Although Butler had never held any position higher than county attorney in Ramsey County, Minnesota, he had worked with Taft during an arbitration case over U.S.–Canadian border issues in Toronto. Taft needed a Catholic alternative to counter Manton, and Butler was his best possibility.

Taft wrote Butler asking him to line up his own panel of archbishops and have them insinuate themselves with President Harding. Butler replied in writing that such an action would be totally improper, and then proceeded to do everything Taft had asked with the archbishops. The strategy had the desired result and Butler was appointed on November 23, 1922. True to Taft's hopes, Butler remained a fervent supporter of Taft's view that the Court should be subordinate to the other branches. Butler served on the Court for seventeen years until his death in 1939.

As a liberal, a midwesterner, and a Catholic, Murphy fit every possible criteria for a Roosevelt appointment. Although a little short on judicial training, Murphy would have hardly been the first nominee to come from a political background. His service as a judge on Michigan's lowly recorder's court actually gave him more prior judicial experience than most of FDR's other eight Supreme Court appointments.

There was just one little problem. Murphy had not the slightest interest in the intellectual mind games the went on in the Supreme Court Building. The job he wanted was secretary of war. Nor was Murphy comfortable with the fact that his nomination chances were being driven on religious grounds. He wrote to one journalist, "The view that one of a certain faith should be succeeded by another of like faith is entirely unworthy."

In an effort to undermine his own appointment, which became increasingly inevitable, Murphy presented President Roosevelt with a star-studded list of alternates, which included such people as former FDR cabinet member James F. Byrnes (an Irishman who had converted from Catholicism to become Episcopalian) and Brennan's former boss in the army, former federal judge Robert Patterson. Murphy told Roosevelt, as he had told the journalist, that religion was not a legitimate basis on which to make an appointment. "Members of the Supreme Court are not called upon nor expected to represent any single interest or group. They speak for the country as a whole. Considerations of residential area or class interest, creed or racial extraction, ought therefore to be subordinated if not entirely disregarded."

Roosevelt never believed for a minute that Murphy's protestations were real. On January 4, Roosevelt made the announcement that Murphy was his choice. The new judge wrote to a friend: "A new honor has come to me which I did not seek and do not deserve. I am totally unworthy." To his parish priest he confided, "I am not too happy about going on the Court. A better choice could have been made. I fear that my work will be mediocre up there, while on the firing line, where I have been trained to action, I could do much better."

Murphy's appointment was almost universally praised. If there were any misgivings from the public or press at all, it was summarized by the lament that the appointment to the Court had sidetracked a man who would have made wonderful presidential material.

Murphy's career on the Court was one of unabashed liberalism. He became a dependable ally of Hugo Black, William Douglas, and Wiley Rutledge. If there was ever a justice who ruled on cases by how he felt rather than what the law or Constitution said, it was Frank Murphy. On the final day of the 1949 term, he wrote, "Law is at its loftiest when it examines claimed injustice even at the instance of one to whom the public is bitterly hostile."

After writing those words at the end of the term, Murphy went home to Detroit, and on July 19, 1949, he died at Ford's Hospital of a heart attack. Seven weeks later, while liberals pondered what move President Harry Truman might make to replace their hero, Justice Wiley Rutledge also died of a heart attack. Although not a crusader on Murphy's scale, Rutledge, only fifty-five at his death, had been a dependable member of FDR's liberal bloc.

At the beginning of his fourth year in the White House since succeeding Roosevelt, Truman was suddenly in a position to make his third and fourth appointments to the court. Always the ward politician from Kansas City, Truman manifested his parochial nature dramatically in his Court appointments. He had already named a nondescript former senator, Harold Burton, to replace Owen Roberts. That had been followed by the Vinson appointment. Two appointments and two Truman chums on the Court. For years presidents had worried about such things as geography, religion, politics, philosophy, and occasionally even excellence. The only geography Truman cared about was the seating chart in the Senate or at his poker table. Those who were despondent over Truman's first two picks were not encouraged by the next two.

Murphy was replaced by Tom C. Clark, a Presbyterian from Dallas, Texas, who had served as a staff counsel on one of Truman's investigating committees. That was enough to qualify Clark to be Truman's attorney general in 1945, the job from which he jumped to the Court.

To replace Rutledge, Truman sank even further. This time, after piously telling a press conference about how seriously he took his judicial appointments, he named former Indiana senator Sherman Minton, whose desk had been next to Truman's in the Senate. Minton's chief contribution to legislation had been his attempt to circumvent the Constitution and to stifle criticism of the New Deal by making it unlawful to transport anti–New Deal literature in interstate commerce.

In an otherwise distinguished presidency, Truman's judicial appointments were inexcusable. Former Truman aide and admirer Clark Clifford confided that it was the weakest aspect of his presidency. *The New York Times*, in an editorial that noted Truman's pronouncements about the federal judiciary, said the appointment of Clark, "a personal and political friend with no judicial experience and few demonstrated qualifications, offers a strange contrast to the President's high ideals." Of the Minton appointment the *Times* said: "Once again the President seems to have allowed personal and political friendship to influence his choice."

In just ten years since Murphy had made a 5 to 4 majority for those who viewed the Court as a possible instrument of social change, Truman, in a few deft strokes, returned the court to the conservatism of the Taft era. The liberal wing was reduced to just two, Hugo Black and William O. Douglas. The four Trumanites, Minton, Clark, Vinson, and Burton, joined with Frankfurter, Robert Jackson, and Stanley Reed to create a substantial seven-member conservative bloc.

Far removed physically and philosophically from the great issues of the day, Brennan was acutely aware of his limitations. He rarely wrestled with any federal issues. The only constitution he bothered with was the New Jersey state constitution. It was often dull and tedious work. But Brennan was a grinder. He could write for days on obscure labor or workers' compensation cases. He became the court's expert on difficult tax and corporate issues.

In his annual summaries of progress in the court plan, Chief Justice Vanderbilt rarely mentioned Brennan. Brennan was very much just one of seven. But Brennan had done one small thing to please Vanderbilt. With Brennan and Jacobs on the court, now four of the seven sitting justices were from Essex County. Vanderbilt asked if Brennan wouldn't mind moving. At first Brennan was slightly taken aback. He and Marjorie had lived in South Orange for nearly fifteen years. He had given up an incredible position to become a lowly judge for $20,000 a year. Now he had to move?

Brennan swallowed hard but could not muster the nerve to say no to Vanderbilt. Marjorie packed up their things and moved forty miles away to a charming converted barn on Conover Lane in the town of Rumson in Monmouth County. Each Monday and Thursday Brennan would drive to Trenton with his law secretary, William Riker, and often his personal secretary, Alice V. Connell, who had come to government with Brennan from Pitney Hardin. There Brennan would join the six other justices of the New Jersey Supreme Court. The rest of the time he resided at his quiet chambers in Red Bank, New Jersey, about an hour south of Newark. His day began at 9 A.M. and was broken by a noon lunch, which Brennan spent at the Old Union House with members of a men's club called the Root Beer and Checkers Club. Inside Monmouth County, Brennan usually wore sport clothes; only on days when he traveled did he don a suit. He preferred gray to blue and always sported a bow tie. Although his personal manner was friendly, his courtroom persona was all business. He had little patience for incompetent or ill-prepared counsel. Fellow judges noted that Brennan's legal mind was quick and decisive. He was said to be able to dictate an opinion from the bench, off the top of his head, as easily as many of the attorneys in his chambers could quote a statute.

Marjorie and Bill Brennan were devoted to each other and seldom socialized in the evenings. When they did, they usually just huddled with each other in a corner talking about their children and sipping a drink. But that was rare. Brennan was a constant reader and preferred to stay home. Marjorie lived the life of the busy housewife. She served on the board of the Rumson Community Appeal and the county's public health nursing organization. While Bill read, she designed and stitched her own needlepoint and watched television. In her entire career as a lawyer's wife, Marjorie had never seen her husband work. She once told New Jersey newspaper reporter Josephine Bonomo: "Sometimes he tells me about a case and asks me what I think. But whatever I say its always the opposite of his opinion. So we leave the legal decisions to him."

The move to Rumson, coming just before the 1952 presidential election, disqualified Brennan from meeting the local residency requirement to vote. Choosing between Eisenhower and Stevenson became a decision he never had to make. That would later prove to be convenient.

On the state supreme court, as on the other courts on which he had served, Brennan was more interested in improving the court system than in crusading for the underprivileged. He worked on reforms to shorten the time it took to get a case to trial. He brooked no nonsense in the courtroom. These were exactly the same things Vanderbilt had cared so much about.

But six months after joining the New Jersey Supreme Court, Brennan was faced with a different issue of justice. On August 23, 1952, police found the body of man named William Prather in the basement of a Newark home. A few hours later police arrested a man by the name of John Henry Tune. At the time of his arrest, Tune admitted to the police that he had committed the crime. He then signed a fourteen-page confession that had been written by a police officer, presumably on the basis of Tune's oral statements. In October, a lawyer was appointed for Tune. Among the first requests of Tune's counsel was that the confession be produced for inspection. In addition, the attorney asked that the prosecutor provide the other evidence that would be used at the trial. He specifically requested an order that the prosecutor disclose to Tune the names and addresses of all persons having knowledge of the facts of the crime.

The New Jersey Superior Court judge overseeing the trial agreed to let Tune's lawyers see the confession. But he rejected Tune's motion to view the rest of their case material.

By May 25, 1953, *New Jersey v. Tune* had worked its way to the New Jersey Supreme Court, and on June 9, 1953, a decision was rendered. A four-judge majority of the court, headed by Chief Justice Vanderbilt, said it could not agree with the proposition that a criminal defendant is entitled to see the evidence that might be used against him before trial. Wrote Vanderbilt: "Such liberal fact-finding procedures are not to be used blindly where the result would be to defeat the ends of justice. The criminal who is aware of the whole case against him will often procure perjured testimony in order to set up a false defense."

Vanderbilt summed up both the view of the New Jersey court and the general view of the law at that time. "Although we are alert to protect the rights of the individual accused, we should also remember that the people of this State must also be protected. In weighing the rights of the individual and those of the State, we must not be carried away to such an extent that the safety of the public is jeopardized."

But Vanderbilt and his four-judge majority did not stop with upholding the lower court's refusal to open up the additional papers. Vanderbilt went so far as to reverse the part of the lower-court ruling that allowed John Henry Tune to view his own confession. The chief justice announced that "to grant a defendant the unqualified right to inspect his confession before trial would be to give him an opportunity to procure false testimony and to commit perjury at the expense of society."

Brennan had sat uncomfortably through the conference on the ruling. He had rarely broken with Chief Justice Vanderbilt. Jacobs was as appalled as Brennan at where the aging Vanderbilt now stood. The man who in his younger days had been a great advocate of liberty, the man who had been the hero for Jacobs and the benefactor for Brennan had turned churlish over the years. It was one thing to uphold the lower court. But to gratuitously reverse the one part of the trial court's decision that was fair, and to thus deny Tune the right to inspect a confession that he had given, was simply too much.

Initially Brennan's objection to the Tune decision came from his court reform zeal. In his work on the bar and in his writings for the *New Jersey Law Journal*, Brennan had always advocated as much pretrial discovery as possible. In short, that meant that in most civil lawsuits, one side could never surprise the other. Real-life trials, Brennan believed, weren't supposed to be like *Perry Mason*. One of the most important facets of speeding up trials had been to demand pretrial depositions and discovery.

If that was the rule for civil cases, how, Brennan wondered, could the same thing be denied for criminal cases, where a person's freedom depended on the result? Brennan's orderly legal mind was offended by the inconsistency. He informed Vanderbilt that he would not be joining the chief's opinion. Jacobs was delighted and asked Brennan to write the dissent, sensing it would have more impact if it came from Brennan, who didn't have Jacobs's liberal reputation.

Brennan worked harder on the Tune dissent than he had on any case in which he had been involved. For the first time as a judge he began to wrestle seriously with the issue of fairness in criminal law. The more Brennan worked on the opinion—and no judge worked harder than Brennan—the more he came to understand that basic fairness was being violated. The more he thought about it, the more unfair it became. Imagine someone not being able to see something that he or she had written!

When Brennan began to write his opinion, he first went on about the laws of discovery and process, things that typically fascinated only himself and his fellow lawyers. His language was convoluted and lawyerly. Then suddenly, on the fifth page of his dissent, something new broke through the fog. The long repressed ghost of William senior seemed to jump through the cloudy, verbose, legal mumbo-jumbo. "It shocks my sense of justice," Brennan wrote, in what was for him, rare plain English, "that in these circumstances, counsel for an accused facing a possible death sentence should be denied inspection of his confession, which, were this a civil case, could not be denied."

He was now going even further than Jacobs had expected. Jacobs urged Brennan to soften his language, telling him that his opinion was "too strident" and "hardly judicial." But Brennan didn't care: his lawyerly shell had cracked; he had become emotionally involved in a case.

Thirty years after the death of his father, Brennan's career of pursuing legal victories for his rich and powerful clients had taken a surprising turn with a realization as profound as Bill senior's to stop the use of nightstick confessions in old Newark.

"In the ordinary affairs of life we would be startled at the suggestion that we should not be entitled as a matter of course to a copy of something we signed," Brennan the younger wrote. "To shackle counsel so that they cannot effectively seek out the truth and afford the accused the representation which is not his privilege but his absolute right seriously imperils our bedrock presumption of innocence."

It was the opening of a dam. In his next four years on the New Jersey Supreme Court, Brennan wrote more than a thousand pages of opinions, many clearly imbued with his found-again liberal social consciousness. In State v. Davis, Brennan held that a policeman could be liable for civil damages after shooting a suspect in a misdemeanor case. "The law values human life too highly to allow an officer to proceed to the extremity of shooting an escaping offender who has only committed a misdemeanor."

In another case, State v. Midgely, Brennan freed a man convicted of burning a house because of errors in the prosecution. "The plea of double jeopardy must be honored though a regrettable defeat of justice may result," he said. He called the decision to free an obviously guilty man "the price of individual protection against arbitrary power."

Those, like President Eisenhower himself, who would later express surprise at Brennan's activism in criminal cases after he joined the U.S. Supreme Court clearly had not scrutinized his record on the New Jersey court system.

On Saint Patrick's Day, in 1954, Brennan was the principle speaker at the annual banquet of the Charitable Irish Society at Boston's Sheraton Plaza. Sharing the stage with Ambassador Henry Cabot Lodge, as well as Massachusetts governor Christian Herter, Brennan stole the show. McCarthyism was rampant as Brennan arrived in Boston. Senator Joseph McCarthy's Permanent Investigations Subcommittee was just part of the problem. Mini-McCarthy committees existed in many states, including Massachusetts. In Boston, then–state senator Silvio Conte had impaneled a Special Commission Investigating Communism in Massachusetts. And if metaphorical witch-hunting weren't bad enough, another state senate committee, also headed by Conte, was dealing with real-life witch-hunts, trying to decide if a woman named Ann Pudeator, convicted of witchcraft in 1692, should be exonerated. Incredibly, even for 1954, Conte's committee voted 14 to 9 to uphold the conviction.

In his address Brennan laid out not only the cornerstones of what would be his philosophy but told much about how he had arrived at it. Remembering the lessons taught by his father and neighbors back in Vailsburg, Brennan, for the first time, identified his commitment to personal freedoms with the struggles of the Irish people. In fact, Brennan said, it was the Irish "love of individual liberty" that was one of the cornerstones of American freedom. In a rare public attack on the anti-Communist witch-hunts of Senator McCarthy, Brennan echoed the lines of CBS newsman Edward R. Murrow, hinting that McCarthy's tactics may have emboldened our enemies. "The enemy deludes himself if he thinks he detects in some practices in the contemporary scene, reminiscent of the Salem witch hunts, any sign that our courage has failed us and that fear has palsied our hard-won concept of justice and fair play."

It was a theme on which Brennan expanded some six months later at the Monmouth Rotary Club:

> A system of inquisition on mere suspicion or gossip without independent proofs tending to show guilt is innately abhorrent to us.
>
> The power to extract answers will beget a forgetfulness of the just limitations of that power. The simple and peaceful process of questioning breeds a readiness to resort to bullying and even to physical force and torture. If there is a right to an answer, there soon seems to be a right to the expected answer, that is to a confession of guilt. Thus the legitimate use grows into an unjust abuse. . . . Intentionally conceived or merely misguided, the result has been to engender hate and fear by one citizen of another, to have us distrust ourselves and our institutions, to have us become a nation afraid. That path brings us perilously close to destroying liberty in liberty's name.

Brennan paused, giving the audience time to swallow the mouthful he had already delivered. Then he continued:

> But there are hopeful signs in recent events that we have set things aright and have become ashamed of our toleration of the barbarism which marked the procedures at some of these hearings. It is indeed reason for pure joy and relief that at long last our collective conscience has sickened of the excesses and is demanding the adoption of permanent and lasting reforms to curb investigatory abuse.

These public outbursts on behalf of civil liberties did nothing to diminish Brennan's standing with Vanderbilt, to whom Brennan was beginning to seem a little quirky but tolerable. Vanderbilt cared more for courtroom efficiency than for ideology. He had rarely come across a judge more organized and hard working than Brennan. At the end of each year, Vanderbilt wrote an annual score card evaluating how many cases had moved through the courts. Brennan was a whiz. Regardless of how liberal his rulings on the criminal side, Brennan moved cases. He enabled Vanderbilt to cite statistics about just how well things were going. And things were going well. Vanderbilt's reforms were, in fact, being looked on by the Justice Department and many state legislatures as the model for the future.

In April 1956, Eisenhower's assistant attorney general, William Rogers, asked if Vanderbilt might come down to Washington and share some of the secrets of his administrative success at a Justice Department conclave on court congestion.

Vanderbilt readily agreed. But several days before the conference was to begin at Washington's Mayflower Hotel on May 21, Vanderbilt began to feel dizzy. He had been in declining health for some weeks and now he was advised by doctors not to travel. Since the topic was court congestion, Vanderbilt knew exactly who he wanted to take his place. Brennan had long been an effective civic club speaker on the benefits reaped by New Jersey's court reform. Vanderbilt placed a call to Brennan's home in Rumson and asked if the judge would mind traveling to Washington in his place. He sent his notes over for Brennan to read. Naturally, Brennan was glad to do it. He hopped on the train to Washington. There at the entrance to the Mayflower, Brennan offered a warm handshake to Herbert Brownell, the attorney general.

Brownell had been Eisenhower's chief adviser on legal affairs since Ike took office in 1952. It was a time when the advocates of restraint maintained the control of the Court that they had gained during the Truman administration. Of FDR's appointments only Jackson, Douglas, Frankfurter, Black, and Reed remained, and neither Frankfurter nor Reed could be construed as expansionist in his Court philosophies.

Brownell had been there with Eisenhower when on September 8, 1953, at 3 A.M., Chief Justice Fred Vinson suffered a heart attack. He died the next day at the age of sixty-three. Eisenhower's first thoughts toward a replacement naturally veered to Vanderbilt, who was, without question, the leading jurisprudential figure in the nation. But before Vanderbilt could be appointed, Eisenhower had to clear things up with California governor Earl Warren. During the Republican convention in 1952, Warren's support for Eisenhower had been purchased with the promise of a Supreme Court appointment. At the time Eisenhower hadn't figured on the first vacancy being the chief justiceship. But according to Warren's memoirs, Eisenhower was good to his word. On September 25, 1953, Warren was contacted by Attorney General Brownell and offered the position as chief.

A year later, on October 9, 1954, sixty-two-year-old Robert Jackson followed Vinson in death. This time Eisenhower and Brownell selected a former Wall Street lawyer, John Marshall Harlan. A man of impecca-

ble integrity, Harlan had a reputation as the most outstanding corporate litigator of his time. The Harlan appointment was almost universally praised. Especially after the Truman years, it was refreshing to see
someone truly selected on merit. But there were some rumblings.
Since the death of Frank Murphy, six appointments had come and
gone. Each had been filled by a Protestant. Eisenhower also began to
hear from state court judges. They were as unhappy as the Catholics.
Not since the departure of Cardozo in 1938 had there been a judge appointed to the Supreme Court directly from a state court. Of the fourteen appointments from Reed's in 1938 to Harlan's in 1955, half were
former office holders, several had been prosecutors, a couple had been
professors. The one bit of experience that seemed to be lacking was experience on the bench, especially from a state supreme court.

Following the confirmation of Harlan, Eisenhower called in
Brownell for a meeting. His next appointment, Ike declared, would
have to be a Catholic, and it would have to be someone presently serving as a state court judge. There was one more thing, Eisenhower told
Brownell. He didn't need to worry about party affiliation. Warren and
Harlan had been dyed-in-the-wool Republicans. Going into the 1956
election, Eisenhower wanted to be able to say that his Court appointments had been made on a bipartisan basis.

Like most of the other Justice Department officials attending the
conference on court congestion, Brownell was disappointed to hear
that Vanderbilt would not be in attendance. Nonetheless he was cordial to the replacement and introduced Brennan warmly, saying New
Jersey had "demonstrated impressively that delays in litigation can be
eliminated." The majority of those in the audience were presidents of
local bar associations and other legal organizations. But no one listened more keenly than Brownell, seated next to Rogers at the head
table.

Using notes, but extemporizing, Brennan spoke convincingly about
the need for court reform, particularly for processes such as pretrial depositions that would speed litigation. He delivered a good speech on
Vanderbilt's behalf. Hardly a rouser like his Saint Patrick's Day oration,
it was mostly about the technical nature of operating a court, based on
the experiences of the New Jersey court eight years after the Vanderbilt constitution had been put in place.

His comments were barely ideological. Brennan talked about the need to abolish jurisdictional controversies, which he declared "delays justice and wastes the time of litigants." He asked that litigation be "promptly decided and that all the courts be administered through a single administration." Most important, Brennan said, was the development of pretrial discovery and pretrial conferences, which tended to weed out frivolous suits, as well as to speed up trials once they began.

The Washington Post, although it covered the conference, didn't mention Brennan at all. The rival Washington Star noted only that he had given a "blow by blow of how justice can be expedited." A brief summary without editorial comment was reported in the U.S. Law Week.

To Herbert Brownell, who believed that the problem of court congestion was the most important legal problem of the time, Brennan's remarks seemed markedly conservative. The judge from New Jersey, it mistakenly sounded to him, was not someone who would entertain technical arguments about constitutionality, especially in criminal matters. Brennan sounded like a judge who wanted to get to the heart of the issue, just as Vanderbilt had urged in his majority ruling in the Tune case. Brownell had never seen Brennan's dissent and simply assumed Brennan and Vanderbilt had been in agreement. As he left the Mayflower Hotel, Brownell expressed some of his feelings about Brennan to Rogers. Both agreed Brennan might be a good person to work into the Department of Justice if something became available. "We might find something for this guy," Brownell observed. Rogers nodded in agreement.

SEVEN

AN UNLIKELY
APPOINTMENT

IN THE FALL OF 1956 THE NATION was preoccupied with politics as Dwight Eisenhower faced the challenge of Democrat Adlai Stevenson. Although in retrospect it appears Eisenhower was a popular president who couldn't lose, the reality at the time was quite different. In the glow of Eisenhower's ultimate victory it was forgotten that shortly after the California primary, the president had undergone major abdominal surgery. Increasingly as the campaign went on, the central issue was not Eisenhower but Vice President Nixon. On that issue, the president's health, and the qualifications of the vice president, Democrats believed Stevenson could win.

Even though New Jersey was seen as a pivotal state, Brennan gave his colleagues no clue as to which candidate he supported. Since the death of his father, Brennan had avoided politics. Not even his closest associates had the slightest idea what his personal politics had become. The issues of war and peace, of civil rights, of the future of the H-bomb, had no resonance in Brennan's reality.

Four months after Brennan had substituted for Vanderbilt at the Justice Department conference, the New Jersey Supreme Court gathered to decide a particularly disagreeable case that would turn out to be Brennan's last on the state court bench.

The issue was one almost as dear to Vanderbilt as court congestion. It was the integrity of the bar. Yet in this case involving a gruesome misuse of an elderly client's estate by a venerable attorney, the court was split 3 to 3. Brennan would cast the deciding vote.

Dougal Herr had once been one of Hoboken's best-known and most respected lawyers. But now, as he neared his eightieth birthday, Herr had destroyed his career. He had been in partnership with a man named William Kaufmann, whose chief client was a German-born businessman, William Breckwoldt, who had three children, including a daughter, Bertha. In 1930 when her two brothers died, Bertha, then sixty-five years old, inherited $450,000.

Bertha frequently came into the lawyers' offices to get legal papers signed. At first Kaufmann didn't seem to mind that his partner, Herr, had taken over Breckwoldt's business affairs. Kaufmann was glad to be free of the nutty old woman. He made a note that Bertha had "slipped pretty badly mentally . . . She wore a continual insipid smile, the same expression such as you would find on a happy child." But he became suspicious of his partner after Dougal rejected a suggestion that a guardian be appointed to manage Bertha's affairs. Instead, Herr had Bertha prepare a "voluntary living trust" granting himself, as her attorney, sole power over her investments and financial matters.

Unhappy with Herr's approach, Kaufmann secretly had Bertha sign a nonsensical document, known in the legal profession as a "crazy-quilt," stating, "I'm as weak-minded and as simple as any human being can be. I don't know one day from another, what I own or owe, who my relatives are, or any of the ordinary things that a normal person would know." Kaufmann hid the crazy quilt in the desk. He could bring it out if it ever became necessary to prove that Bertha didn't know what she was doing when she signed over her money to Herr.

A year after the living trust was signed Herr began to borrow liberally from Bertha's accounts. While Bertha lived frugally in a $50-a-week Hoboken apartment, Herr's office documents showed her expenditures at more than $65,000 per year. Even more questionable was Herr's decision to advance $100,000 into an airport development project in which the he was a principal.

In 1956, two years after Bertha's death, an investigation by her cousins revealed the extent of Herr's mismanagement of her accounts. A complaint was filed with the state bar of New Jersey. In such a case it was up to the state supreme court justices to determine if Herr should be disbarred and dishonored.

Brennan had spent a considerable amount of time agonizing over the briefs and conflicting statements of Kaufmann and Herr. Finally he told Vanderbilt that he had decided to cast the deciding vote to disbar. From the bench in Trenton, Brennan read one of the finest, and most ignored, statements about the ethics of lawyers:

> There is no profession, save perhaps the ministry, in which the highest morality is more necessary than that of the law. There is in fact no vocation in life where moral character counts for so much or where it is subjected to a more crucial test by citizen and public than is that of members of the bar. There is no profession apart from the legal profession where there is a greater disparity between true character and reputation. The fault lies in the lack of understanding of the public, provoked by the transgressors among us—not so much by the flagrant violators, by those members who by unconscionable conduct tip the delicate balance in which trust and confidence in a lawyer's action hang; not by malefactions which are criminal but rather from those in the twilight of low morality.

The *Herr* case was typical of the narrow, local issues Brennan usually found himself deciding. As he sat down at his desk to study the cases that he would use to write his opinion, he hardly noticed that on September 7, U.S. Supreme Court justice Sherman Minton, who had been suffering from anemia and circulatory problems, had resigned.

Minton had never particularly enjoyed his judgeship anyway. Under Justice Felix Frankfurter's persistent prodding, the Indianan had turned from a New Deal senator into an almost reactionary judge. Yet Minton had certain sensibilities and a self-awareness of his weaknesses. Almost immediately after submitting his resignation, he began feeling regret. "When one contemplates retirement," he wrote to Hugo Black, "it sometimes seems most attractive. But when it comes to consummating the act, there is much pulling at the heartstrings."

If nothing else, Minton's decision was well timed from Attorney General Brownell's point of view. Shortly before the 1956 election, it provided an excellent opportunity for the savvy former Eisenhower campaign manager to solidify the president's position with some recalcitrant constituencies. There is nothing so loved in Washington as a vacancy. By appointing a Catholic from a state court, Eisenhower could satisfy two of his most nettlesome critics, the Catholic hierarchy and the Association of State Court Judges. In point of fact, three weeks before Minton's retirement, Francis Cardinal Spellman had met with Eisenhower to talk about the lack of a Catholic voice on the Court. "Mr. President. It isn't that I want a Catholic on the Supreme Court," Spellman said. "But I want someone who will represent the interests and views of the Catholic church."

Eisenhower nodded yes and asked his aide, Bernard Shanley, to "remind me about what the cardinal wants when the time comes."

Shanley didn't need to remind Eisenhower. The president had been clear that a Catholic judge from a state court was what was needed. Brownell and his deputy attorney general, William Rogers, sat down to discuss the possibilities. It was Rogers who first remembered the impressive performance Brennan had made at his conference. They both agreed that on the important issue of court congestion, Brennan's presentation at the conference had by far been the best. The more Rogers talked, the more convinced Brownell became that Brennan was the man. Attorney General Brownell was sold, but the party issue still troubled Rogers.

"There's only one problem, Herb," Rogers told him at the Justice Department. "Brennan is a Democrat."

"Eisenhower doesn't care about that," Brownell replied. "I want to make sure he's really a member of the Catholic church."

Rogers called Cardinal Spellman to verify Brennan's fitness as a Catholic.

"Who is his parish priest?" Spellman asked.

Brownell admitted he had forgotten to ask.

Spellman said not to worry, he would find out and call back.

Brennan's bill of health from his priest was good: he attended Mass virtually every week. Spellman called Brownell back and said he had to admit that Brennan was a legitimate practicing Catholic.

Brownell called Brennan on Friday night and asked him to come down to Washington the next morning. According to recollections by Mrs. Brennan, the family excitedly rushed around the house to get Justice Brennan packed for his trip to Washington. "We were so caught by surprise that we had to borrow a suitcase from a neighbor." Brennan boarded the Congressional Limited at 5 A.M. He arrived at Washington's Union Station and insisted on carrying his own bag when Brownell met him at 8 A.M. He was driven to Brownell's home to freshen up, then told the president wanted to see him at 9:30 A.M. Brennan was literally in a daze as Brownell whisked him past the White House guards and into the Oval Office. Eisenhower was cordial and asked little of substance. Brownell recalled that they had a short conversation about hats and Brennan's war job. For Ike the meeting was just a formality. He assumed that Brownell had already asked the important questions. After just a twenty-minute meeting, without so much as even consulting New Jersey's two senators or its governor, Eisenhower offered Brennan the job. "I am honored to serve," Brennan replied.

In the middle of a vigorous reelection campaign, Eisenhower was just about to leave for a swing through the Midwest and simply didn't have a lot of time to worry about it. To make the process even more rushed, Minton's announcement left only a month before the Court's traditional opening on the first Monday in October.

What was important to Brownell was that Stevenson was about to begin a six-day tour of seven electoral-vote-rich eastern states, a trip that included a considerable amount of time in New Jersey. The ever-political attorney general relished the prospect of Brennan's appointment coming just as Stevenson was flying into Newark. The Democratic candidate had been all too confident lately. A speech in Minneapolis had been greeted by wild enthusiasm from a crowd of 15,000, and Stevenson's aides were sure their candidate was turning the corner.

As they left the Oval Office, Brownell said they would make the announcement over the weekend.

Eisenhower staffers were not so enthralled at the haste, or the choice, despite Eisenhower's repeatedly erroneous insistence that Brennan was "Vanderbilt's boy." One typed a warning memo to her diary page exclaiming, "He is Roman Catholic *and* a Democrat."

After emerging from the White House at 10:30 A.M., Brennan phoned Marjorie but she was out. He called his mother, then later reached his wife as she was preparing a dinner of baked ham and cauliflower. As Brennan later observed: "She was as astounded as I was." She was also perplexed. Friends were coming over for dinner, yet neither Marjorie nor Bill was supposed to tell anyone until it had been announced by the White House. "What will I tell them?" Marjorie asked.

Brennan chuckled. "Well, they are all good friends of ours. Just ad lib as best you can." But by the time the guests arrived, Brennan had not yet returned, and Marjorie was so exhausted she told the party to go on without her and went upstairs to bed.

Eisenhower had instinctively liked Brennan, surprising even his press secretary, James Hagerty, with how quickly the decision was made. Not knowing the gist of Brennan's opinions in criminal cases was just the tip of an iceberg of ignorance in the administration. The following morning, when Hagerty announced the appointment to the press, he realized there was not even an official bio sheet on the new justice. Privately, Hagerty insisted that the suddenness was Brennan's fault rather than Eisenhower's. "I've never seen a man accept a job so fast," Hagerty said.

Brennan's hometown *Newark Evening News* called the action "so sudden that all the usual procedures were swept aside."

It was widely and erroneously reported that the White House appointments secretary, Bernard Shanley, had played a strong role in Brennan's selection. He was a fellow Newark native whose family had known the Brennans for nearly fifty years. It seemed logical that he would have intervened, but Shanley himself acknowledged that he wasn't asked about Brennan until after Brownell had made the push. By then Shanley said, "Eisenhower knew more about Bill Brennan than I did."

Even though Brennan's local priest had vouched for the judge's good churchgoing habits, no one was more upset about the appointment than Spellman. He was irritated that Brownell had chosen a Catholic he had never met and who owed him no favors. According to John Cooney's book *The American Pope*, Spellman blamed Shanley for what he termed "a fiasco." Wrote Cooney, "In an effort to help Shanley among both Catholics and his friends in New Jersey, Brownell spread the word that Shanley had played a key role in Brennan's selection (although Shanley hadn't). Spellman believed Brownell and thought Shanley had betrayed him." Interestingly, many people, including

Brennan, have clung to the erroneous information that it was Shanley who engineered the appointment.

According to Cooney, Spellman came back to the White House and gave Shanley a dressing-down the likes of which Shanley had never experienced. Shanley tried to explain that he had no significant role in the appointment, but Spellman didn't believe him. Writes Cooney, "The Cardinal continued his tongue-lashing until he turned and left."

It fell to Brownell to break the news to Vanderbilt that Brennan had been selected. Although Vanderbilt had done much to advance Brennan's career, it seemed to Brownell that the chief justice of New Jersey was stunned that the lightning that had always danced all around him had scored a direct hit on his fifty-year-old colleague. Ironically Brennan was not even the bright light on the New Jersey court. That, of course, was Jacobs. As far back as 1931, when Jacobs had first gone to work for Vanderbilt, he had been carrying on a correspondence with Felix Frankfurter about the progress of the New Jersey court reforms. Jacobs, as a former top Frankfurter student and Paul Freund's predecessor as *Harvard Law Review* editor, was a personal favorite of the great Frankfurter. Ironically, Frankfurter's presence blocked Jacobs's deserved advancement to the Supreme Court. Just as Brennan was being promoted because of his religion, Jacobs was once again being ruled out because of his Jewish faith.

A friend of Brennan's who was in Vanderbilt's office when the call came described Vanderbilt as "really stricken" by the news about Brennan. Almost every account of Brennan's appointment gives Vanderbilt credit for intervening on Brennan's behalf. But that was not the case, according to the man who knows best, Herbert Brownell. One exception to the general misconception appeared in an unauthorized biography of Earl Warren written in 1967 by Leo Katcher. Katcher's version, which seems to be correct, says: "All took it for granted that since Brennan appeared to be a protégé of Vanderbilt, he must share Vanderbilt's judicial philosophy. But no one had asked. Now Vanderbilt, like the wife of a philandering husband, became the last to know. And his reaction was much the same: immediate shock and disbelief, followed by a sense of outrage. According to Katcher, an American Bar Association official heard Vanderbilt say, 'He [Ike] has done it again. He's pulled another one.' "

Over the years that followed, and even in his memoirs, Eisenhower would repeatedly refer to the fact that Brennan had come with Vanderbilt's highest recommendation. In a farewell conversation two years later with Justice Harold Burton, who was leaving the Court, Eisenhower expressed amazement that Vanderbilt could have recommended such a man. Eisenhower's impression, that Brennan was "Vanderbilt's boy," was simply never the case.

Brennan later told Justice Frankfurter that even though Vanderbilt had said with bravado that he would only take the chief justiceship, Vanderbilt still wanted an appointment to cap his judicial career. According to a letter Frankfurter later wrote on the subject, Brennan claimed that Vanderbilt was sure Eisenhower would at least give him the courtesy of asking him to serve, because Vanderbilt had been actively attempting to set up a memorial for Eisenhower through the American Bar Association's state chapters.

To his credit, Vanderbilt quickly recovered and never voiced his wistfulness that it was Brennan and not himself who would go on the Court. In his public comments to the press, Vanderbilt was statesmanlike, praising Brennan as an excellent choice. But having seen his destiny escape him so many times, and then having it go to the lightly regarded Brennan, was almost more than he could bear. Just a year later, on June 14, 1957, Vanderbilt died of heart failure.

If Brennan's so-called mentor was not happy, one might have thought that his old classmates at Harvard Law would be ringing a church bell in celebration. But at Cambridge there was an equally stunned silence. No one was more surprised than Brennan's classmate, now Harvard law professor, Paul Freund. He was sure that Brennan's good fortune had damaged his own chances of attaining the Court, having always imagined that he would replace his mentor and idol, Felix Frankfurter. It was still possible, but the appointment of Brennan dimmed his chances. How many Harvard Law School graduates could Ike be expected to name to the court? he wondered.

Freund's disgust was apparent in an October 9, 1956, letter to Frankfurter. "I am chagrined to say that I don't remember him as a classmate." He had even checked with Professor Milton Katz, another graduate of the class of 1931. Katz had not known Brennan as a student either. Another black mark noted by Freund was that Brennan had failed to show for the class's twenty-fifth reunion dinner.

Freund finally found one colleague who had met Brennan during his war service and described him as man of "ability and affability." Freund noted: "I am led to hope that he will be as companionable as his predecessor [Minton]."

Freund also checked on Brennan's grades, wryly noting that constitutional law was not in his program. "Maybe he gave himself the pleasure of listening in," Freund wrote sarcastically. But in the most revealing portion of the letter, Freund took pains to apologize for his prediction in a Harvard student newspaper that Brennan would make "a great justice." "I seem to recall that you too have learned how dangerous it is to jest with reporters," Freund said. He called his prediction "spurious." After consulting with Brennan's far better-known colleague Nat Jacobs, who vouched for Brennan's intelligence and diligence, Freund wrote again to say the best they could do was "keep their fingers crossed."

Harvard Law School dean Erwin Griswold also barely knew Brennan. Although a fairly close friend of Brownell's, Griswold had not even been consulted on the appointment. When he read the widespread accounts that Vanderbilt had been behind the choice, Griswold was distraught. Years earlier, he had opposed Vanderbilt in a proceeding at New York University involving the firing of a law professor, Alexander Sachs. Ever since, Vanderbilt had given Griswold the cold shoulder. Any friend of Vanderbilt's, Griswold concluded, was no friend of his.

At Yale Law School, where the faculty was known to be a little more liberal than at Harvard, Brennan's appointment also brought concern. Here the hero on the court was not Frankfurter but William Douglas. Yale Law professor Fred Rodell wrote of his concern to Justice Douglas. Rodell said he didn't know enough about Brennan to be sure, but "the odds were against his being great" because he was "chosen for all the wrong reasons." Like many others, Rodell was not all that familiar with Brennan's state court record, and wrongly assumed that Brennan was part of Frankfurter's Harvard establishment, and that he would be taken over ideologically by Frankfurter.

The public reaction to the appointment of the unknown judge from Newark was more positive. His service on the New Jersey courts had erased his antiunion, antipicketing reputation. Writing in *The New York Times*, powerful columnist Arthur Krock called Brennan's appointment "inspiring." He went on to write: "It is an important proof of democracy when a Supreme Court justice is representative of what an American can, with honor and industry, achieve without the birthright of social and economic privilege."

A *Times* profile identified Brennan as "a moderate liberal and a defender of civil rights. He is regarded as a strict judge in insisting that lawyers be prepared, but [he] is well liked. He is much in demand as an after dinner speaker."

The Washington Post editorialists were also pleased. Though noting that Brennan was "largely unknown," the *Post* said his speech on court congestion "had not gone unnoticed." As for the appointment itself, the *Post* called it "a fine example of a great tradition of a qualified and independent judiciary."

In its brief profile, *U.S. Law Week* cited Brennan's "noticeable interest in the protection of civil rights." Even so, *Law Week* observed, "more noticeable has been Justice Brennan's enthusiasm for reforms in court rules and administration."

Such praise from those who endorsed more court activism make it hard to believe that Republicans could later claim that Brennan "changed." Thomas Dewey, for example, told a biographer that Brennan had been investigated "backwards and forwards."

"The guy just changed on us," Dewey said.

But that was an uncharacteristic misstatement by the renowned prosecutor and investigator. All he really needed to do was to have checked with Brennan's colleagues.

Writing at the time of the appointment in the *New Jersey Law Journal*, a New Jersey lawyer, J. L. Bernstein, proved that it wasn't impossible to predict that Brennan would ultimately be more in tune with Earl Warren than with Felix Frankfurter. "Prediction in print is a preoccupation of the foolhardy," Bernstein wrote. "But we have a notion that Justice Brennan, son of a former labor leader, will become a valuable assistant to Chief Justice Warren, son of a former railroad mechanic. As Warren seems to have inherited the practical bent of mind that goes with use of the hands, so has Brennan. Such a man is apt to exalt form over substance. Judged by ability and industry and by the qualitative and quantitative estimate of his work in New Jersey, Brennan seems destined to join the libertarian group on the U.S. Supreme Court of Warren, Black, and Douglas.

"In one respect alone, the appointment of Brennan was a great one," Bernstein wrote. "He succeeds Sherman Minton, a man of conspicuous judicial shortcomings, whose votes against civil liberties exceeded those of any other man on the Court, and who wrote comparatively few opinions of other kinds. The spokesman against freedom has been replaced by a spokesman for freedom, and the man who shied away from work has been succeeded by a workhorse."

The fact that Brennan, a Democrat, was nominated by a Republican was noted as an oddity but only a slight one. In those days Supreme Court appointments did not have the partisan taint they later acquired. It was Republican Taft who appointed Democrat Cardozo. Democrat Roosevelt had promoted Republican Stone to the chief justiceship; and Democrat Truman had named Republican Burton.

A week after his appointment, Brennan was standing in the backyard of his Rumson home, posing for pictures for a *Life* magazine photographer. Brennan's total lack of sophistication shone through his comments to the *Life* reporters, while he pushed seven-year-old Nancy in a swing. "I'm not much of a do-it-yourselfer," Brennan joked. "But I did manage to sink the frame of this swing in concrete, so I guess it's here for the next fellow to swing his kids on."

He had made preparations for his just-married son, Hugh, to move into the house while he, Marjorie, and Nancy took an apartment in Washington. Asked what he stood for, Brennan replied, "Fewer cases brought to trial, and those quickly. Delayed justice is bad justice, for time has a way of blurring memories and killing witnesses."

Brownell clipped the comments and showed them to Eisenhower. It had been exactly what they hoped for.

The two weeks from appointment to his swearing in had been a whirlwind. Brennan returned for one last time to the state courthouse in Trenton, the city where his father had first lived when he came to America. He was already fifty years old, young by Court standards but approaching the age at which William senior had died. Brennan walked to his chambers and took his black state court robes out of the coat rack. Slowly he folded them and put them in a box. He bade his colleagues good-bye and hugged Jacobs. Then he descended the courthouse steps and walked onto the national stage as the most unlikely Supreme Court appointee of the century.

AS CITY COMMISSIONERS CAST BALLOTS

1

AS A YOUNGSTER, and the oldest male, Bill Brennan was very much his mother's son, although he would later say that his character was molded by his politician father, William Brennan, Sr. All three are shown here voting in a Newark election.

BILL BRENNAN at the University of Pennsylvania.

AS A COLONEL in the U.S. Army, Brennan played an important role in calming labor problems at companies producing war-time matériel.

WILLIAM BRENNAN during his tenure as Supreme Court justice on
October 16, 1956.

CARDINAL SPELLMAN had lobbied President Eisenhower heavily for a Catholic justice, but when Brennan (RIGHT) was named he complained that Ike has chosen the wrong one. Nonetheless, after the appointment, Spellman visited the Court to pay his respects to Brennan.

JUSTICES FELIX FRANKFURTER (LEFT) and Hugo Black (RIGHT) were in the midst of an intense personal and professional rivalry when Brennan arrived on the Court. They immediately engaged in a battle for Brennan's soul, of which Black clearly prevailed.

THE INTERIOR of the Supreme Court chamber as it looked when Brennan announced his historic ruling in *Baker v. Carr*.

PICTURED HERE are eight of the justices of 1962. FROM LEFT TO RIGHT, TOP: Byron White, William Brennan, Jr., Potter Stewart, Arthur Goldberg. BOTTOM: Tom Clark, Hugo Black, Earl Warren, William Douglas. Missing is John Harlan.

BRENNAN'S SON, William J. Brennan III, became a partner in a Princeton, N.J., law firm and president of the New Jersey Bar Association.

JUSTICES WARREN BURGER (LEFT) and Harry Blackmun (RIGHT) were both from Minnesota and had known each other since childhood. They were prejudged as "Minnesota Twins," until Brennan's influence persuaded Blackmun to follow a more progressive legal path.

JUSTICES BRENNAN and Marshall became so close that clerks jokingly referred to them as "Justice Brennan-Marshall." They appeared together outside of court in 1985 at the dedication of a new courthouse in Marshall's hometown of Baltimore.

12

SHOWN HERE at his eightieth birthday party on April 25, 1986, Brennan is surrounded by clerks dressed in T-shirts silkscreened with a mock order from the Court to commemorate the occasion.

JUSTICE BRENNAN working in his Supreme Court office.

CONFIRMATION AFTER THE FACT

O<small>N</small> M<small>ONDAY</small>, O<small>CTOBER</small> 1 6 , 1 9 5 6 , without so much as a confirmation hearing, Brennan took his place on the Supreme Court. The procedure for seating a justice on the Court while Congress was in recess had lain dormant for 150 years before President Eisenhower employed it to seat Governor Warren in 1952 and now Brennan in 1956. The recess appointment had fallen into disuse after President Washington's ill-fated attempt to use it in the appointment of his friend John Rutledge. In September of 1795, Washington had named John Rutledge to succeed John Jay as chief justice. Rutledge served an interim appointment for some four months before the Senate convened in December to take up his nomination. Rutledge proved to be a controversial choice. Unhappy that he had opposed the Jay Treaty with England, the Senate rejected his nomination and forced him to leave the Court. Rutledge was so humiliated that he attempted suicide and later went insane.

Until Eisenhower, that had been the end of recess appointments. But when Ike decided to name Earl Warren as chief justice in 1953, he

ignored the advice of aides who said a recess appointment was potential trouble. Despite the problems Rutledge had encountered, Eisenhower was convinced that a few months of service would enhance
confirmation prospects for his nominees by showing they could do the
job before coming before the members of the Senate Judiciary Committee.

His reasoning, however, is rather difficult to accept. Brennan's elec-
tion-year appointment, like Warren's, was in no danger. It wasn't reasonable for Eisenhower to call Congress back into session during an
election year to approve Brennan's appointment. That would merely
give political opponents an opportunity to take potshots. The usual
course of action would be to wait until after the election and then announce Minton's replacement. But that approach had political costs.
There was no way to predict how long the process might be dragged
out by Senator James Eastland, who controlled the committee and who
was known to wheel and deal.

Brownell, however, did not want to wait. Why waste an opportunity
to use the appointment for political gain? Here was a chance to make
inroads with Catholic, eastern voters, the very people with whom
Eisenhower was weakest.

Thus it was that without even a confirmation hearing Brennan took
his robes out of the box into which he had carefully folded them, then
slowly slipped them on over his suit. They were the same robes he had
worn to his first swearing in as a judge a short seven and a half years
ago. As he entered the Court's conference room with his family for
photographs, he was garrulous. "How would you like us to line up,
gentlemen?" he called out. During one photo, Brennan's seven-year-
old daughter Nancy impulsively reached up and kissed her mother.
Shushed back to her place, Nancy said, "I guess I made a boo-boo." In
addition to Nancy, Brennan was joined by his two sons, William III, a
second lieutenant with the U.S. Marine Corps, and twenty-year-old
Hugh, then a student at Monmouth Junior College.

Brennan's swearing in was attended by his former law partners Wal-
dron Ward and Donald Kipp, as well as Attorney General Brownell
and Brownell's chief deputy, William Rogers. From the New Jersey Bar
Association, a delegation included the president, vice president, and
secretary of the association. Arthur Vanderbilt did not attend.

At ten o'clock on the morning of October 16, Chief Justice Warren

gaveled the proceedings to their beginning. He announced the retirement of Justice Minton with a warm farewell. "We shall miss both your
wise counsel and our constant companionship with you," Warren said.
"While you no longer will be with us daily, you will continue to be one
of us."

After reading an equally sweet note to the justices from Minton,
Warren formally welcomed Brennan to the Court, and the clerk, John
Fey, read the letter of appointment from the president. Brennan then
took the oath:

> I, William Joseph Brennan, do solemnly swear that I will administer
> justice without respect to persons, and do equal right to the poor and
> to the rich, and that I will faithfully and impartially discharge and per-
> form all the duties incumbent on me as associate justice of the Supreme
> Court of the United States according to the best of my abilities and un-
> derstanding, agreeably to the Constitution and the laws of the United
> States. So help me God.

After taking the oath Brennan called Shanley. "I want to thank you
for all you have done for me," Brennan said.

Shanley replied: "I have done nothing for you."

The slight pause that followed led Shanley to the feeling that Brennan didn't believe him. But in any event, Brennan did have a favor to
ask.

"I'd like to see the president's office," Brennan said. Shanley was
puzzled. He reminded Brennan that he had met the president in the
Oval Office just two weeks earlier.

"I know," Brennan said, "but when I was told that I was appointed
to the Supreme Court, I was so overwhelmed that I don't remember
what the room looked like and I'd like to see it."

No one was more aware than Brennan that he made a sharp jump in
class by coming to Washington. "I'm the mule in the Kentucky Derby,"
he admitted to a friend. "I don't expect to distinguish myself but I do
expect to benefit by the associations."

In reply to a letter of welcome from Justice John Marshall Harlan,
Brennan continued the humble-pie routine. "I think you are right that
our paths have not crossed, although I have some recollection that I
may have been introduced to you in the late '30s. . . . What mutual

friends have said of you gives me the very comfortable feeling that I will not be without a friend, and approaching a task, which believe me, now appears hugely formidable to my capabilities."

It was a schtick that didn't sit well with everyone. A circuit court of appeals judge named David Bazelon, later to become one of Brennan's closest friends, first met Brennan at a birthday party for Justice Douglas, fifty-eight. "To tell the truth," Bazelon noted to his wife on the way home, "I thought he had a bit of the blarney in him."

"We'll have to wait and see," she replied.

The Warren Court that Brennan joined was hardly the united and purposeful Warren Court that it would later seem. It was a sharply divided court with Frankfurter leading one wing and Black the other. But the wings were hardly equal. On one side, interested in maintaining the limited power of the federal government against the states was Frankfurter, Harlan, Burton, Clark and the soon-to-retire senior justice of the court, Justice Stanley Reed. On the other side were the two bona fide activists, Black and Douglas, eager to expand the protections of the Constitution. Warren certainly appeared to be leaning in their direction, although in 1956 the extent of his leftward drift was by no means certain. If Frankfurter were to have his way, Brennan would become the sixth vote in a firm conservative majority. Justice Frankfurter was not subtle about putting on the pressure. At a Federal Bar Association luncheon to honor Brennan's appointment, someone noted that both Brennan and Douglas had the first name Bill. Asked by Tom Clark what he would call Brennan, Frankfurter replied, "I've got to see how he's going to vote first."

As the Court's master manipulator, Frankfurter did not intend to leave Brennan's voting record to mere chance. His approach was cynical and calculating. In the past, with weak Truman appointees such as Minton, Clark, and Burton, flattery had been a totally successful maneuver. He would flood the justices with notes of false praise and encouragement. If that failed, Frankfurter would resort to brow-beating and intimidation. His efforts to influence fellow justices through their clerks was legend, especially when those top law school graduates were Harvard men. Any Harvard graduate, regardless in whose chambers he worked, was considered by Frankfurter to be his own. They were invited to dine and lunch with him. They let him know what the other justices were thinking. Frankfurter let them know what their bosses *should* be thinking. The justice from Harvard was so brilliant and confident that he was quickly able to dominate anyone of weaker intellect. Conversely, anyone not from Harvard was considered by Frankfurter to be not worth talking to.

Frankfurter's "Brennan Project" had begun even before Brennan arrived in Washington. He had had Paul Freund pull Brennan's collegiate record to find out what courses he had taken and what his marks were. He had received an evaluation from Nat Jacobs about Brennan's service on the New Jersey Supreme Court.

No sooner had Brennan been appointed to the Court than Frankfurter began to woo him with sweet notes of welcome. To the first one written on October 3, 1956, Brennan replied: "My Dear Justice Frankfurter. Your warm note was most especially welcome. I cannot hope that you would remember one so inconspicuous in your classroom, but my recollections of your good self are most vivid and your imprint has been permanent. I count with confidence upon having a 'friend in court' indeed in what you will appreciate is a task I approach not without trepidation as to my capacity to measure up."

Encouraged by Brennan's respectful tone, Frankfurter began a more active phase of his attempt to win over the new justice. Ensconced in the chambers immediately adjacent to Brennan, Frankfurter began consulting with him on a variety of professional and personal matters. Most important, he arranged for the Brennans to move into half of a frame house owned by NBC correspondent Richard Harkness across the street from his own house at 3037 Dumbarton in Georgetown. Harkness offered to sell Brennan the entire home, but Brennan demurred. He told Harkness he didn't know how long he would stay in Washington and Marjorie wanted to keep the house in New Jersey.

Unaware of the doubts Freund had privately expressed about him, Brennan accepted Frankfurter's suggestion that he use Freund, who had stayed at Harvard to teach, as a supplier of law clerks. In 1957, Freund sent Brennan two of his students, Daniel O'Hern and Edward W. Keane. Brennan rarely bothered to interview Freund's selections. As he always had with other justices, Frankfurter pounced on the clerks as if they were his own. But with Brennan's clerks, Frankfurter was only marginally successful. Brennan was so personable, so friendly. He was not an easy man to betray.

Frankfurter, who had lived in Washington for thirty years, knew everyone of import. Part of his strategy, Brennan quickly deduced, was "to make you feel it was an honor to be associated with his crowd of giants." To his clerks, Brennan was less diplomatic. He repeatedly complained to them of Frankfurter's "condescending nature." To another, Brennan said: "He makes me so damn mad sometimes."

One particularly annoying episode occurred at a dinner at Frankfurter's Dumbarton Street home. Guests included two giants of the Washington, D.C., bar, John Lord O'Brien and former secretary of state Dean Acheson, both partners at Washington's prestigious firm of Covington & Burling. The conversation was steered toward the work habits of Justice Brandeis, for whom Acheson had clerked. As Acheson told his stories of Brandeis's methods and attitudes, as if on cue, Brennan realized the whole conversation was concocted to inculcate certain judicial propositions in Brennan's mind. He left the party fuming.

To work in the chambers of Justice Brennan quickly became recognized as one of the plums of the Supreme Court. Although clerks were not allowed in the conference meetings of the justices, where they hashed out the issue and cast their preliminary votes, Brennan was open and friendly from the beginning. Unlike Douglas, who was distant and even mean to his clerks, or Black, who wrote most of his own decisions and did not depend very heavily upon them, Brennan made a point of giving O'Hern and Keane a strong sense of importance and a complete rundown of who said what.

Best of all, Brennan was easily the warmest and most natural of the justices. In conversation, Brennan moved in close, LBJ style. He talked with his hands and frequently touched whomever he was engaging. He got to know not only the clerks but the elevator operators and the security guards. An inveterate note writer, Brennan sent letters of thanks or appreciation to almost everyone he met. He had inherited many of his father's natural political instincts. Just as he had an uncanny memory for cases, Brennan never forgot a name. Those were some of the sweet qualities that initially led D.C. Circuit Court of Appeals judge David Bazelon to his conclusion that Brennan was full of "blarney." After he had gotten to know Brennan better and even steered the justice into some business deals and real estate investments, Bazelon decided his initial impression had been totally wrong. Brennan was the same to everyone and treated everyone equally. There was nothing false about him, Bazelon concluded.

John Marshall Harlan, Frankfurter's chief philosophical ally—and the only other conservative on the Court whom Frankfurter truly respected—also did what he could to cultivate Brennan. Harlan pulled strings at the powerful Century Association in New York to get Brennan admitted. Harlan asked Brennan for the names of some friends who might write letters of recommendation. It was symptomatic of Brennan's obscurity that one of those Brennan suggested, William Foster Dewey, replied to Harlan that he had never heard of Brennan. Nonetheless, Harlan, who had once been a powerful Wall Street lawyer, got Brennan into the club. He and his wife also invited the Brennans to spend weekends at their Connecticut estate.

For all Frankfurter's efforts, it was Earl Warren whom Brennan found more personally appealing, just as J. L. Bernstein had predicted in the *New Jersey Law Review*. The chief justice and Brennan developed an almost immediate kinship. Brennan was a big baseball fan. He loved the Dodgers, and when he arrived at the Supreme Court to meet his colleagues he was delighted to be told by Warren that they were in a third-floor conference room watching the Dodgers-Yankees World Series. Entering the room, Brennan was greeted by his fellow justice with the cry, "Sit down so we can see the game." Another called, "Turn off the light." He felt immediately at home.

At the age of sixty-five, Warren was some fifteen years older than Brennan and shared many personality traits with Bill's father. Like William Brennan, Sr., Warren was an incorruptible former lawman, disgusted with mobs, gambling, and vice. They both shared an equal contempt for corrupt police and truncheon-wielding tactics. Just as Brennan had seen police beatings and abuse in Newark, Warren had fought it with equal fervor in California. Both men were strict disciplinarians in their personal and professional lives. As time would pass, the chief justice would do such fatherly things as taking his young protégé to Griffith Stadium to see the Washington Senators play baseball. Yet through their entire relationship, Brennan never referred to Warren by his name, he was always "The Chief."

For Brennan's school-age daughter Nancy, the chief justice became the grandfather she never had. Warren's personal papers at the Library of Congress are littered with notes, birthday greetings, and thank-you notes from little Nancy. She even took the liberty to occasionally clip a cartoon and send it to the chief justice. The granddaughterly tone of the correspondence is warm. Oddly, Brennan's own correspondence with the chief, as his inability to call Warren "Earl" showed, was stiffer and more formal, just as his relationship with his own father had been.

Brennan's almost instant rapport with Warren, his sense of Warren as a family member, almost a surrogate father, multiplied his bitterness toward Frankfurter. Much of Frankfurter's pitch was predicated on making cutting remarks about the chief behind his back. Each jibe made Brennan's blood boil. Ultimately he would rebel at Frankfurter's manipulative efforts. After one particularly condescending lecture about the need for judicial restraint, the specific nature of which seems to have been forgotten, Brennan lost his temper and turned red as a berry. He bluntly told Frankfurter to stop treating him as a student.

Mortified, Frankfurter wrote Brennan a profuse apology: "I suppose it is the professor in me that makes me talk that way."

But his efforts did not stop. Shortly thereafter, Frankfurter, angry at Brennan's increasing closeness to Warren, lectured the junior justice about showing too much deference to the chief.

"Any encouragement in a chief justice that he is the boss, that he differs from the other members of the Court in matters other than administrative, must be rigorously resisted."

Frankfurter added: "I, for my part, will discharge what I regard as a post of trusteeship—not the least of which is keeping the chief justice in his place, as long as I am around."

But the bond between the chief justice and the Court's new member had a synergy that could not be turned aside. If Brennan's reasons for seeking a relationship were instinctive or familial, Warren's were practical. Warren had been a district attorney, an attorney general, and finally the governor of California. As a man well versed in leadership, he had long ago recognized the value of having good assistants and a loyal bureaucracy. But the position of chief justice offered little in the way of perquisites or staff. Traditionally the members of the Court, as Frankfurter's missives indicated, did not consider the chief as their superior in any way. He was simply the one justice who had the headaches of administrative matters. For his trouble, in 1956 the chief was awarded a flat annual salary of $40,000 instead of the $39,500 received by the others.

In influencing the direction of the Court, the chief did have one significant power, granted only by Court tradition. It was the chief who assigned the writing of opinions for the side on which his vote fell. Even that was no awesome power. The fact was that Warren was a politician, accustomed to barking orders to which others jumped. Even on an average Supreme Court, that wasn't about to happen. But this Court was dominated by extraordinary men like Black, Douglas, Frankfurter, and Harlan who weren't about to show deference to the chief. And the weaker members like Clark and Whittaker tended to listen more to Frankfurter than to Warren. They were advocates of judicial restraint with little interest in furthering the agenda of a man interested in fixing society's problems.

When Warren arrived on the Court just three years before Brennan, he too had walked into the middle of the Frankfurter-Black feud. And even though he aligned himself philosophically with Black—as Brennan ultimately would—Warren never considered himself Black's superior. Black, who had been on the Court since 1937, was a man of tremendous fortitude and fitness, a demon on the tennis court until the age of eighty-three. He never compromised. His belief in the truth of the U.S. Constitution and in the sanctity of the Bill of Rights was religious in its fervor.

Much of what was said about Black also applied to William O. Douglas, except that Douglas was more impossible to work with. He was rude to his clerks, totally unpredictable and unpleasant with his colleagues. He was a man, it was often said, who loved humanity and hated people. Black himself told his clerks that Douglas was the most brilliant man he had ever met. He was also the laziest, Black would add.

The arrival of John Marshall Harlan on the Court in 1954 did little to solve Warren's need of a deputy. A gentle patrician, Harlan was a self-confident and wealthy Wall Street lawyer. Before his appointment to the federal bench, Harlan was recognized as one of the great lawyers in the United States. But his instincts were conservative. He, too, was more comfortable with Frankfurter's philosophies.

William Brennan was different. His views were unformed. He had no fanatical devotion to any philosophy in 1956. His reputation, although large enough for New Jersey, was not national, as was Harlan's. At the age of fifty, Brennan was the youngest member of the Warren Court. And throughout his career, Brennan had always fostered mentors. In law practice it had been Shelton Pitney. During the war it had been Robert Patterson. On the New Jersey bench it had first been Nat

Jacobs and later Arthur Vanderbilt. Now his mentor seemed destined to be Earl Warren, and both men seemed to intuitively know it right off the bat.

Amid the storm of personalities, friendships, and philosophies that swirled around him, Brennan's performance in his first few months proved to be anything but predictable.

The first case in which Brennan sat, *Butler v. Michigan*, challenged the arrest of a Detroit bookseller for peddling an allegedly obscene book called *The Devil Rides Outside*. The first lawyer to argue a case in front of Justice Brennan was Manuel Lee Robbins, Butler's New York City lawyer, who unsuccessfully asked the Court to void Michigan's century-old antiobscenity statute. Brennan asked only a couple of questions, leaving the lion's share of the interrogation to Frankfurter.

His first written opinion came in a relatively obscure tax case, *Putnam v. Commissioner of Internal Revenue*. The issue was whether a loss incurred by a Des Moines, Iowa, businessman could be taken as a deduction on his income taxes. It was virtually unanimous that he could not take a full loss. Only Justice Harlan dissented, and sheepishly at that. He sent Brennan a note apologizing that he had to dissent on Brennan's "first."

From his seating on the Court until the beginning of his confirmation hearings in February, Brennan was as likely to vote with Frankfurter as against him. In fact, Brennan's first dissent, published in his own name, came on January 14, in *LaBuy v. Howes Leather*. Bucking the Warren, Douglas, and Black alliance, Brennan's dissent was joined by Frankfurter, Burton, and Harlan. The case was technical, but the point was that his opinion stressed the limits of judicial power in a case involving a Minnesota federal judge.

In *Fikes v. Alabama*, another case heard in Brennan's first two months on the Court, Brennan again took a more conservative stance, even though the matter involved the rights of a criminal defendant. The Fikes case involved the coerced confession of a black Alabamian. Although Brennan was as appalled as Black at the outrageous details of a police beating, he felt obligated to join Frankfurter's opinion, rather than Black's. In his separate concurrence, Brennan explained that while the facts in this particular case were outrageous, and he did vote to overturn the conviction, "a state court's judgement of conviction must not be set aside by this Court where the practices of the prosecution do not offend what may fairly be deemed the civilized standards of the Anglo-American world." He did not want the ruling to be a precedent.

But in a trio of other cases handed down on February 25, Brennan cast his vote with Black, Douglas, and Warren in a losing block of four. Each of the three cases—In re *Groban*, *Pollard* v. *U.S.*, and *Nilva* v. *U.S.*—involved the rights of the defendant against the power of the states. In re *Groban* questioned whether a fire-department investigator had to notify a witness of a right to counsel. The Pollard case allowed the imprisonment of an embezzler on a state charge, after he had been released from federal prison where he served time for the same crime. Brennan agreed with Black and Warren that this constituted double jeopardy. *Nilva*, the least important of the three, allowed the conviction of a slot-machine executive despite errors by the prosecution at his trial. As he had in the Tune case, Brennan felt errors at the trial were cause to void a conviction.

But in *Breithaupt* v. *Abram*, decided the same day, Brennan deserted the bloc to support Frankfurter's view that the state had the right to extract a blood sample from an unwitting traffic accident victim, then use the sample against the person in court to prove drunken driving.

Those hoping to identify a trend in those first decisions were badly disappointed.

The day these decisions were released, February 25, 1957, after he had served nearly two thirds of the Court's October to May term, the Senate finally got around to confirmation hearings. Although not endangered, Brennan's appointment was hardly universally welcomed. South Carolina senator Olin Johnston threatened to challenge what he feared were Brennan's "integrationist tendencies." Shortly after coming on the Court, Brennan had joined in a unanimous vote upholding a ban on segregation in Montgomery, Alabama's bus system. "I would like to look into Brennan's background and check on some of his beliefs and disbeliefs with a fine-tooth comb before taking a stand," Johnston said.

Mississippi senator James Eastland, chairman of the committee, postponed the first scheduled public hearing on Brennan, a move designed as a bargaining chip against Eisenhower's civil rights program. Eastland could indeed be difficult. When Eisenhower had presented

Eastland with Solicitor General Simon Sobeloff as a prospective judge on the Fourth U.S. Circuit Court of Appeals in 1955, Eastland had told President Eisenhower that the only way the appointment would be heard by the committee was if the administration promised not to send up any civil rights bills in 1956. When Eastland initially failed to get a response, he continually postponed hearings on the nomination. Explaining one of the delays to Greenville, Mississippi's *Delta Democrat Times*, he said: "I had the committee staff prepare a lengthy brief. Then in the committee I recognized Senator Johnston, who spent five weeks of our committee sessions reading it. Then I told the administration that they could have Sobeloff as long as no further civil rights measures were offered and on July 1, they agreed." They had to.

Eastland said in March that if the administration hadn't finally agreed to his demand, he wouldn't have scheduled the next hearing until July 9. "And I wouldn't have made that one," Eastland said, " 'cause I had to learn about a new irrigation system down on my farm." Sobeloff was finally confirmed by the Senate in late July, almost a full year after his nomination.

Eastland would ultimately vote for Brennan, but only after making clear to Brownell that the Eisenhower administration owed him a few more favors.

More determined than Eastland to wreak havoc on the Brennan nomination was Wisconsin senator Joseph McCarthy. McCarthy's network of informants and supporters had not neglected to take note of Brennan's speeches at both Boston and Red Bank. McCarthy viewed Brennan's Red Bank speech as particularly challenging, since it was at nearby Ft. Monmouth that McCarthy was investigating alleged Communist infiltration into the army.

Just as worrisome to the extreme right, although less of an issue to McCarthy, was a speech Justice Brennan delivered to the Legal Aid Society of New York three weeks before his hearings. In that address Brennan spoke eloquently of the importance of justice to the poor. "Nothing rankles more in the human heart than a brooding sense of injustice," Brennan said. "Illness we can put up with. But injustice makes us want to pull things down. When only the rich can enjoy the law, and the poor can not have it because expense puts it beyond their reach, the threat to the continued existence of a free democracy is not imaginary, it is very real."

On February 25, 1957, a jammed hearing room of 150 people gathered to hear the confrontation between two very different Irishmen. Outside the room representatives of the National Liberal League, an organization which advocated the independence of the Court but feared papal domination, passed out literature claiming that a Catholic was unfit for the Court. Someone called out, "What about Justice Murphy?"

A leafleteer's face turned red. "Murphy did all right," he conceded. But the league members were nervous about having their luck hold through a second Catholic appointment.

Inside the hearing room, Senator McCarthy himself passed out pamphlets. He told spectators that he wondered whether Brennan could "distinguish between Americanism and communism." McCarthy then swept into the room dropping a large red-covered volume on his senate desk.

"I have never personally met Mr. Brennan," McCarthy began his interrogation. "Anything I say here is not motivated by personal feelings. I have asked to appear before this committee for one reason and one reason only. As the committee is well aware, the Supreme Court will have a number of cases before it in the months ahead concerning the Communist conspiracy and concerning congressional efforts to expose the conspiracy. Whether Congress will be able to pursue its investigations of communism will depend, in a very large measure, upon how those cases are decided. I think therefore that it is of the utmost importance for this committee, for the Senate, and for the American people to know if the judges that will decide those cases are predisposed against congressional investigations of communism. On the basis of that part of the record that I am dealing with, I believe Justice Brennan has demonstrated an underlying hostility to congressional attempts to expose the Communist conspiracy. I can only conclude that his decisions on the Supreme Court are likely to harm our efforts to fight communism. I shall therefore vote against his confirmation unless he is able to persuade me today that I am not in possession of the true facts with regard to his views. I shall want to know if it is true that Justice Brennan, in his public speeches, has referred to congressional investigations of communism, for example, as 'Salem witch-hunts' and 'inquisitions,' and has accused congressional committees of 'barbarism.' "

Brennan stared intently at the Senate's grand inquisitor. The one thing he didn't want to do was irritate McCarthy any more than necessary.

The Wisconsin senator continued: "I have evidence that he has done so. And such views, in my opinion, reflect an utterly superficial understanding—putting it mildly—of the Communist threat to our liberties as well as an underlying contempt for the Congress of the United States. I believe that before a vote is taken on this matter, this committee and the Senate and the American people have a right to know whether Justice Brennan can be counted on to help or hinder the fight against communism.

"I don't have any high hopes of being successful in opposition to Justice Brennan's nomination. I have great fear that the left-wing—and I emphasize left-wing—Democrats and the so-called moderate Republicans, just what that means I don't know, but the moderate Republicans will roll over and play dead and approve his nomination."

Democratic senator Joseph O'Mahoney, yet another Irishman, interrupted. "You made reference to your possession of certain documents," he said. "Would you identify the documents?"

McCarthy: "I would be glad to. They are statements that come from the mouth of Justice Brennan."

O'Mahoney: "Pardon me, senator."

McCarthy: "Can I finish, senator?"

O'Mahoney: "No."

McCarthy: "Let me finish my answer."

O'Mahoney: "You can't answer it."

McCarthy: "Senator O'Mahoney, let me answer your question."

O'Mahoney: "You can't answer it until you know what it is."

McCarthy: "I heard your question."

O'Mahoney: "But you don't understand it . . . "

Just minutes into the process, Brennan's confirmation was in danger of becoming a circus. Brennan breathed deeply and took a drink of water. O'Mahoney continued: "Let me say for the record, senator, that the documents you have in your hand are mere typewritten papers. I don't want you to read them. I want you to identify them."

McCarthy: "I was about to identify them, Mr. O'Mahoney."

O'Mahoney: "Please do."

McCarthy: "And I might say that these were gotten from Mr. Brennan's office as a result of news statements about them, so I assume they are accurate."

O'Mahoney: "Oh, you assume. I want to know. Are they accurate?"

McCarthy: "When they come from him, senator."

O'Mahoney: "What is your proof?"

McCarthy: "When they come from him?"

O'Mahoney: "What is your proof that they come from him?"

McCarthy: "His letter stating that he was sending them to me. If he questions them, I would be glad."

O'Mahoney was finally satisfied. "Now you are identifying them," he said.

But a moment later they were back at it.

"The documents I refer to are speeches made by Mr. Brennan."

O'Mahoney interrupted again. "Your say-so doesn't make it so."

McCarthy: "I think my say-so may mean something. I just told you that they are speeches of Mr. Brennan."

O'Mahoney: "If you would only identify them, then we would know if your say-so is correct."

McCarthy: "Could you give me one second's time to identify them?"

O'Mahoney: "You have all the time there is, sir. I just want you to proceed in an orderly manner, not in a disorderly manner."

McCarthy: "If I didn't have this interruption I would be proceeding in an orderly manner."

O'Mahoney: "Well, for the record you stated that you had a lot of books on the table. I see only the *Congressional Record* and some concealed pamphlets."

McCarthy's face turned bright red as the audience erupted in laughter.

"I may say, Mr. Chairman, that some of the audience may think this is humorous. There is nothing humorous about appointing a justice to the Supreme Court and I don't think it is humorous. You may have a great sense of humor, senator, but I am just trying to answer your question and I will answer it if you will just be quiet for thirty seconds."

O'Mahoney: "Please answer the question and I will be quiet."

McCarthy held up copies of the two speeches, the one from Boston and the one from the Rotary Club in Red Bank. "I must say that Mr. Brennan is a very erudite gentleman and gives very good speeches,"

McCarthy allowed. "But I am not going to discuss the overall speech of Mr. Brennan. I intend to question him about some of the items he brought forth."

His jousting with O'Mahoney over, McCarthy turned to confront Brennan, who had sat silent through all that had so far transpired. "Do you approve of congressional investigations and exposure of the Communist conspiracy?" McCarthy had gotten right to his point.

"Not only do I approve, senator, but personally I cannot think of a more vital function of the Congress than the investigatory function of its committees, and I can't think of a more important or vital objective of any committee investigation than that of rooting out subversives in government," Brennan replied.

McCarthy: "You, of course, I assume, will agree with me—and a number of the members of the committee—that communism is not merely a political way of life, it is a conspiracy designed to overthrow the United States government."

Brennan: "Will you forgive me an embarrassment, senator? You appreciate that I am a sitting justice of the Court. There are presently pending before the Court some cases in which I believe will have to be decided the question what is communism, at least in the frame of reference in which those particular cases have come before the Court. With that qualification, whether under the label communism or any other label, any conspiracy to overthrow the government of the United States is a conspiracy that I not only would do anything appropriate to aid suppressing, but a conspiracy which, of course, like every American I abhor."

It was Brennan at his lawyerly best. Not a person in the room understood what Brennan had just said. The murmur of "huhs?" was audible. That was of course because he had said nothing except that a conspiracy is a conspiracy and all Americans abhor conspiracies.

Even McCarthy scratched his head. "Mr. Brennan," he said, "I don't want to press you unnecessarily, but the question was simple. You have not been confirmed yet as a member of the Supreme Court. There will come before the Court a number of questions involving the all-important issue of whether or not communism is merely a political party or whether it represents a conspiracy to overthrow the government."

Brennan: "Well, let me answer it, try to answer it, this way. Of course my nomination is now before the Senate for consideration, nevertheless, since October 16 I have been sitting as a member of the Court. The oath I took as unreservedly as you took your own, and as I know every senator took his. And I know, too, that your oath imposes upon you the obligation to ask just such questions as these. But I am in the position of having an oath of my own by which I have to guide my conduct and that oath obligates me not to discuss any matter presently before the Court because I have actually sat in consideration on such matters and the only way the mouth of a member of the Court may be opened in expression of an opinion in respect of any of them is a formal written opinion when that is finally written and filed. I do hope you will not feel that in saying what I do, I am doing any more than taking what I am sure is your own position that each of us has to be faithful to his own oath."

McCarthy: "Mr. Brennan, we are asked to either vote to confirm or reject you. One of the things I have maintained is that you have adopted the gobbledygook that communism is merely a political party, not a conspiracy."

Brennan: "I can only answer, senator, that, believe me there are cases now pending in which the contention is made, at least in the frame of reference to which cases come to the Court, that the definitions which have been given by the Congress to communism do not fit the particular circumstances."

McCarthy: "Will you repeat that?"

Brennan: "I say the contention is being made in those cases that the congressional definition does not fit the particular circumstances presented by the cases."

McCarthy: "I don't want to interrupt you, but could you tell us where and when?"

Brennan: "I can't say anything to you, senator, about a pending case."

McCarthy was flabbergasted.

"You just did," he exclaimed. "You said the Congress, the definition of the Congress does not fit—what is the word you used?"

Brennan: "I said the contention made in the particular case—and for that reason the issue which is presented to the Court for decision— is whether on the particular facts in the case now before the Court that definition does or does nor fit."

Not since his appearances in the postwar army hearings had Brennan so tongue-tied a congressional committee. McCarthy asked the clerk to read it all back.

"You know that Congress has defined communism as a conspiracy, you do know that," McCarthy said.

"I know the Congress has enacted a definition, yes," Brennan replied.

McCarthy bellowed. "I want an answer to this. I want to know whether or not the young man who is proposed for the Supreme Court feels that communism is a conspiracy or merely a political party. [Brennan, at fifty, was actually two years older than McCarthy.] Now just so you won't be in the dark about my reason for asking that, the *Daily Worker*, all of the Communist-lip papers, and the Communist witnesses who have appeared before my committee, I assume the same is true of Senator Eastland's committee, have taken the position that it is merely a political party. I want to know whether you agree with this. That will affect your decision. It will affect my decision on how to vote on your confirmation. I hope it will affect the decision of the other senators."

"I appreciate that what to one man is the path of duty may to another be the path of folly," Brennan responded. "But I simply cannot venture any comment whatever that touches upon any matter before the Court."

Stymied in his attempt to get Brennan to differentiate between communism as a mere party or an international conspiracy, McCarthy moved on to the Brennan speeches, challenging him to explain his remarks about the possible excesses of congressional committees. Here Brennan retreated.

"I was not concerned primarily with any committee as such," Brennan squirmed. "What troubled me was largely this: I think that committee investigations are so vital a part of congressional work that it is awfully important that what those committees do in the discharge of their work has the complete confidence of all of us, because I think when people become more interested in how the job is done, rather than that the job is done, we have symptom of a condition which threatens to impair the vitality of the job and the job is too important."

Brennan continued: "The symptom in this instance, as I saw it, was also in a form in which aspects of fair play came in. By that I mean this: I suppose there is no American heritage that all of us cherish more than that of the right to fair play. And I mean not only do Americans expect fair play of their courts and administrative agencies but I think as well of investigating committees. I don't think Americans distinguish justice in that sense as court justice or agency justice or legislative justice and they are the things I commented upon in that speech."

McCarthy: "Do you find any evidence of Salem witch-hunts?"

"I couldn't say that of any congressional committee," Brennan replied. "What I was thinking of was this: There was a general atmosphere that bothered me and I think a lot of other Americans about this time. This was in 1954 and before that when we seemed generally to be highly hysterical, as I think I quoted in my speech, did I not, and quoted Ann O'Hare McCormick something to the effect that a picture of ourselves as a nation petrified by the fear of communism is neither true nor flattering. It was the general notion—not congressional committees—but there was a general feeling of hysteria that I felt was very unfortunate and many things were symptoms of it, not congressional committees. I want to make it clear, I never said that congressional committees were embarked on Salem witch-hunts."

McCarthy thought for a moment.

"Have you ever approved an investigation of the Communist exposure?" he asked. "If you will think back and you have made speeches saying you were against communism—have made some high-sounding speeches along that line—while you have been making those speeches against communism generally, can you tell us of when you have approved a single investigation of the same Communists you were talking about?"

In the audience the Brennan supporters squirmed. J. L. Bernstein, thought Brennan was dead. "It's one thing to explain away things you did say, but how do you explain things you didn't say," Bernstein muttered about the unfairness of it all.

"I don't know quite what you mean, where I have approved," said Brennan, buying time while he got his wits together. "I say and say again that we cannot do enough to make sure this fight is won. We can't do enough to see that anything like it within or out of government is exposed. What I was talking to was a premonition I felt that unless it were approached differently than it was being approached, we would lose our eyes, get our eyes off the target and on other things which would dissipate our energies to do it."

Brennan didn't even know what that meant. But it sounded good. "That's what I was talking about," he added.

McCarthy wasn't going to be fooled.

"I have a rather long memory," he said. "I think at least three minutes, so I remember the question I asked you. Have you ever approved an investigation of the Communist exposure. If you will just think back, have you ever approved by one little word the exposure of Communists, either by the Internal Security Committee, the House Committee, the investigating committee or any other committee?"

"I had no occasion in either of these speeches," Brennan said. "I don't recall I have had any other occasions when I affirmatively in public got up to say what I just said now. I can only say that if I ever had I would have said precisely what I said now: That I was very much for it, very, very much for it. I just want to be certain we don't dissipate our energies by not doing it as effectively as we could."

McCarthy: "What did you mean when you referred to barbarism of the investigating committees? I would like to know where we have been barbaric in exposing communism? You talked about epithets hurled at hapless and helpless witnesses. Can you give us an example?"

Brennan continued to waffle. "No. These, senator, were honest illustrations, a little artist's license, if you please, of what it is I was getting at. I can't tell you exactly what it was I had in mind, but I know that there was certainly an impression abroad, and believe me I think actually the appearance for this purpose is as bad or almost as bad as the actuality, that witnesses in some of these instances were not being treated as I am presently being treated."

His answer irritated Republican senator William E. Jenner of Indiana. "Did you ever hear some of the epithets that were hurled at the committee members?"

"No, sir," Brennan answered meekly.

"Some of those were pretty bad too," returned Jenner.

McCarthy: "People were entitled to think that when you made a statement you were basing it on fact. Do I understand now that when you talked about epithets being hurled at hapless and helpless victims you had no incident in mind, that you were merely speaking from what you thought might have been an impression created?"

Brennan: "No, I probably did but I don't now remember."

Brennan was tiring. But McCarthy bore in with one more assault. "I would like to hand you a copy of the rules under which the investigating committee acted. Is there anything barbaric in that or is there anything barbaric that you know of by any other committee?"

McCarthy prepared for his zinger. "And, Mr. Brennan, just so there is no doubt in your mind, I have been reading in the *Daily Worker*—and I don't intimate that you are even remotely a Communist or anything like that."

"I have never read a copy of it," Brennan muttered.

"I do," McCarthy hollered. "I read it. I have been reading in every left-wing paper the same type of gobbledygook that I find in your speeches talking about the barbarism of the committees, the same Salem witch-hunts. I just wonder if a Supreme Court justice can hide behind his robes and conduct a guerrilla warfare against investigating committees."

Brennan's performance had been anything but courageous. Liberal columnist Murray Kempton described Brennan as "too soggy for sympathy!" Instead of rising to the challenge like a man, Kempton wrote, "Brennan assumed a bearing that my own inflamed sensibilities could only take for abjection."

Following his first day's inquisition, McCarthy promised to drag Brennan through a second day of the rack and screw. Brennan's friends used McCarthy's unrelenting examination to second-guess Brennan's decision to personally appear before the Senate. On the evening of his first night of testimony, some of his confidence had dissipated. He had been treated with relative politeness by McCarthy and the Senate. Yet the questioning had been withering. Brennan wondered what it must be like to get the full treatment.

On the following morning, Brennan pushed through the crowds of Capitol visitors to resume the joust. But to his relief, McCarthy didn't show. Instead he sent Eastland a letter:

"I am convinced after yesterday's session that there is no further doubt about the accuracy of my initial conclusions. I believe that the written record of the committee now confirms Justice Brennan harbors an underlying hostility to congressional attempts to investigate and expose the Communist conspiracy and I am doubtful that further questioning on the subject would serve any useful purpose."

It was truly McCarthy's last hurrah. Three months later the most

infamous character in the history of the U.S. Senate died of liver disease at Bethesda Naval Hospital.

There was, however, one last matter to clear up that didn't involve
McCarthy. That was the issue of Brennan's Catholicism. Although
Catholics had served on the Court since 1836, there were still questions about Brennan's allegiances, just as there would be four years
later when Democratic senator John F. Kennedy of Massachusetts
sought the presidency. The president of the National Liberal League,
concerned that Cardinal Spellman had persuaded Eisenhower to appoint someone who would do nothing but follow the dictates of the
Catholic church, had continued to press the committee to read the
following question to the nominee.

"You are bound by your religion to follow the pronouncements of
the Pope on all matters of faith and morals. There may be some controversies which involve matters of faith and morals but also matters of
law and justice. But in matters of law and justice you are bound by
your oath to follow not papal decrees and doctrines but the laws and
precedents of the Nation. If you should be faced with such a mixed issue, would you be able to follow the requirements of your oath or
would you be bound by your religious obligations?"

Senator O'Mahoney, who himself was Catholic, decided to go ahead
and read the question. "I am sure the justice will be happy to answer,"
he said.

Senator Estes Kefauver of Tennessee wasn't happy, but did not object. "I do dislike the idea and I hope this won't be considered as estab-
lishing a precedent of having political considerations," Kefauver said.
"I mean religious consideration. Let me say that the very basis of our
country is that one's religion and politics and thoughts are supposed to
have freedom in connection with them. I would hate for this precedent
to start a wave of religious considerations pro and con with connection
with issues or with nominees."

"I think it would do more harm than good for the committee not to
have the question propounded," O'Mahoney answered.

After a few more moments of debate, when O'Mahoney read the
question, Brennan was ready with his answer. "Senator, the oath that I
took is the same that you and members of the Congress, every member
of the executive department up and down all levels of government
take to support the Constitution and the laws of the United States. I

took that oath just as unreservedly as I know you did and every member and everyone else of our faith in whatever office elected or appointed he may hold.

"My answer to the question is categorically that in everything I have ever done, in every office I have held in my life or that I shall ever do in the future, what shall control me is the oath that I took to support the Constitution and the laws of the United States and to act upon the cases that come before me for decision. It is that oath and that alone which governs."

With that assurance from Brennan, the nomination moved to the floor of the Senate. With only the one dissenting vote from McCarthy, Brennan was formally approved.

A ROCKY BEGINNING

Wʜᴇɴ ɴᴇᴡs ꜰɪʟᴛᴇʀᴇᴅ ꜰʀᴏᴍ ᴀᴄʀᴏss the street that Brennan was at last a permanent, and official, member of the Court family, Hugo Black was among the first to offer his congratulations. Just as Chief Justice Warren had seen Brennan as the answer to some of his shortcomings, Black, too, saw traits in Brennan that would be most valuable. For several months he had watched and weighed Brennan's attitude and moods. And Black had read and been impressed by Brennan's opinion in the New Jersey *Tune* case.

Although Black considered Warren "a wonderful guy," as he often put it to his clerks, the chief was not considered the brightest fellow in the world by the other judges. Douglas, whom Black believed was the most brilliant man he had ever met, drove the Alabamian crazy with his laziness. Douglas simply didn't want to spend time on Court work. He was involved in politics and clung to a hope that somehow he might one day be president.

Brennan, Black judged, was certainly not lazy. The new justice seemed to thrive on work. As for his mind, Black told his clerks, Brennan was no Douglas, but he wasn't Warren either. If there was anyone on the Court whom Brennan resembled, Black felt, it was Harlan. Neither of them seemed to believe in absolutes. Black described Brennan to his clerks as "a weigher." "Both Brennan and Harlan want to weigh everything," Black observed on one occasion. He attributed this to the fact that, unlike Douglas, Frankfurter, and Warren, both Harlan and Brennan had served as judges before coming on the Court. Instinctively Black distrusted judges, fearing that a balancing act would inevitably result in compromise. "If you start weighing the public interest against a constitutional right," Black would say, "you might rule against the right."

What Black found so encouraging was that although Brennan wanted to balance interests, as did Harlan, he invariably came down on the side of the constitutional right, rather than on the side of the state as did Harlan.

As a former southern politician, Black understood the power of subtle persuasion far better than the professorial Frankfurter ever could. He had watched and waited before making his approach. After the Senate hearing Black asked Brennan if he would like to join his country club in Virginia. Brennan was pleased to accept. In addition, Bill and Marjorie began receiving frequent dinner invitations to the Black home in Alexandria. It was a relief to find that there was no hidden agenda, no Dean Acheson's delivering lectures on how it all ought to be done. On Saturdays Black and Brennan would often walk across First Street to the Senate cafeteria for lunch.

The more Black knew of Brennan the surer he was that despite his flirtations with Frankfurter in such cases as *Breithaupt* and *Fikes* Brennan had the stuff to be one of the great justices. Bill Brennan, Black predicted to his clerk George Saunders, "is going to be my heir."

Never before in the history of the Court had the line been drawn so clearly between two conflicting ideologies. In shorthand, Frankfurter was the conservative, although there is an element of unfairness in portraying the defender of Sacco and Vanzetti, a founder of the American Civil Liberties Union, and a close friend and supporter of Franklin Roosevelt as a conservative in the modern popular sense. But as a justice, Frankfurter was not expansive in applying the federal Constitution to the states. The long-held position of the Court was that federal laws, statutes, and prosecutions must adhere to the letter of the Constitution. But state laws and procedures were another matter.

Despite his admirable record as a private attorney and teacher,

Frankfurter in no way connected the role of being a "justice" with the concept of "justice."

"I do not conceive that it is my function to decide cases on my no-tion of justice," Frankfurter wrote Brennan, urging him not to fall prey to the camp of Warren and Black. "If it were, I wouldn't be as confi-dent as some others are that I knew exactly what justice required in a particular case."

Yet Black's moral appeal was persuasive. It was his absolutist view that no state law infringing on any of the guarantees in the Bill of Rights could be lawful. He was a truly a Democrat with a small "d." And for many years, long before his appointment to the Court, he had held the simple belief that in America anybody should be able to say anything or write anything that he or she wanted to. And if other peo-ple didn't like it, that was tough. They didn't have to listen.

Until 1868, when the Fourteenth Amendment was ratified, the Supreme Court had held that the Bill of Rights did not apply to the states. Even something as basic as the constitutional provision that pri-vate property shall not be taken without just compensation was ruled inapplicable to state action until 1897. It wasn't until 1925, in a land-mark case called *Gitlow* v. *New York*, that the basic guarantees of the First Amendment were seen to be protected from state infringement. Gitlow was convicted of anarchy in 1920 for distributing left-wing lit-erature. But even though the Court ruled that states could not im-pinge on the basic right of political expression, Frankfurter and others clung to the view that Gitlow was an aberration and that most of the guarantees of the Bill of Rights did not have meaning for the states.

The philosophical underpinning for this view came from action taken at the Constitutional Convention in 1789. James Madison had proposed an amendment to the Constitution specifically binding the states to the Bill of Rights. "Restrictions on state power," Madison had argued, "is of equal if not greater importance." His suggestion was overwhelmingly rejected by the other Founding Fathers, who feared federal power, not state power. Thus it was that state legislatures had historically been able to restrict rights, while the federal government could not.

By the time Brennan arrived at the Court, Black and Frankfurter had been bickering over this issue for at least sixteen years; ever since the historic decision in the case of *Minersville School District v. Gobitis* in 1940. As expertly told in James Simon's work, *The Antagonists*, schoolchildren Lillian and William Gobitis were members of the Jehovah's Witness sect and had been taught by their parents not to bow down before idols. Thus when their local elementary school in Minersville, Pennsylvania, asked them to salute the flag in the morning, they refused. The refusal was met with expulsion. Their father then sued the school district.

Both the U.S. District Court judge who heard the case and the U.S. Court of Appeals that subsequently ruled on it, found the expulsion to be a pointless denial of freedom of religion. The patent unfairness of making someone salute the flag in school was almost unquestioned and nearly all major bar and academic organizations supported the Gobitis family.

But rather than view the case from the perspective of religious freedom, Frankfurter chose to view it as an issue of state and local power. Did a state not have the ability to ask its citizens to show respect for the flag?

At the Court's conference on the case, Frankfurter, a foreign-born patriot, upheld the expulsion, declaring that public schools have a right to instill "love of country" into our young people. Frankfurter was chosen by the chief justice to deliver the 8 to 1 opinion of the Court. Although Black had deferred to Frankfurter, he had been virtually silent on the case. Then three months after the decision had been announced, in June 1940, Black announced that he had made a mistake. Writing in a second Jehovah's Witness case, Black said the ruling had suppressed the free exercise of religion. Writing for himself, for Justice Douglas, and for Frank Murphy, Black declared, "the Bill of Rights has a high responsibility to accommodate itself to the religious views of minorities, however unpopular and unorthodox those views may be."

That Black had been able to persuade Douglas and Murphy to follow his thinking rather than Frankfurter's enraged the former professor. He accused Douglas of acting on his desire to become president. He questioned Murphy's intelligence and denounced Black as a manipulator. Harlan Fiske Stone, who had been the original dissenter, was spared from a Frankfurter diatribe. When Roosevelt appointee Wiley Rutledge joined the court in 1943, Black suddenly had a five-man majority in opposition to Frankfurter's views on judicial restraint. Later that year when the court heard a similar case on religious freedom from West Virginia, Black's views won out by a 6 to 3 vote.

Frankfurter reacted with one of the most remarkable personal statements ever to appear in a Court opinion. Writing his dissent, Frankfurter virtually cried out in pain at the antireligious-freedom position into which he had maneuvered himself. "One who belongs to the most vilified and persecuted minority in history is not likely to be insensible to the freedoms guaranteed by our Constitution. Were my purely personal attitude relevant, I should wholeheartedly associate myself with the general libertarian views in the Court's opinion, representing as they do the thoughts and actions of a lifetime. But as judges we are neither Jew nor Gentile."

From that critical dividing point in judicial history, it was the Madisonian Black who became the leader and darling of the liberals. Frankfurter's path became consistent in the opposite direction. He would repeatedly defer to state and legislative power no matter how unreasonable the statutes and laws might be.

Totally unsuspecting, totally naïve to the infighting on the nation's highest court, Brennan walked into the middle of the feud. Frankfurter hardly wasted a moment trying to sweep Brennan into his pocket. For Frankfurter the stakes were high because the new chief justice was becoming an unabashed disciple of Democrat Black. On a personal level their friendship was warm. On the road, Warren wrote long pen-pal type letters to Hugo.

As chief justice, Warren had something to offer Brennan that Frankfurter was not willing to give. Under the customs of the Supreme Court, the senior justice of the majority assigns the writing of the opinion. If the chief justice is in the majority, he assigns the opinion. While Frankfurter wanted Brennan's vote, he was not willing to give Brennan many opinions to write. Frankfurter had no confidence in any other judge, especially a newcomer, to write important decisions of the Court he worshiped. The chief justice, on the other hand, was more than willing to assign the actual work to Brennan. Warren was most definitely not a legal craftsman. He was a politician, and the Court would be his instrument for social change. As the senior justice, Black endorsed the idea of giving Brennan more than the usual number of important early decisions. He determined it might be nice to be on the winning side more often. "Maybe he can do better than I at bringing over someone from the other side," Black admitted on one occasion. Brennan, who was intrigued with trying to find consensus, liked the idea. As a former judge, the only former state court judge on the Court, Brennan also enjoyed opinion writing.

It was in three landmark cases, all announced in June 1957, that Brennan established himself as a serious contributor to the Court's business. It was also in those three cases—one involving antitrust, criminals' rights, and pornography, respectively—that Brennan made clear that his first allegiance would be to the chief justice and Black rather than to Frankfurter.

In early 1957, Warren persuaded Brennan to his side in the nation's most watched antitrust case, one involving the purchase of General Motors by the Du Pont Corporation. Since three of the "conservatives" on the court—Harlan, Clark, and Whittaker—had to recuse themselves for various reasons, Brennan's support gave the alliance of Warren, Black, and Douglas a four-man winning majority in a result that deeply disturbed big-business interests. The case was *United States v. E. I. Du Pont* and it was considered "the" monumental antitrust case of the century. The original federal court trial alone had lasted seven months and created an 8,283-page transcript.

The idea today of two companies as mighty as Du Pont and GM being merged would send shock waves through even the most hardened observer of American megabusiness. But the two giants weren't always totally separate.

In 1907, the Du Ponts, who had originally made their fortune in explosives, had seen the need to diversify their business. The U.S. Army, which had been the firm's major purchaser, had decided to open its own munitions plants. In anticipation of this change in the essential nature of their business, scientists in Delaware began experimenting with nitrocellulose, the principal raw ingredient in the making of many bombs. This work led to the discovery of numerous nonmilitary applications, especially in the production of synthetic fabric. In 1913, Du Pont purchased the Fabrikoid Company as a vehicle through which to manufacture synthetic leather. Three years later Du Pont expanded into the tire business by purchasing Fairfield Rubber Company. In 1917, just before their resources were turned back to war production, Du Pont added divisions in paint, color processing, and varnish.

None of this, of course, was by chance. Pierre S. Du Pont was already thinking about the automotive industry. As far back as 1914, he began buying stock in General Motors, a little conglomerate put together by William C. Durant from the Buick, Cadillac, Oldsmobile, and Oakland car companies. Subsequently, Chevrolet was added to the company. Durant fought numerous battles for financing with his banker, and in 1915 Pierre Du Pont had been appointed by a creditor's committee to serve as chairman of the General Motors board. On a personal level, Du Pont got along so well with Durant that he was encouraged to continue to buy an increasing interest in GM. On December 19, 1917, Du Pont happily complied, purchasing $25 million worth of stock in the company. It was a move that not only would provide tremendous profits from the investment itself but virtually guaranteed a steady market for Du Pont's synthetic seat covers, paints, and varnishes.

By 1921, four of GM's eight automotive divisions were buying almost exclusively from Du Pont, and tremendous pressure was exerted on the other four to follow suit, even though some independent suppliers could provide the same materials more cheaply or efficiently. Companies that had been long established suppliers to the GM divisions quickly capitulated. Flint Varnish and Chemical sold out to Du Pont for almost nothing. For the most part the only time any subsidiary of GM bought from a non-Du Pont source was when the tremendous demand simply outstripped Du Pont's ability to produce.

By the 1950s the government had attempted on numerous occasions to slow the tremendous power of the Du Ponts. But in case after case, the probusiness bias of the Supreme Court had resulted in Du Pont victories. The current action involving Du Pont's association with General Motors had been filed by the United States in 1949. The government's allegation was that Du Pont's ownership had given Du Pont an illegal preference over competitors. After the lengthy federal court trial, the judge had dismissed the government's action as totally without merit.

On November 14 and 15, 1956, at the end of Brennan's first month on the bench, the herd of lawyers for Du Pont and GM trooped into the Court in an attempt to preserve their lower-court victory.

In stating the government's argument, Assistant Solicitor General John F. Davis claimed that Section 7 of the Clayton Act prohibited one corporation from buying stock in another, if the result of that was to lessen competition or restrain commerce. Du Pont's answer was that the Clayton Act was intended only to restrain purchases of stock in a competitor, not in a customer or supplier. No one could argue that Du Pont and GM were competitors. Du Pont didn't make cars.

Davis told the Court that Du Pont's intent in buying General Motors was to obtain "illegal preference" with respect to GM's purchases of materials. He presented a 1917 memo from a Du Pont official stating that "ultimately Du Pont would control and dominate the whole General Motors situation."

Brennan interrupted: "This is all you have as to intent?"

Davis patiently explained to Brennan that the government's case was based on three legs: the first was power; the second, intent; the third, restraint of trade. Davis acknowledged to Brennan that Du Pont had not acted nefariously. "I'm sure they thought what they were doing was good for Du Pont, good for General Motors, and good for the United States."

"You are getting dangerously close to a famous epigram," Frankfurter said cheekily.

The case for Du Pont was made by noted corporate attorney Hugh B. Cox. He denied that Du Pont companies got preference in supply contracts and orders. Some GM divisions, he argued, would buy all their paint from Du Pont, others very little. He said there was also competition in fabric purchases. If that was true, Justice Stanley Reed asked, why did General Motors buy such a higher percentage of its paint from Du Pont than the other car companies did? Cox answered that up until 1939 Ford did buy as much Du Pont paint. But after that time, he said, Ford began a policy of making its own paint and fabric. Chrysler, he added, made a decision to buy all its paint from Pittsburgh Plate Glass Company. Again Brennan interrupted.

"Is there any evidence whether decisions to buy paint from Du Pont were arrived at after tests of comparable paint?" He asked.

"They constantly tested," said Cox.

Chief Justice Warren jumped in: "Are there Du Pont products that are not used by General Motors or that are used in small quantities?"

"Yes, we sell more Du Pont products to others than we do to General Motors," Cox said.

Three days later the justices entered their conference room to figure out which side would prevail. Justice Harlan, who had been a lawyer for

Du Pont, did not join them. To Warren there was little question that
the opinion of the federal judge had been completely wrong. "When
Du Pont went into this," Warren told the justices in their weekly conference, "it did so for the purpose of controlling a channel for the out-
let of its products and it gave them control." Black and Douglas
agreed. Frankfurter and Burton, as expected, quickly came out to affirm the decision in favor of Du Pont. There was certainly no conspiracy and the Court had no right to interfere with the progress of
business. Brennan initially, as might befit a newcomer, did not stake
out a definitive position. But he was not silent either.

Brennan said he wasn't sure the antitrust had been violated, but he
had a feeling that Du Pont's motives in its GM investments might have
been to guarantee their markets. But unlike Black and Douglas, Brennan was circumspect about ordering Du Pont to sell its stock. Indeed,
he seemed to be in support of the corporations when he observed that
both Du Pont and GM "had tried hard not to abuse their relationship."
Frankfurter was confident Brennan would wind up on his side.

But under Warren and Black's constant prodding, Brennan began to
come around to the chief's point of view. As always Warren cared little
about the precise intent of the Clayton Act. For him court decisions
did not fall on narrow legal technicalities. The merger of two giants
was not desirable. It couldn't help but lead to abuse, even if it wasn't
obvious from the record. Brennan found himself sympathetic to Warren's conclusion. Although Brennan had been antiunion for most of
his life, he was not particularly for big business. His opposition to the
labor unions had been for precisely the reason that they had become
too powerful, too big. He felt the same about private business. In his
speeches, Brennan had repeatedly stressed the importance of the individual. Supporting a merger of two giants would not have been in his
character.

As in many of his early decisions, Brennan tried to find as much a
middle ground as possible. True to his nature as an accommodationist,
Brennan did not go so far as to order an immediate sale of the stock, as
Douglas and Black wanted, but sent the case back to a lower court for
"the equitable relief necessary." It would be several years before the
Court would finally order Du Pont's divestiture of GM stock.

In subsequent conference sessions, Brennan assured the chief that he would join a majority along with Black and Douglas. With Harlan not participating, and with Reed retired, that made the vote 4 to 3 against Du Pont and for the government. Since Brennan's was the deciding vote, Warren and Black rewarded the convert with the important assignment of writing the opinion. Otherwise a more strident opinion by Justice Douglas, for example, might push Brennan back to the Frankfurter side and instead of winning, Warren and Black would lose by a 4 to 3 vote.

On June 3, 1957, Brennan read from the bench what would be the first of two major decisions that day.

> We hold that any acquisition by one corporation of all or any part of the stock of another corporation, competitor or not, is within the reach [of the Clayton Act]. . . . Thus although Du Pont and General Motors are not competitors, a violation of the section has occurred. . . .
>
> We agree with the trial court that considerations of price, quality and service were not overlooked by either Du Pont or General Motors. Pride in its products and its high financial stake in General Motors' success would naturally lead Du Pont to try to supply the best. But the wisdom of this business judgment cannot obscure the fact, plainly revealed by the record, that Du Pont purposely employed its stock to pry open the General Motors' market to entrench itself as the primary supplier of GM's requirements for automotive finishes and fabrics.

Frankfurter and Harlan were appalled by Brennan's about-face.

As Brennan read his decision and Warren looked on approvingly, Harlan passed Frankfurter a note: "Now that my lips are no longer sealed, if there was ever a more superficial understanding of a really impressive record, I would like to see it. I hardly recognize the case as I listen to him speak. Harold's [Burton] and your dissent at least puts the Court record something towards redeeming what (between you and me) for me has been the most disillusioning blot in the Court's processes."

Frankfurter nodded to Harlan in disgusted agreement.

In the dissent fashioned by Frankfurter and Burton, Brennan's opinion was denounced as "too sweeping." He was accused of ignoring the simple fact that there was no proof of, indeed no allegation of, any intentional misconduct. But the reaction of Frankfurter and Burton was mild compared to that of the business establishment. *Fortune* magazine punched:

> Justice William Brennan's sweeping majority opinion ignored 40 years of precedent and administrative experience, enunciated radical new concepts of antitrust theory and did almost nothing to clear up ambiguities in the [Clayton Act] law. On the contrary, Justice Brennan's opinion introduced uncertainties into the law and placed virtually every large company under a cloud of suspicion.
>
> Most ominous of all, the decision represents an extraordinarily exacting definition of what constitutes effective competition within a given market.
>
> Justice Brennan's sweeping assertion of the government's right to outlaw intercorporate relationships of long standing—even where no monopoly exists and where none is alleged—immensely strengthened the Clayton Act. Indeed it is difficult to see why the Justice Department should henceforth trouble to prove monopoly or restraint under the Sherman Act, when it can prove merely the possibility of restraint under the newly interpreted Clayton Act.

But Du Pont wasn't the only controversy in which Brennan became embroiled on June 3, 1957. Warren had given his new lieutenant another charge, one to which Brennan was a little bit more attuned from the beginning. As a former prosecutor, Warren was interested in few things so much as cleaning up the nation's atrocious record on defendant's rights. While it would be glib to assume that a prosecutor would want to strengthen criminal laws, actually the converse was true. Warren had seen all the prosecutorial abuse he could stand. And on the court, he was determined to do something about it.

For Brennan's part, overzealous police work was something he had seen since his childhood. His father had warred against it for thirteen years as Newark's commissioner of public safety. As a justice on the New Jersey Supreme Court, Brennan was extremely proud of his vigorous dissent in the New Jersey murder case of John Henry Tune. More than anything he had done in his professional life, the *Tune* dissent had honored the memory of William Brennan, Sr. The only thing that would have honored that memory more would have been if Brennan could have convinced Vanderbilt to go along with him, to make it a landmark majority ruling. But now, on the U.S. Supreme Court, a case had come along that would provide the opportunity to do exactly that in *Jencks v. United States.*

Clinton Jencks had been president of the International Union of Mine, Mill, and Smelter Workers. As required by law at the time, April 28, 1950, Jencks's position compelled him to file a statement with the National Labor Relations Board that he was not a member of the Communist party. It was one of the provisions [section 9 (H)] of the Taft-Hartley Act that Brennan, while a private attorney, had supported in his speeches condemning Communist interference in the labor movement. Jencks filed the affidavit swearing that he was not affiliated either with the Communist party or with any front organizations.

But an FBI investigation of Jencks's past showed some associations that he had not revealed. According to a man named J. W. Ford, who himself claimed to have been a Communist from 1946 to 1950, Jencks had been a party member. Ford said he could recall at least five Communist party meetings that Jencks had attended. Another paid FBI informant, Harvey F. Matusow, verified Ford's recollections. He told the agents that while at a ranch in New Mexico, Jencks had urged people to read the *Daily Worker* and that he had heard Jencks praise a Soviet plan for world disarmament. Another witness testified that Jencks was once present at a closed Communist party meeting in Colorado, where Jencks, who was a veteran of World War II, urged other veterans to "spread out" and radicalize a wide variety of organizations. Based on the testimony of Ford and Matusow, as well as other informants, Jencks was indicted and charged with perjury in his affidavit.

When the case came to trial, it was revealed during the cross-examination of Ford and Matusow that they had made written statements about Jencks to the FBI. Believing that such material might provide some basis to impeach their oral testimony—perhaps their stories had changed—Jencks's lawyer asked that the documents be made available to the judge, and that those details pertinent to Jencks be made available to the defense. Government lawyers objected to the production of the confidential FBI reports, and the trial judge denied the motion virtually without comment. A U.S. Appeals Court upheld the trial judge's exclusion of the evidence saying that Jencks's attorneys had not shown there was inconsistency between Matusow's testimony and his written statements.

Jencks's appeal, which asked that Jencks be allowed to inspect the documents and get a new trial, was heard by the Court on October 17, 1956, just two days after Brennan's arrival. As was the custom before the Supreme Court, the lawyers' arguments were limited to half an hour for each side of the case. Then on either Wednesday or Friday at five minutes before 9:30 A.M., a buzzer sounds calling the judges to the conference room. There, seated around the table on high-backed leather chairs on rollers, with a crystal chandelier overhead, the justices would do their business, screening petitions for new cases, deliberating the cases that had just been argued, or doing internal Court business. No one except the justices are present at the conference: no clerks, no secretaries, no visitors.

The conference of the Supreme Court is the most secretive deliberation in Washington. All that is known about the sessions has come from reading the notes that justices have made while discussing cases. The most extensive collection comes from Justice Douglas, who deposited his notes in the Library of Congress. Justice Black, on the other hand, ordered his destroyed.

In conference the judges shake hands with one another and take their seats at a long rectangular table, the chief at one end and the senior justice, Hugo Black, at the other. Along the sides of the table the three more senior justices sat on one side, while Brennan took his place, on the crowded side, with Whittaker, Clark, and Harlan. The most junior justice, Whittaker, sat closest to the door and opened it when there was a knock to deliver a message.

By custom, the chief justice always spoke first. It was his role to review the facts and to recite the holdings of the lower courts. Chief Justice Warren then stated his view that the conviction should be overturned. He argued that it was just basic fairness that Jencks have the judge examine the reports, "particularly when he says he has no recollection of anything in them." Following Warren, the justices moved around the table in order of seniority. The only argument was over whether everything in the reports should be given to the judge or only what the government deemed relevant. Justices Burton and Clark both supported the more restrictive approach.

Finally, after seven justices had spoken, Brennan's turn came. He hardly suffered from any rookie nervousness, but jumped right in. Brennan announced that he not only agreed with Warren but that he felt the Court should go even further. It wasn't enough, Brennan said, to let the judge screen the materials. It should all be handed to the defense. "Statements should be made available to the parties," Brennan said. "I don't like this examination by the judge only." Because Brennan appeared to feel so passionate about the issue, because it was so close to the feelings he had already written about in the New Jersey prosecution of John Henry Tune, and because he wanted to see what Brennan could do, Chief Justice Warren announced after the conference that Brennan would write the opinion. He eventually wrote a far-reaching opinion that incorporated the concepts he had expressed at the conference. "The practice of producing government documents to the trial judge . . . is disapproved," Brennan wrote. "Only after inspection of the reports by the accused must the judge determine admissibility." He then circulated a draft of his opinion to the other justices. They would make comments and return them to Brennan. Often they would be accompanied by statements like, "I'm still with you" or, "You are going too far. I am reconsidering my vote for affirmance."

Since the Jencks prosecution was a federal one, not a state action, Frankfurter continued to concur in the result, although he was nervous about Brennan's inclination to make a ruling that went beyond what even the defense attorney had asked for. Frankfurter suggested that Brennan make the narrowest possible ruling and that he forget about his idea to make the reports available to the defense. But supported by Douglas, Black, and Warren, Brennan ignored Frankfurter's advice. Frankfurter, not wanting to lose Brennan in the future, made a calculated judgment to let the new justice go ahead. Even though Frankfurter was sure it was bad law, he did not want to anger Brennan, whom he might need in the future.

Tom Clark, one of two remaining Truman appointees, was distraught at the scope of Brennan's conclusion. Clark said he could support disclosure to the judge, but to hand the materials over to the defendant was too much. Brennan did nothing more to accommodate Clark's feelings than he had for Frankfurter. As a newcomer to the court, Brennan had not yet learned the damage that even one angry dissenter could cause.

So on June 3, 1957, the same day he announced the decision in *Du Pont*, Brennan announced the Court's remarkable ruling in *Jencks*. Not only must the materials be turned over to the defense, Brennan declared, but if the prosecutors choose not to comply, there would be no alternative but to dismiss the indictment.

When Brennan finished, Justice Burton issued a short opinion, disagreeing only with the contention that the case should be completely dismissed rather than sent back for a new trial. Then an angry Tom Clark lit up the chamber's press gallery. "Even the defense attorneys did not have the temerity to ask for such a sweeping decision," he declared. "They only asked that the documents be delivered to the judge for his determination of whether the defendant should be permitted to examine them. Perhaps with a recanting witness the trial judge should have examined the specific documents called for, as the defense requested, and if he thought justice required their delivery to the defense order such a delivery to be made. But as Brother Burton points out this would not require a reversal but merely a vacation of judgment and a remand to the trial Court."

Now he had the Court's attention.

"Unless the Congress changes the rule announced by the Court today, those intelligence agencies of our government engaged in law enforcement may as well close up shop, for the Court has opened their files to the criminal and thus afforded him a Roman holiday for rummaging through confidential information and vital national secrets."

The gaudy language of Clark's dissent, his call for action and his "Roman holiday," caught the national headlines. The phrase quickly became a rallying cry for a public that was truly stunned by how far Brennan had taken the case. At the Justice Department there was shock. In the federal courts there was confusion. And in Congress there was just raw political anger and demagoguery.

J. Edgar Hoover put together a dossier of supposed confidential informants and sent a summary to every cabinet-level office in Washington. The packet revealed information that the Communist party USA was "jubilant." According to a book on the FBI and the Court, entitled *Cloak and Gavel* by Alexander Charns, Hoover found the threat of the ruling so serious that he had memoranda about the case put in a file along with memos about the FBI's "Intrusion Detection System." One

day after the ruling, Hoover told callers that he was already working
with legislators to overturn the Brennan doctrine.

A confused President Eisenhower called the ruling "hard to understand." At a dinner party Ike told guests, "I've never been as mad in my
life" as he was at the decision to "open secret FBI files to accused subversives."

Attorney General Brownell also began to have his first doubts about
the man he had gotten appointed to the court. He issued a public
statement saying Brennan had caused "an emergency in law enforcement." In the days following the ruling public passions were inflamed
by a deluge of reports that criminals were going free because of Brennan's *Jencks* ruling.

Illinois congressman Harold Collier took the well of the House on
July 10 to vent his feelings: "FBI files were in effect declared sitting
ducks in open hunting season by the Supreme Court of the United
States in the now famous *Jencks* case. The court told every criminal
and his lawyer that they have the right to examine the sealed files of
the FBI if they think that through such examination they can find
documentary evidence to support whatever nefarious position they
choose to take. Under the new Court edict their mass of material is
open to the prying eyes of lawyers and outright criminals—men who
would and could use it to their own advantage and without regard for
those whom it might needlessly hurt."

South Carolina senator Olin Johnston declared, "Red spies will not
be brought to trial because the Justice Department will not risk giving
up files to the Communist defendant's lawyer." Senator Everett Dirk-
sen of Illinois summed up the feelings for many colleagues when he
said, "We hold up our hands in Holy Horror. Something has to be
done. The government is about to topple."

A newspaper in Columbia, South Carolina, even found a way to
link the rookie's two villainous rulings. Wrote an editorial-page editor
at the *Columbia State*: "In freeing convicted communists on technicalities [the Court] may have endangered national security. In applying
the Antitrust Act to vertical corporations for the first time, as in the
Du Pont–General Motors case, it has caused grave concern and mis-
giving throughout the nation's corporate structure."

Oddly, Brennan was rarely mentioned by name. Warren had already become the whipping boy of the right. A columnist in *The Washington Evening Star* demonstrated that quite aptly in a column of June 24, 1957:

> Led by Chief Justice Warren and Associate Justices Douglas and Black, the court has dragged in every technical rationalism to reverse decisions of lower courts in Communist or contempt cases. In one of the most recent decisions—the Jencks Case—the conviction of the labor leader for falsehood in signing a non-Communist affidavit was set aside because he had not been given access to FBI reports. Communists and fellow travelers have been trying for years to destroy the effectiveness of the FBI. They have tried every trick and subterfuge to deal a fatal blow to our top investigating agency by forcing it to reveal its intelligence sources. Now they appear to have succeeded."

Two weeks after Brennan's *Jencks* ruling, the Court announced a host of decisions that further inflamed the "Better Dead than Red" constituency. Those decisions placed even tighter restrictions on the government's ridiculous attempts to identify domestic Communists. In one of them, now known as the *Yates* case, the Court weakened the federal law making it a crime to advocate the overthrow of the government. In another case decided on June 17, 1957, the *Watkins* decision, the Court overturned the contempt conviction of a former labor official who had refused to provide a committee with names of alleged Communist colleagues. In nearly all of the decisions, only Tom Clark dissented, just as he had in *Jencks*.

But of all the cases decided by the Court, none stuck in the craw of Congress more than Brennan's ruling in *Jencks*. Even *New York Times* columnist Arthur Krock, who only a year earlier had been such a supporter of Brennan's, felt the justice had made a grave error. "Of the seven recent Supreme Court decisions which have come under heavy fire," Krock wrote. "the ruling in the *Jencks* case is the only one in which the necessity for immediate legislation was demonstrable and the power of Congress to grant it was unquestionable."

He continued: "Justice Brennan's opinion for the Court, granting the defendant more than he sought, gave the Department of Justice the alternative of abandoning prosecution in a large number of critical security, kidnapping, tax evasion, and narcotics cases or turning over to the defendants all the confidential FBI reports that governmental witnesses drew on for testimony. This posed a simultaneous threat to the essential function and value of the FBI and to the protection of the people from heinous crime."

He added gratuitously: "Brennan's language was so broad and generalized that the lower courts at once began to interpret it in various ways."

Even Ervin Griswold, dean of the Harvard Law School, was mystified that Brennan could have slipped so badly. "It is puzzling to me," he wrote Frankfurter, "that Justices of the Supreme Court do not see in advance the dangers of writing important opinions in sweeping terms. Much of the trouble of this spring could have been avoided with just a little more care in the opinions."

Although he never let on to his clerks, Brennan's personal notes to other justices illustrated that he was distraught that his opinion had been singled out as the most poorly written and confusing of the group. And the honor of having Congress countermand a ruling with legislation was no honor at all.

Shortly before going on recess in August, Congress passed a bill that became popularly known as the Jencks Act. It provided that no statement of a witness be made available to a defendant until that defendant had testified. Furthermore, it allowed for a judge to conduct an inspection of the documents before passing them on to the defendants.

The passage of the Jencks Act did less damage to the spirit of Brennan's ruling than it did the authority of the Court. No one on the Court, except perhaps Clark, wanted to see his decisions altered by action in the U.S. Capitol across the street.

On August 29, 1957, after the bill had become law, Frankfurter attempted to soothe the Brennan's wounded feelings. "The fact is that I largely blame myself for all the dust that has been kicked up," he wrote. "I firmly believe that if I had not allowed my good colleagueship to suppress my good sense, the rumpus would have been avoided. For if I had let my wisdom govern, I would have written a short concurrence with your opinion, sticking my pen into Tom's hot air and puncturing his balloon."

In his private letters to Griswold, Frankfurter was less humble. "I do justifiably blame myself regarding *Jencks*, for I can say with complete confidence that if the majority opinion had contained what I wanted to put into it, there would have been no Clark opinion to help kick up a rumpus. Without the Clark dissent the rumpus could not have been kicked up."

To which Griswold replied, "I do not think you should blame yourself. You cannot write an opinion in every case."

Brennan, normally full of jolly self-confidence and rarely given to introspection, revealed a side of himself that even his clerks say surprised them. "The regrets should not be yours but wholly mine," he wrote in a private note to Frankfurter. "Because you suggested not once but several times that something be done to answer Tom's approach. I confess to considerable concern over the summer that I may have been the instrument (and in my first year) for demeaning the standing of the Court."

BRENNAN DEFINES PORNOGRAPHY

IF THE PRESS AND LAW SCHOOL
community were finding plenty to criticize in Brennan's early writings,
Chief Justice Earl Warren was not. Personally he had taken an instinctive liking to the New Jersey Irishman. But professionally, Warren was
quick to realize that Brennan could serve a useful function. As illustrated by the tone of Frankfurter's notes to Brennan about the chief
justice, the rivalry between Warren and the senior justice was already
in full bloom by late 1956. If Black and Frankfurter were eager to fight
for Brennan's vote in their fierce ideological battles, Warren's interests
were more practical. The former governor needed a deputy he could
trust. The forces on the Court were entrenched and difficult. The arrival of Harlan in 1954 had hardly helped. A Wall Street lawyer, Harlan had quickly found his way to Frankfurter's chambers. But Brennan
seemed a man whom Warren could bring into his confidence. Each
week before the Court's full conference with all nine judges, Warren
called Brennan to his chambers. There they went over the cases that
would be discussed on the following day. And it was there that Warren
had asked Brennan to write the important opinions in *Du Pont* and
Jencks.

Rarely had a new justice been given such landmark rulings in his first term. Hardly had Brennan arrived before the other justices recognized that the chief justice, who was much more of a politician than a legal scholar, had found himself a workhorse. Brennan began to hear himself referred to by the others as "the deputy chief."

In early 1957, the Court agreed to hear an appeal of a conviction of a bookseller named Samuel Roth. As one of the first Supreme Court cases to deal seriously with the legal limits on obscenity, *Roth* v. *United States* was exactly the kind of case Frankfurter expected to write. Indeed, until 1919, in *Schenck* v. *United States*, the Court had never heard a free-speech case. And it hadn't been until 1942 that the Court ruled that obscenity and lewdness were not protected under the First Amendment. But state and federal governments were clearly abusing their authority to determine what speech could be curtailed, and in *Roth*, the justices felt they could exert a little more authority. Privately, as his notes in *Jencks* showed, Frankfurter felt that he was the only justice truly capable of writing important constitutional decisions. But as he had in *Du Pont* and *Jencks*, Warren turned once again to his new protégé to author the opinion. In their weekly Thursday meeting, Brennan was confident in his ability to deal with the complicated dilemma of obscenity. He was planning to write an opinion that would restrict, at least to some degree, the pornographer's right to sell and distribute whatever he wished.

As a judge on the New Jersey Supreme Court, Brennan had delivered an important obscenity ruling in a case called *Adams Theater Co.* v. *Keenan*. In that case the Adams Theater in Newark had been denied a license to operate burlesque shows. Brennan ruled that the Adams Theater couldn't be denied a permit before a show had been performed. The state had no right to presume that something was obscene before a performance had even been put on. But in ruling for the theater, the pre–Supreme Court Brennan had emphasized that he did not yet share Black's absolutism when it came to the First Amendment. He acknowledged that protection of free speech was not unlimited and that "there are narrowly limited classes of speech" which are not given the protection of the First Amendment.

It was just the kind of approach Warren thought might enable the Court finally to set some kind of standard on obscenity, to decry outright lewd pornography, but at the same time protect literature. As he had in the earlier cases, Brennan threw himself into the assignment with an intensity and completeness that Warren appreciated.

Samuel Roth was a native of Austria who had moved to the United States in 1903, at the age of seven. As a child he had written poetry for Yiddish magazines and newspapers. Later, as a student at Columbia, he published a campus magazine that featured writings by such controversial writers as D. H. Lawrence. Later still, Roth opened the Poetry Bookstore in Greenwich Village and continued to publish controversial and sometimes banned literature in a magazine called *Two Worlds Monthly*. In 1927, Roth was prosecuted and sent to jail for publishing parts of James Joyce's classic banned work *Ulysses*. Three years later, in 1930, Roth was again jailed, this time for publishing a pirated version of *Lady Chatterley's Lover*.

Jail time did little to dampen Roth's enthusiasm for publishing, and by the 1950s he was still in business, with a mailing list of 400,000 customers. Although much of what Roth was harassed for was considered classic literature, he was once prosecuted for publishing an essay by Benjamin Franklin entitled "To a Young Man on How to Choose a Mistress." He was arrested on seven occasions and convicted four times. A well-known figure in the New York literary world, Roth wrote for *Harper's* and the *Nation* magazines. In addition he published material under sixty-two different pen names.

In 1955, Roth was indicted by a federal grand jury for publishing a magazine called *American Aphrodite*. He was convicted in January 1956 on one count of sending obscene materials through the mail and sentenced to five years in prison. A federal appeals court upheld the conviction, although admitting reservations about the severity of the sentence. Judge Jerome Frank set the stage for an appeal to the Supreme Court by saying that although he felt constrained by previous rulings to uphold the conviction, he believed the conviction was unjust. Wrote Frank: "To vest a few fallible men with vast powers of literary or artistic censorship is to make them despotic arbiters of literary products. If one day they ban mediocre books as obscene, another day they may do likewise to a genius."

This was not to be a case in which Justice Brennan would distinguish himself as a great civil libertarian. When it came to cases involving pornography, Chief Justice Warren, a former California prosecutor, had little sympathy for the defendant. In his preconference conversations with Brennan, Warren talked about the fact that they both had daughters. As Brennan later told Yeshiva University law professor Edward de Grazia, "Warren was a terrible prude. Like my father was. If Warren was revolted by something, it was obscene. He would not read any of the books. Or watch the movies. I'd read the books and see the movies and he'd go along with my views." The last comment was more Brennan blarney than anything else. In fact, it was Brennan who, despite intense pressure from Black and Douglas to support their view that there could be no exceptions to the First Amendment's guarantees of free speech, agreed to go along with Warren and write the opinion that would affirm Roth's conviction.

As he worked on the case in the spring of 1957, Brennan had to contend with a pile of pornography the Justice Department had shipped to his chambers as evidence of what might happen if the Court ruled in Roth's favor. The stack had been stored at the old Post Office Building in downtown Washington, a structure known as the Chamber of Horrors. Postmaster General Arthur Summerfield pressured the solicitor general to bring the material to the Court, and during the oral argument Justices Douglas and Clark began passing it up and down the bench. Much to Brennan's relief, no one in the press noticed what was going on. When the hearing was over the material was brought to Brennan's chambers. Virtually every morning in the spring of 1957, when he came to work, Brennan shook his head at the embarrassing material."What am I going to do with these?" he would moan to one of his clerks. Never in his career as a state judge had Brennan ever had anything like this in his office.

In addition to the Roth appeal, Brennan also worked on a companion case dealing with another seller of supposed pornographic literature. The defendant, David Alberts, had committed offenses similar to Roth's but had been prosecuted under a state of California statute rather than a federal one.

As Brennan worked on his opinion, Frankfurter, as usual, peppered him with notes and memos, urging that the opinion be as strong as possible. The states, Frankfurter believed, had to have an absolute right to ban obscenity. In the *Alberts* case, Frankfurter felt certain that the federal government, and the Supreme Court in particular, had no right to interfere with California laws on the subject. Although it was one of those rare times when Warren was on Frankfurter's side, Brennan became increasingly concerned that Frankfurter's suggestions were going too far. He worried about the right of the government to ban literature, especially the controversial works of fellow Irishman James Joyce, whose writing was banned and seized by the U.S. Post Office in the 1920s. Warren agreed that censoring Joyce or D. H. Lawrence was hardly what these cases were about. He assured Brennan that he had no desire to protect the public from Joyce, just dirty pictures.

The arguments in the *Roth* case had been among the first heard by Brennan. After receiving the assignment from Warren to write the opinion, he wrestled with it nightly. Unlike his father, who had come down so hard on the "hygiene" movie some thirty years earlier, Brennan was uncertain how to proceed. So rather than present the case from front to back, Brennan worked on his conclusion, then constructed the reasoning that would fit the goal both he and Warren wanted.

Ultimately, Brennan felt he had found a formula that would prohibit real pornography while protecting literature. Foremost, it was important to answer the question, for the first time, whether obscenity was protected by the Constitution. "The question is whether obscenity is utterance within the area of protected speech and press," Brennan wrote. "Although this is the first time the question has been squarely presented to the Court, expressions found in numerous opinions indicate that the Court has always assumed that obscenity is not protected by the freedoms of speech and press." He noted that thirteen of the first fourteen states provided for the prosecution of libel and all of those states made either blasphemy or profanity, or both, statutory crimes.

"In light of this history," Brennan declared, "it is apparent that the unconditional phrasing of the First Amendment was not intended to protect every utterance. There is sufficiently contemporaneous evidence to show that obscenity was outside the protection intended for speech and press."

But obscenity was the only exception, Brennan said. He wrote: "All ideas having even the slightest redeeming social importance—unorthodox ideas, controversial ideas, even ideas hateful to the prevailing climate of opinion—have the full protection of the guaranties.

"But implicit in the history of the First Amendment is the rejection of obscenity as utterly without redeeming social importance. This rejection . . . is mirrored in the universal judgment that obscenity should be restrained."

Then the key words, the phrase that would later give Brennan nightmares: "We hold that obscenity is not within the area of constitutionally protected speech or press."

Having tried to define obscenity as something that generated no sense of ideas, Brennan took pains to explain that not all sexual material was obscene. "Sex and obscenity are not synonymous," he wrote. "Obscene material is material which deals with sex in a manner appealing to the prurient interest. The portrayal of sex in art and literature and scientific works is not itself sufficient reason to deny material the constitutional protection of free speech and press.

"Sex, a great and mysterious motive force in human life, has indisputably been a subject of absorbing interest to mankind throughout the ages; it is one of the vital problems of human interest and concern. It is therefore vital that the standards for judging obscenity safeguard the protection of freedom of speech and press."

Under those parameters, Brennan ruled, the proper test as to whether material is obscene or not, and thus subject to exemption from constitutional protections, is "whether to the average person, applying contemporary community standards, the dominant theme of the material as a whole appeals to prurient interests."

It was an argument that united himself and the chief justice with the conservatives on the Court. But it was not welcomed by Black and Douglas, who wrote separate dissents critical of Brennan's thinking.

"Government should be concerned with antisocial conduct, not utterances," wrote Douglas. "Thus if the First Amendment guarantee of freedom of speech and press is to mean anything in this field, it must allow protests even against the moral code that the standard of the day sets for the community."

Brennan was also criticized by Justice Harlan, who concurred on the conviction of Alberts but felt Roth's prison sentence should be overturned. States may well have the power to ban pornography, Harlan believed, but the federal government did not. The essence of conservative judicial thought was that the federal constitution protected citizens only against federal action. He said of Brennan's reasoning, "I fear it may result in a loosening of the tight reins which state and federal courts should hold upon the enforcement of obscenity statutes." In defending his view that states have more latitude to ban whatever they desire, he said, "The fact that the people of one state cannot read some of the works of D. H. Lawrence seems to me, if not wise or desirable, at least acceptable. But that no person in the United States should be allowed to do so seems to me to be intolerable."

The community-standards issue seemed to be the best that the Court could come up with. Like his *Jencks* ruling, Brennan had tried so hard to find middle ground that the federal courts had trouble understanding exactly what he meant. Obscenity was hard to define before his ruling; and just as hard after his decision.

The six to three decision upholding Roth's conviction condemned the sixty-two-year-old bespectacled bookseller to spend five of his last years of life in Lewisburg Federal Penitentiary.

Yet scholars would later argue that Brennan's ruling, rather than being an attack on freedom of expression, was actually an important crack in allowing it. It guaranteed that true works of literature could not be banned. As Edward de Grazia described it, "a freedom-favoring tail that would wag the censorship dog. . . . Sex yes, obscenity no, seems to be about what Roth stood for."

Brennan was not so charitable to himself. Sixteen years later, in *Paris Adult Theater I* v. *Slaton*, his middle-of-the-road position in *Roth* would be replaced by an older Brennan, who was far closer in thought to Black and Douglas. Brennan would write, "The approach initiated 16 years ago in *Roth* v. *United States* cannot bring stability to the area of the law without jeopardizing fundamental First Amendment values." Rejecting his own formulation, Brennan concluded that it was simply demanding too much to ask communities to distinguish between what is merely sexual and what was obscene.

"The essence of our problem in the obscenity area," he wrote, "is that we have been unable to provide sensitive tools to separate obscenity from other sexually oriented but constitutionally protected speech, so that efforts to protect the former do not spill over into suppression of the latter. . . . Our experience with the Roth approach has certainly taught us that the outright suppression of obscenity cannot be reconciled with the fundamental principles of the First and Fourteenth Amendments. For we have failed to formulate a standard that sharply distinguishes protected from unprotected speech. . . . "

Although he still believed that the government should somehow be able to control hard-core pornography, the later Brennan would never be able to figure out how to do it. He reluctantly concluded that Black and Douglas had been right all along, adding, "I do not pretend to have found a complete and infallible answer to what Mr. Justice Harlan called 'the intractable obscenity problem.' "

Ironically, Brennan's recantation came in a losing effort to allow an Atlanta, Georgia, adult movie theater to show pornographic films. A majority of a more conservative court banned the films, citing the earlier Brennan rule on community standards as a major part of their rationale.

But in 1957, in *Jencks*, in *Du Pont*, and finally in *Roth*, Brennan was a new justice desperately trying to find his way. On his path to an illustrious career, Brennan had found the early going extremely difficult. Yet his image problems were largely confined to the academic and Court communities. Warren was content to take all the criticism and heat from the general public. All Brennan had to do was the work.

SPEEDING DESEGREGATION

THE SUMMER OF 1958 PROVIDED A
much-needed rest for Bill and Marjorie. As was their custom, they
spent much of the summer at the Cape, then Brennan left to meet
Chief Justice Warren and Justice Clark in New York City for a conference. Their stay in New York was unexpectedly cut short when the Little Rock school crisis escalated into a Court battle that had to be
settled before the scheduled opening of school in September. On August 28, 1958, Justices Brennan, Clark and Warren boarded a train in
New York City destined for Washington. It was on that ride that the
chief justice asked Brennan to get up to speed on desegregation cases.
He had in mind what would be Brennan's most difficult and possibly
controversial task.

Brennan had arrived on the Court too late to participate in the historic school desegregation case of *Brown v. Board of Education*. Nor
had he had ever been much involved with the civil-rights movement.
But there was never any ambiguity in how Brennan felt about race relations. The example that William Brennan, Sr., had set in hiring
blacks to work on the police department was the standard that guided
young Bill's life. There was never any question in the Brennan home

that blacks should be entitled to lives of dignity with full civil rights. But typically, Brennan had not been involved in any political movements to further such a goal. That void in his background would not stop him from coming to rule in several decisions that would put teeth in the illusory promises made to the nation's blacks by Earl Warren.

But in *Cooper v. Aaron*, the most controversial and prominent integration case to come before the court since the *Brown* decision itself, Brennan found himself further troubled by the erosion of the Court's authority that he had helped to bring about by his unpopular ruling in *Jencks*. The passage of the humiliating Jencks Act had been followed by congressional threats to rein in the authority of the court further. Indiana senator William Jenner had proposed a bill that would severely restrict the authority of the Court to strike down laws made by Congress. His proposal also challenged the Court's ability to rule in cases involving civil rights. Its supporters called it "the most fundamental challenge to judicial power in twenty years." More important, the attack on the Court from a midwesterner tended to widen the criticism of the Court from beyond arenas that were strictly racial or strictly regional. In a floor vote on Jenner's proposal, taken on August 20, 1958, the Indianan had lost only by a 49 to 41 roll-call vote. That slim margin was very much on the minds of the justices.

Warren's decision in *Brown v. Board of Education* was certainly a landmark and hailed as a turning point. But it did not immediately translate into results. In his effort to forge unanimity among his colleagues, Warren had bent to the concept that the South not be rushed into desegregation. The language of his decision ordered that integration of the schools be accomplished "with all deliberate speed." Many southern politicians hoped that that language might enable them to postpone desegregation for another century.

When the Court did return to desegregation it seemed invariably to occur in short pro forma rulings that were often released without explanation. Public beaches, golf courses, and buses were desegregated by the Court, strictly by decree. Warren's propensity for what his critics called "dictatorship" perplexed more than a few law school professors. In a 1957 article, Frankfurter's former student and alter ego, Alexander Bickel, wrote, "Since handing down its judgment in the segregation cases, the Court has declined to write further on the general subject, disposing by per curiam orders of a number of other cases which can only in the loosest way be held to be governed by the decision of May, 1954. . . . This is not to say that they could not be founded in reason; only that the Court has made no effort to do so."

If there was any place in the South that figured to accommodate desegregation peacefully it was Little Rock, Arkansas. No capital city in the South had a more progressive local business community and newspaper. The *Arkansas Gazette*, run by Harry Ashmore, had won awards for its attitude on racial tolerance. The state chairman for industrial development was Winthrop Rockefeller, brother of New York governor Nelson Rockefeller. Little Rock was represented in Congress by an out-and-out liberal named Brooks Hays. The state's senator was J. William Fulbright. Even Governor Orval Faubus had been elected as a moderate.

It was thus not surprising when the Little Rock School Board, of which William Cooper was president, prepared a desegregation plan that would have been among the first in the South to place black students in a previously all-white high school. Adopted by the school board on May 24, 1955, just a year after Warren's *Brown* decision was announced, the Little Rock plan would have fully integrated its city's schools in just seven years. Little Rock civic leaders had hoped to be examples for the rest of the country on how integration could be peacefully accomplished. Unlike the programs that ultimately worked in many southern cities, Little Rock's idea was to integrate high schools first, then the junior highs. The third and last phase was to integrate the elementary schools. The plan was to commence in September 1957.

But despite the best hopes of Little Rock's moderate establishment, it was the pressures of elective politics that complicated matters. Being the first southern governor to preside over integrated schools would have sent Faubus into political oblivion. So rather than do what he knew was right, Faubus blocked the integration of Little Rock's Central High School by calling out the state's National Guard. Faubus's defiant act brought ugly white rioters and antiblack protesters to the high school in support of Faubus and the guard. A constitutional crisis loomed. It seemed clear that even if a federal court ordered the black students admitted to Central High, Faubus would defy them. The authority of the Court, which after all has no army or police, had never been in more doubt.

In an effort to solve the crisis, Congressman Hays arranged a meeting between Faubus and President Eisenhower on September 14, 1957. According to reports of the meeting by Eisenhower aide Sherman Adams, Faubus was conciliatory. He acknowledged that the Brown decision was the law of the land and must be obeyed. When the meeting ended, Eisenhower assumed Faubus would return to Little Rock and allow the integration of Central High to take place. But on his return Faubus took no action. On September 20, 1957, a federal judge issued an order demanding that the students be admitted. Faubus again defied the Court, and it took troops sent to Little Rock by a furious Eisenhower to admit the nine black children.

In a speech to the nation, Eisenhower stressed that personal opinions could have no bearing on his decision. Ike was a chain-of-command president. "Our personal opinions about the decisions have no bearing on the matter of enforcement," he declared. "The responsibility and authority of the Supreme Court to interpret the Constitution are very clear. . . . We are a nation in which laws, not men, are supreme."

Although Eisenhower had won the first round by nationalizing the guard and escorting the black students into the school, Little Rock's business and education leaders feared the president had moved too quickly. Citing the tense public mood, the Little Rock School Board in February 1958 postponed its plans for further desegregation. In a petition to the federal court in Little Rock, the school board asked that the plan be put on hold until "tempers had cooled." On June 20, 1958, U.S. District Court judge Harry Lemley agreed to delay integration of the Little Rock schools for an additional thirty months, until the 1960–61 term. But Lemley's order was immediately challenged by the NAACP's chief legal counsel, Thurgood Marshall, who argued that the threat of violence could not be used to block an order of the highest court in the land.

In response, Faubus only became more difficult. Casting off his moderate image, presumably for political reasons, on August 20 he told the people of his state that Supreme Court decisions are not the law of the land. (Winthrop Rockefeller claimed that he "begged" Faubus not to get involved in the Little Rock school situation. According to Neil Pierce in the The Deep South States of America, Faubus replied, "I'm going to run for a third term and if I don't do this, I'll be torn to shreds.")

Led by Thurgood Marshall, the NAACP argued that the state of Arkansas could not be allowed to defy the Supreme Court. "It's one thing for a politician to disagree with the Supreme Court," Marshall said. "But it's another thing for a lawyer to stand up and argue that there is doubt about it. . . . The issue is whether or not a federal district court can delay an integration plan already in progress, solely because of violence and threats of violence." A three-judge federal panel agreed with Marshall, ruling that "the time has not yet come in these United States when an order of a federal court must be whittled away, watered down, or shamefully withdrawn in the face of violent and unlawful acts of individual citizens."

With the start of the 1958 term only a week away, the Little Rock School Board appealed the result to the Supreme Court, still hoping that its legitimate fear of violence would move the Court to allow some time to pass. Although most of the justices were still on their summer vacations at the time, Chief Justice Warren called the brethren back to Washington for what was only the third special session of the Court ever held. As the Court prepared to meet, defiance was in the air throughout the South. The Arkansas legislature passed a state constitutional amendment commanding that officials of the state oppose "unconstitutional desegregation decisions." On August 26, the Arkansas legislature passed a host of bills designed to strengthen the state's position, including a law requiring that the governor close any school facing integration; and in the event schools were integrated, it transferred all money destined for public education to private schools.

The Little Rock crisis reverberated nowhere as dramatically as at the Supreme Court building. On August 28, a prehearing was held at the Court to decide whether or not to hold the session. At that hearing Richard Butler, the attorney for the school board, told the justices, "If the governor of any state says that a United States Supreme Court decision is not the law of the land . . . the people of the state have a right to have a doubt."

Warren virtually exploded with rage. "I have never heard such an argument made in a court of justice before and I have tried many a case through many a year. I never heard a lawyer say that the statement of a governor as to what was legal should control the action of any court." He then asked the parties to submit briefs and set the full hearing for September 11, 1958.

Four days later, in a letter to Justice Harlan, Frankfurter expressed concern that Warren would ultimately exacerbate racial tensions in the South. "His attitude toward the kind of problems that confront us is more like that of a fighting politician than that of a judicial statesman."

On September 11, Brennan and the other justices took their places on the bench. As usual, Warren saw the battle in political rather than legal terms. It was a test of wills, a test of authority. Warren may have lost the presidency, but he would show Faubus who had the power. Between the positions of Clark and Frankfurter on one side and Warren on the other, it once again fell on Brennan to find the legalistic reasoning that would satisfy both extremes on a badly divided court.

In the federal lower-court rulings, the case had turned on substantive issues relating to integration itself. In the federal district court and the appeals court, the judges had centered on what seemed to be the central issue: Was the disruption and violence of Little Rock a legitimate reason to delay the implementation of desegregation? Now, midway through the opening argument of Little Rock School Board attorney Richard Butler, Brennan interrupted in his thick New Jersey accent to begin reading the supremacy clause of the U.S. Constitution. "I know that you are familiar with Clause Three of Article Six of the federal Constitution," Brennan said, "which requires every state legislature and every state official, executive or judicial, to take an oath when he enters upon his service to support the federal Constitution. I think the actual language is, 'to support this Constitution.' You are familiar with that?"

Barely waiting for a reply, Brennan continued: "I think your brief also suggests something, some action on the part of your state's judiciary—not on the side of enforcement of the Constitution but opposed indeed in every way that the state can contrive to that enforcement. Just how is this Court in a position to allow, or sanction, or approve a delay sought on the grounds that responsible state officials, rather than being on the side of enforcement of these constitutional rights, have taken actions to frustrate their enforcement?"

Butler had little response, except to claim that the school board seemed to be caught in the middle of the fight between the Supreme Court and the state government. "I have that later in my argument," he stammered weakly.

By the conclusion of the oral argument, Brennan's opening on the supremacy clause had become the centerpiece of the case. Attorney Thurgood Marshall, arguing on behalf of the NAACP, astutely picked up the thread woven by Brennan and carried it out in his rebuttal. "The one single issue in this case," he said, "is whether or not a federal court can delay an integration plan, desegregation plan, already in progress, solely because of violence and threats of violence. I believe it's the only question in this case."

When the argument was over, the judges trooped back to the conference room. In a brief thirty-minute conference it was decided that Brennan's supremacy clause comments would become the focus of the Court's decision. Once again, Brennan was asked to draft the opinion. This was not a case in which any of the arguments about desegregation of the schools was to be considered. This was to be a statement of the Court's power and authority. It was to be an answer not just to Faubus but also to Senator Jenner and his friends. No one was more anxious to do what he could to restore that authority than Brennan, acutely conscious that he may have "demeaned" the Court with his earlier mistakes.

Not that the justices were united. Tom Clark, the Texan who was often the Court's most nettlesome dissenter, repeatedly pointed out that "all deliberate speed" didn't mean you had to integrate overnight. Warren had pushed up the timing of the Court's hearing and decision making to make sure that it all happened before the schools actually opened. That made no sense to Clark, who didn't see what it would hurt if the schools weren't integrated until the following year.

But it was Brennan, not Clark, who was to write the words that would become the statement of law in the land. "The federal judiciary is supreme in the exposition of the Constitution," he said. "Every state legislator and executive and judicial officer is thus solemnly bound not to wage war against the Constitution. He is obligated rather to obey its relevant commands as defined by this Court, and whatever his station, he may not consider himself free to act in his official capacity in a way at variance with those commands."

In his writing of *Cooper v. Aaron*, Brennan made one other contribution to the debate over race mixing in the schools. Although the word had not been officially used much in Court hearings, Brennan chose to substitute the word *desegregation* in his ruling in place of the more commonly used word *integration*. For years Supreme Court tea-leaf readers wondered why the change had been made. For twenty years Brennan said nothing about it, although volumes of speculation had been written about the subtle differences between the two words. In 1987, Brennan finally cleared up the mystery. He revealed that he had been writing the opinion on the porch of his Georgetown home when his next-door neighbor and landlord, NBC correspondent Richard Harkness, stopped by to say hello.

When Harkness heard what Brennan was doing, he had offered a suggestion. The word *integration*, Harkness told Brennan, was inflammatory. Southerners might accept *desegregation* a little more easily. Brennan accepted Harkness's advice. "I was taken with his suggestion that it made a difference to people in the South, and after all we were writing an opinion that we had hoped would find understanding and acceptance in the South as well as in the rest of the country," he said.

At high noon on Monday September 29, Warren read Brennan's decision in *Cooper* v. *Aaron* as a unanimous statement of the Court. Few outside the inner circle knew that it was Brennan who had written the important words for which Warren was now taking credit. But even Warren's biographer, Bernard Schwartz, has acknowledged, "Chief credit for this must go to Brennan, who justified the Chief's reliance on him for this most important decision since Brown."

But like his previous decisions, *Cooper* v. *Aaron* came under immediate attack. This time the opposition was not just from segregationists, unappeased by the linguistic compromise on *integration*. Conservative professors accused the Court of wrapping itself in the cloak of infallibility. Alexander Bickel, the Yale professor who only a few years earlier had clerked for Frankfurter, derided the decision sarcastically. "Whatever the Court lays down is right, even if wrong, because the Court and only the Court speaks in the name of the Constitution. Its doctrines are not to be questioned; indeed they are hardly fit subject for comment. The Court has spoken. The Court must be obeyed."

University of Chicago professor Philip Kurland called the opinion an example "of a Court carried away with its own sense of righteousness." The nut of the opposition to Brennan's opinion was its strident nature. Sure enough, on the day the decision was issued, Faubus announced that all the senior high schools in Little Rock would be closed.

With more diplomatic language, Frankfurter believed, such harsh reactions could have been averted. He longed to give Brennan a lecture on the damage he had done to the future of race relations but decided against any personal appeal. He told Harlan, "I have decided to curb my temperamental spontaneity and not talk to Bill Brennan. Too much ego in his cosmos. When Paul Freund was here recently—and Paul Freund is as wise as any member of the profession whom I know, he asked, 'Is Bill Brennan as cocksure as his opinions indicate?' Cocksure begets sensitiveness and as his erstwhile teacher, I have to be particularly careful with Bill."

At Frankfurter's request, Harlan had agreed to play the Trojan horse for Frankfurter's philosophy. But despite Brennan's friendship with Harlan, and an extremely close friendship between their wives, Marjorie and Ethel, Brennan ignored Harlan's advice as well.

Although Frankfurter had concurred with the result in *Cooper v. Aaron*, he decided to write his own, much more conciliatory, opinion. As he explained his reasons: "Implementation [of the *Brown* decision] will come not through court decrees but by winning the minds of the leading influences of the recalcitrant states. Some of the brethren, particularly the Chief and Brennan, aren't only awry in perception, but cockily so, and have a poor limited understanding of public relations."

Frankfurter thought the officials of the school board should get some credit for at least trying to accommodate desegregation. He had wanted language that would have buttered them up a little bit. Frankfurter explained that Brennan's opinion had failed to take Southern sensibilities into mind. Frankfurter declared that he had a special gift of communication "in view of my rather extensive association by virtue of my years at Harvard Law School, with a good many Southern lawyers and law professors."

Naturally Frankfurter immediately won the love of the academic community. Catherine Drinker Bowen, admirer of Oliver Wendell Holmes, wrote a letter to Frankfurter, describing Warren as "a dangerous man. He runs whatever he is in charge of." Prominent New York lawyer John J. McCloy wrote that the majority opinion "did not put the issue clearly." Former secretary of state Dean Acheson wrote to Frankfurter: "I wish the Court had let you speak for it."

Frankfurter's interjection into the opinion infuriated Brennan and Black. The Irishman was not without a temper, but his clerks had

never seen him as angry as he was at Frankfurter's insistence on stepping on what was to have been unanimous. Warren had always considered it of paramount importance that decisions on integration come
from a united Court. Tom Clark had been persuaded by Warren to stifle his urge to dissent in the spirit of unity, in the spirit of moving the
country ahead. But now Frankfurter, even though he agreed with the
result, was muddying the waters. Brennan had slaved over the opinion.
Yet he would receive no credit for writing it. And to make matters
worse, he had to accommodate every suggestion of the Brethren, many
of them additions he could have rejected if the opinion had been solely
his. He complained to clerks that this was carrying opinion by committee too far. If the opinion was poorly written, Brennan certainly didn't
feel that this time it was his fault.

Black and Brennan decided not to let Frankfurter's opinion go
unanswered. They threatened to issue a statement that would reveal
the deep schism in the Court. The statement read: "Mr. Justice Black
and Mr. Justice Brennan believe that the joint opinion of all the justices handed down on September 29, 1958, adequately expresses the
view of the Court and they stand by that opinion as delivered. They
desire that it be fully understood that the concurring opinion filed this
day by Mr. Justice Frankfurter must not be accepted as any dilution or
interpretation of the views expressed in the Court's joint opinion."
Such a statement would have caused a stir in the press. It was not often that differences inside the Court were made public. That was considered bad form. But before the rebuttal could be issued, Justice
Harlan urged them to calm down and let the matter drop. "It is a mistake to make a mountain out of a molehill," he counseled. "*Requiescat
in pace.*"

Before Brennan's ruling in *Cooper v. Aaron*, there were those, like
Bickel, who still argued that a Court decision was not a ukase but
could be applied only in the wake of specific litigation. Others went
further and argued that although the supremacy of the Court was not
seriously in doubt, its rulings applied only to the litigants in that particular case. After Brennan, it was clear that a ruling was more than
just a statement of result for a case. The Court's ruling had become indisputably the law of the land. Earl Warren had begun the process of
desegregation with *Brown*. But it was Brennan who stated the principle that the Court's decisions were a binding part of federal law, law

that must be obeyed even by the governors of states, states that once had been led to believe that they had the exclusive control over their schools.

Cooper had impressed even the Court's most personally difficult member, liberal William O. Douglas. Responding much after the fact to Yale professor Fred Rodell's concerns about Brennan, Douglas concluded triumphantly that Brennan had "licked the odds," by finally being able to defy the manipulative Frankfurter.

THE FRANKFURTER FEUD

COOPER V. AARON HAD BEEN THE last major decision heard by Truman appointee Harold Hitz Burton. In June of 1958, Burton had been diagnosed with Parkinson's disease. For thirteen years he had been one of Frankfurter's most reliable allies. And in no area of the law had Burton been more consistently conservative than in upholding the government's authority in national-security matters, regardless of the implications to personal freedom.

On July 17 at 2:30 in the afternoon, Burton went to the White House to inform Eisenhower of his resignation. According to Burton's handwritten diaries, a bewildered Eisenhower expressed disappointment at the decisions of Warren and Brennan, particularly in national-security cases such as *Jencks*. The president told Burton he just didn't understand how Vanderbilt could have been so "off-base" as to recommend Brennan for the Supreme Court. It was those comments by Eisenhower that later translated through the rumor mill to a statement that Eisenhower said: "I have made two mistakes and they are both sitting on the Court." The truth was that Eisenhower didn't say it exactly that way to Burton. But the thought was there.

Admitting that he had erred in appointing a man about whom he knew so little, Eisenhower emphasized to Burton that in naming his replacement, ideology would play an important part. He wanted someone who would not continue to hamper the ability of government and business to fire suspected Communists. In his diary Burton wrote, "The president said he wanted a conservative attitude."

Eisenhower did not immediately name a successor, and on September 19, shortly after the Court's decision in the Little Rock case, William Rogers, by now Brownell's successor as attorney general, stopped by Burton's office to ask him to reconsider and to stay on the Court. The trend in Brennan's rulings had set off a crisis in the White House. But Burton said that was simply impossible. Less than a month later the appointment was given to Potter Stewart, a Republican judge sitting on the U.S. Court of Appeals in Cincinnati.

It did not take long for the wooing of the newest justice to begin. By the beginning of the 1959–60 term, the Court was clearly divided into two warring camps. Just as Brennan had danced in his first few years on the Court, Stewart had to move gingerly from side to side. But more often than not his instincts were to go with Frankfurter.

In January 1959, Stewart's swing role became clear in *Irvin* v. *Dowd*. A relatively obscure legal battle from Indiana, the *Irvin* case would nonetheless come to have a profound impact on Brennan's relationship with Frankfurter and his alma mater, the Harvard Law School. Starting in 1954, a series of murders rocked the vicinity of Evansville, Indiana. Two were committed in December and another four in March. On April 8, 1955, under intense public pressure to convict somebody, police arrested Leslie Irvin and announced he had confessed to the crimes.

Although the trial had been moved to an adjoining county where it was thought passions were less inflamed, Irvin's attorneys sought a second change of venue to a still more distant locale. That motion was denied. The process of jury selection began on November 14, 1955. Each day for four weeks, Irvin's lawyers continued to file motions for a change of venue, claiming an impartial jury simply couldn't be picked. Four of the twelve jurors were finally seated despite statements by them saying in their opinion the defendant was guilty.

A guilty verdict was delivered on December 20, 1955, and on January 9, 1956, Irvin was sentenced to death. Nine days later, Irvin escaped from the county jail, where he was being held, but left a note for his attorney: "I know this is the wrong thing to do," Irvin scribbled. "But I just can't go up to Michigan City and wait. If they ever give me a new trial, I'll come back and face it. Maybe the jury will then believe the truth.

"I appreciate it if you go on with the appeal. That was why I asked you the last time I saw you if I had to be here when you filed for a new trial. I know that you are doing everything you can for me. It's a hard fight. But all three of us knows that the police lied and I was convicted before I was even tried. I haven't given up hope, but it sure is hard. As I said above, if and when I get a new trial, I'll try again. Thanks for everything you have done for me. Yours very truly, Les."

In accordance with Irvin's wishes, his attorney did file a motion for an appeal. But the Indiana courts were not amused. Even though Leslie Irvin was recaptured three weeks after his flight, the Indiana Supreme Court rejected the motion for a new trial. The court ruled that the act of escaping from custody forfeited his right to an appeal. In its opinion the Indiana Supreme Court wrote, "Courts should not coddle those who are defiant of its authority and the law, and who yet ask for its relief." That was supposedly the issue that the U.S. Supreme Court would be asked to decide. Irvin's lawyer requested that the court issue a writ of habeas corpus, an order of the court to a sheriff or warden demanding that Irvin be immediately produced, so that a court could determine if he was being lawfully detained. The idea that a federal court could issue a writ of habeas corpus in a state prosecution was seen by the restraintist bloc of justices, especially, as the worst kind of meddling in federal-state relations.

But when Brennan and Warren began discussing the case on January 15, 1959, it was not the escape that bothered them so much as the impaneling of jurors with preconceived notions of guilt. When Warren and Brennan got together, Warren's advice to Brennan was fairly constant. The Court existed for fairness, Warren would say. It was a message that Brennan took to heart, although the concept was initially novel to him. On the New Jersey Supreme Court original approaches weren't encouraged. State court judges were expected to follow precedents.

By the beginning of the 1959–60 term, Brennan was no longer considered a swing vote. An analysis of his voting record showed that although he had agreed with Frankfurter as often as not in his first couple of terms, by this time Brennan rarely agreed with Frankfurter. With the almost always certain vote of Black and Douglas, Warren and Brennan needed only to persuade the new justice, Potter Stewart, of their approach. That usually took some doing. But Brennan and Stewart had quickly become friends. From watching Frankfurter, Brennan had learned how not to woo a new ally. Although Stewart was nine years younger, the two men had comparable professional backgrounds. While Brennan had been practicing corporate law in Newark, Stewart had been in private practice in Cincinnati. The two men became frequent lunch companions at the Methodist Home cafeteria across the street from the Court.

In the *Irvin* case, as he would in many of his decisions, Brennan learned that Stewart's instincts leaned to the liberal side, if the opinions could be written narrowly enough that his natural reluctance to expand judicial power could be accommodated. Stewart complained that while he felt there was a wrong to be corrected, previous court precedents, particularly a case called *Brown v. Allen*, seemed to preclude the Supreme Court from getting involved in the state prosecution. Brennan assured Stewart that the *Brown* case "didn't bear on this situation." And to make sure there was no misunderstanding, he promised to put that in his opinion. With that concession, Stewart gave Brennan the fifth vote to force the state of Indiana to consider Irvin's appeal.

As he sat down to write his opinion, Brennan concentrated almost exclusively on the jury issue. He finally concluded that Irvin was entitled to a new trial because the state had not ruled on the jury claims. As far as the escape argument was concerned, said Brennan, "we do not reach the question."

For the four judges in the minority—Frankfurter, Harlan, Clark, and Whittaker—it was yet another example of the Court overstepping its bounds. Brennan had interposed federal court review over state criminal actions, and once again Frankfurter was beside himself with indignation. In his dissent, Frankfurter repeated what had become his dominant theme: "The federal judiciary has no power to sit in judgment upon a determination of a state court. . . .

"Something that thus goes to the very structure of our federal system in its distribution of power between the United States and the state is not a mere bit of red tape to be cut, on the assumption that this

Court has general discretion to see justice done. . . . Even the most benign or latitudinarian attitude in reading state court opinions precludes today's decision."

Stewart, who was walking a fine line between the two camps, wanted to make sure his agreement with Brennan wasn't misinterpreted. He asked Brennan to add one line to the opinion: "Mr. Justice Stewart concurs with the judgment and the opinion of the Court, with the understanding that the Court does not here depart from the principles announced in *Brown* v. *Allen*." Brennan's ability to size up people quickly had paid dividends with Stewart. It was an approach Brennan would use over and over again with the new justice.

Had Frankfurter's dissent been the end of the matter, the issue perhaps would not have escalated. But *Irvin* v. *Dowd* had an unintended side effect. It became yet another lightning rod for academic and public criticism of Brennan's opinion writing. Frankfurter was not about to let the matter drop. With every word Brennan seemed to be writing, Frankfurter kept seeing what he believed was more bad law. He then encouraged a distinguished Harvard professor, Henry Hart, to focus on the case in the 1959 edition of the *Harvard Law Review*. Frankfurter and Hart had collaborated before. In 1933 they had coauthored the *Harvard Law Review*'s annual summary of Supreme Court actions. But that had not been sub rosa.

Hart's article began innocuously enough, pretending to "address itself not to any especially noteworthy decisions or events of the past term, but rather to problems of the Court's administration which are common to every term—problems of the volume of the Court's business and the ways in which business is done." Brennan, no doubt, didn't miss the coincidence that this was a constant refrain of Frankfurter's and a subject of an annual beginning-of-term memo that Felix sent to his brethren. Hart's article wandered around such topics as the time available for judges, the mechanics of the oral arguments, the Friday conferences, the consideration of the writs of certiorari, the study of records and briefs. But it was after sixteen pages of this setup, that Hart zeroed in for the kill.

"The opinions of the Justices," he wrote, "if one turns to them, confirm the conclusion that the Court is trying to decide more cases than it can decide well. Regretfully and with deference, it has to be said that many of the Court's opinions are about what one would expect could be written in 24 hours. Few of the Court's opinions, far too few, genuinely illumine the area of law with which they deal. Other opinions fail by even more elementary standards. Issues are ducked . . . technical mistakes are made. . . . First rate lawyers," Hart declared, "are losing confidence in the Court."

Thereupon, Hart, with Frankfurter's approval, launched into the most vicious ad hominem attack ever made in the *Harvard Law Review* on a sitting justice, certainly on a justice from Harvard Law School itself. Describing *Irvin v. Dowd* as an example of all he had cited wrong with the Court's decision-making processes, Hart wrote: "Mr. Justice Brennan, speaking for a bare majority of the Court, approached the case without paying any attention to the historic function of the freedom writ, or to the developments which have been outlined, or to the difficulties those developments posed. . . . To explicate all that is wrong . . . is not easy."

It was clear to Hart that Brennan had decided what he wanted to do first, then wrote the decision to accomplish that result. The alternative at the Court had usually been to study the law and the precedents and then make a determination based on them. Hart charged that Brennan's opinion "gave gratuitous aid and comfort to the most extreme of its critics who say that it twists facts and words at its pleasure in order to reach the results it wants to reach." Again, a constant refrain of Frankfurter.

Initially Brennan was not sure if he should respond. He had come to view Frankfurter and his friends with some degree of humor. With his clerks, Brennan rarely revealed any pique at his brethren's antics. It was Brennan's friend Judge David Bazelon who advised that a response was necessary. He offered to arrange a rebuttal through the good services of Arnold, Fortas & Porter. Filled with good Yale men, Arnold, Fortas & Porter was more than willing to come to the aid of an enemy of Frankfurter's. At the request of Bazelon and William Douglas, who also urged a response, Thurman Arnold himself agreed to pen a response, one that was published in a succeeding issue of the *Harvard Law Review.*

"To say that this result, clearly just and clearly reasoned in the majority opinion, shows judicial incompetence, as Professor Hart does, is fantastic," Arnold wrote. He added that the so-called "first-class lawyers" of whom Hart wrote were the same people who had chal-

lenged the constitutionality of such progressive legislation as child labor laws. "The growth of the law is a painful process," said Arnold.
"Professor Hart's reaction is a classic example of such growing pains."

The Hart article stung Brennan as badly as anything that had been
said about him. But three years later he showed he was not about to be
intimidated. It was Brennan himself who got the last word. When the
case eventually came back to the Supreme Court, with Irvin still on
death row, Brennan ruled definitively that pretrial publicity had poi-
soned the jurors in the case. He ordered the state to commute Irvin's
death sentence. In the late 1980s Irvin finally died, but of cancer
rather than electrocution.

Irvin v. Dowd marked the end of any meaningful relationship between Frankfurter and Brennan. Although they remained civil, Brennan almost never joined a Frankfurter dissent. Conservatives had
continued to hope that Brennan's alliance with the liberals was not ir-
retrievable, but after *Irvin v. Dowd* it was. Hart's article drove Brennan
irrevocably into the Warren camp, where he had always felt more comfortable anyway. Brennan had absorbed much criticism for his opinions
since he joined the Court. But no justice, he confided to clerks, should
have to endure such daggers from the steps of his own law school. And
he had no doubt that Frankfurter's hand had directed Hart's pen.

By the beginning of the 1961–62 term, Brennan's allegiance to
Black and Warren was complete. He was no longer following the ideological lead of Justice Warren but taking an active leadership role in
trying to find cases that would promote his reforms. Despite the difficulties he had encountered in the *Jencks* case, Brennan was anxious to
push the *Jencks* doctrine, as well as the incorporation of the other
amendments, onto the states.

It was just as often Brennan as Warren who began to advance an
ideological agenda. There was no better example of his effort than
when a robbery case called *Ashe v. Tennessee* came up in which the
state authorities refused to give the defendant evidence needed to prepare a defense. Showing his stubborn streak, Brennan wrote Warren
on March 2, 1961: "The above case on the conference list this week
presents an ideal opportunity for the extension of *Jencks* to the states.
It involves a jewelry store robbery. At the time of trial in the state
court the two principal witnesses testified that they had given state-

ments to the local police and FBI agents. Demand for their production on the authority of *Jencks* was made. An order of production was denied on the ground that the defense had not proved that the statements still existed and were in the possession of the prosecution."

Brennan noted that state courts, especially in Tennessee, had ruled that the *Jencks* principle was not a constitutional principle but "rested on our supervisory authority over the administration of justice in the federal courts.

"I suppose there would be a vehement protest," Brennan wrote, "and the probabilities are we would lose out on the merits. The latter probability may be good reason to pass up this opportunity, but I do think we'll wait a long time before we get a question as sharply presented." Warren persuaded Brennan to pass up the case. But other opportunities would soon come along. The chief and the "deputy chief" vowed to watch for them. Then, they believed, they would make history.

January 20, 1961, was one of the coldest days in Washington's history. The wind-chill factor was way below zero, and yet all of Washington was preparing for the inauguration of President John F. Kennedy. Brennan's morning, as always, had started in Georgetown with the justice cooking the bacon. He would then sit and read. Shortly after seven one of his clerks would come to drive him to the Court. President Kennedy's inauguration was special to Brennan. Kennedy had endured many of the same questions about religion that had confused his own nomination. JFK's election had freed Catholics from the stigma that they were in office only to serve the interests of the Pope and the Catholic church.

Shortly before noon, Brennan and the other justices walked across the street to the Capitol Building for the inauguration. Brennan was escorted to the platform, where he shook hands with the country's first Catholic president. Brennan couldn't help but feel a surge of pride in Kennedy. When it was over, he went back to the Court and met with his clerk for the ride home. Just behind the White House, in the blizzard conditions, the car broke down in traffic. Brennan hopped out of the back and helped push it to the side, much to the discomfort of the mortified clerk. When the car was safely out of harm's way, Brennan turned to his aide, shook his head, and said simply: "You know, you really ought to get a new car." There wasn't the slightest chance that anyone witnessing the scene would realize that this graying, diminutive man was a justice of the U.S. Supreme Court. In a city of famous people, Brennan was as close to anonymous as one could be.

Less than a month after the Kennedy inaugural, on February 15, 1961, Brennan made one of the most important speeches of his judicial career. Although three years earlier there had still been considerable debate about his ultimate ideology, an address at New York University made it abundantly clear that Hugo Black had won the mind of the judge from New Jersey. Brennan had been selected to deliver NYU's second annual James Madison Lecture. The first had been given by Black a year earlier. Since the 1947 case of *Adamson* v. *California*, Black had been fighting a lonely losing campaign to "incorporate" the Bill of Rights, or to make them applicable to the states. Contrary to Frankfurter, who had so long controlled the Court, Black took the position that not only did the Bill of Rights apply to citizens against tyranny of the state but also that the guarantees of the Bill of Rights were absolute.

In his James Madison Lecture Black had said that there were no circumstances under which rights could be abridged. Such abridgment, Black believed, in itself outweighed the injury with which the public might be threatened. "It is my belief," Black had said, "that there are absolutes in our Bill of Rights and that they were put there by men who knew what words meant and meant their prohibitions to be absolutes."

Reading the remarks Black had sent him before delivery, Brennan reflected on his own heritage and upbringing. He was a descendent of the oppressed Irish, a child of immigrants, and he had seen exactly the tyranny of bad government of which Black so clearly warned. He was delighted when NYU followed up the Black address with an invitation for Brennan to deliver the James Madison Lecture the following year.

It was clearly the speech in which he laid out his framework for what would be the next six years of decisions: the period in which the Bill of Rights was changed from an abstract document to a steady friend and protector of the American people. It was clear to Brennan that the Founding Fathers had not meant to apply the protections of the Bill of Rights to the states. But he had come to believe, as Black did, that the Fourteenth Amendment provided the mechanism through which they could be extended. In his NYU speech, Brennan openly declared his alliance with Black:

> Mr. Justice Black believes that the Court fell into error in failing to sufficiently consult the history of the Fourteenth Amendment. He reads that history as demonstrating that the Framers of the Fourteenth Amendment intended to enfold the Federal Bill of Rights within its commands.
>
> Three other justices shared this view with Mr. Justice Black in 1947, but it has yet to command the support of a majority of the Court.
>
> However, the rejection of the incorporation theory has not closed every door in the Fourteenth Amendment against the application of the federal Bill of Rights to the states. The Court has opened a door through the Fourteenth Amendment's due process clause.
>
> True, it is often insisted that the application to the states of a safe-guard embodied in the first eight amendments is not made because those rights are enumerated in the first eight amendments but because they are of such a nature that they are included in the conception of due process of law. . . . It is reason for deep satisfaction that many of the states effectively enforce the counterparts in state constitutions of the specifics of the Bill of Rights. But too many state practices fall far short. Far too many cases come from the states to the Supreme Court presenting dismal pictures of official lawlessness, of illegal searches and seizures, illegal detentions attended by prolonged interrogation and co-erced admissions of guilt, of the denial of counsel and downright bru-tality. Judicial self-restraint which defers too much to the sovereign powers of the states and reserves judicial intervention for only the most revolting cases will not serve to enhance Madison's priceless gift of the great rights of mankind secured under this Constitution. For these se-cure the only climate in which the law of freedom can exist.

Brennan was fifty-five years old. At last, a philosophy had emerged. But to make Black's dream of incorporation reality, the liberal bloc still needed one more solid vote.

BAKER V. CARR

No CASE WOULD ILLUSTRATE BLACK
and Brennnan's commitment to expand the power of the Court at the
expense of the fifty states as did *Baker* v. *Carr*. It was this landmark
ruling that led to the transfer of political power in the United States
from rural America to the cities. Earl Warren himself would often call
it the most interesting and significant case of his tenure.

At the heart of the controversy over *Baker* v. *Carr* was the continuing disagreement among the justices about the role, scope, and power
of the Court. The surface issue was whether the federal courts of the
United States could mandate relative equality of legislative districts.
Justice Frankfurter, the advocate of judicial restraint, had long believed that the Court had no power over the legislative branch, and especially not over the legislatures of the separate states. In 1946
Frankfurter, in one of his most personally prized rulings, *Colegrove* v.
Green, had dramatically ruled that the Supreme Court had no power
to interfere with issues regarding apportionment of state legislatures.

"To do otherwise," Frankfurter had declared in one of his most famous declarations, "would embroil the Court in issues of a peculiarly
political nature. . . . Courts ought not to to enter this political

thicket." Over the next fifteen years, the words "political thicket," became as well known as any judicial phrase, constantly uttered by those interested in minimizing the power of the Warren Court.

But as deeply and passionately as Frankfurter believed the Court should stay out of the political thicket, Justice Black believed the Constitution mandated that every citizen's vote have the same weight. Article 1 of the Constitution, Black would point out, guaranteed that each citizen had a right to vote and to have that vote counted. Yet because of malapportioned legislative districts, a citizen living in a district of 900,000 people has a much smaller percentage of a vote than someone living in a district with 112,000.

In his dissent to Frankfurter's *Colegrove* opinion, Black had said that while the Constitution contained no express provision requiring that districts be of equal size, "the constitutionally guaranteed right to vote and to have one's vote counted clearly imply the policy that state election systems should give approximately equal weight to each vote cast."

Had Frankfurter's victory in *Colegrove* come from a full Court, the tradition of stare decisis, that prior decisions be allowed to stand, might have prevailed, and the prior ruling would not have been reconsidered. But in 1946 two justices had been away at the time of the ruling. Chief Justice Stone had just died. Justice Robert Jackson had taken a leave to serve as chief prosecutor of the Nuremburg trials. Frankfurter's victory had been eked out by a narrow 4 to 3 vote. Such a shaky, four-man majority was not considered nearly as sacrosanct and gave Black hope that the day would come when *Colegrove* could be overturned.

For fifteen years groups interested in good government could get little help from the federal courts in apportioning legislative and congressional districts. In most states their redress had to be through state constitutions or ballot initiatives. Only in rare cases did the Court enter the political thicket. One exception came in a 1960 case called *Gomillion v. Lightfoot*, in which it was shown that the boundary lines of Tuskegee, Alabama, district had been deliberately drawn to flout the voting rights of black residents. Frankfurter himself had written the decision in *Gomillion*. It was an opinion designed to protect *Colegrove*, for if *Colegrove* was allowed to justify blatant racial gerrymandering, it would not last long. *Gomillion*, Frankfurter decided, wasn't a Fourteenth Amendment reapportionment case at all, but rather a Fifteenth

Amendment case of specific racial discrimination.

Despite Frankfurter's care to keep *Gomillion* from threatening his political-thicket argument, Black saw an opening. Just one week after Frankfurter's *Gomillion* ruling on November 14, 1960, Black persuaded his colleagues that they should also be willing to hear arguments in *Baker* v. *Carr*, the case of a Tennessee voter who claimed that his state's antiquated reapportionment scheme denied him due process under the more significant and more general Fourteenth Amendment. A three-judge federal panel in Tennessee had dismissed the lawsuit, saying that the federal courts had no jurisdiction over the legislature.

On November 21, 1960, Black persuaded Warren, Brennan, and Douglas to join him in granting certiorari to *Baker*. It was just possible, Black thought, that one of the two new justices, either Stewart or Whittaker, might be persuaded to join them, based on the opening *Gomillion* had provided. It was a longshot, but one that Black figured was worth taking. Still, although four votes was enough to have the case considered, it did not bode well for overturning *Colegrove*. All five of the other justices, including Stewart and Whittaker, initially supported Frankfurter's contention that *Baker* v. *Carr* was a political case outside the jurisdiction of the Supreme Court. Frankfurter, Harlan, Whittaker, and Clark seemed certain to vote together to uphold the principles of *Colegrove*. The only possible way Black could win was if Justice Stewart could somehow be persuaded to join his bloc.

On Wednesday, April 19, 1961 the Court held its first of two oral arguments on *Baker* v. *Carr*. Charles S. Rhyne, the attorney for the eleven plaintiffs, spoke first. He claimed that Tennessee's system of apportionment "systematically nullified" the voting rights of Tennessee's urban dwellers. He pointed out that one third of the state's residents elected two thirds of the legislators. This in spite of the fact that the state constitution required reapportionment every ten years.

Hardly had Rhyne gotten started when he was interrupted by Frankfurter. "What is the bearing of this provision on the federal question?" Frankfurter asked pointedly.

"Our argument is that the appellants are deprived of equal protection under the law, so it is important that the law of Tennessee creates the right."

Stewart, the only judge who hadn't predecided the case before the argument, asked many of the questions. He wondered, for example, if the result of reapportionment would be to create urban dominance of the legislature. Rhyne insisted it would merely create balance, not dominance for the cities.

Following the two-day argument, Warren convened a conference to discuss the case. As was his custom, he called on each justice to speak in order of seniority. Frankfurter spoke for nearly two hours, pulling law books off the oaken shelves. By the time Warren called on Stewart, the most junior justice, there was an even four to four split among the others. All heads turned toward Stewart. But he was not ready to decide. In that case, Warren announced, he would hold the decision on the case over for the next term and ask the attorneys to reargue it.

Frankfurter immediately began working on Stewart. He wrote to him: "I feel so strongly the gravity of the implications, particularly for the Court, that one disposition of this case rather than another involves. . . . To open up these undetermined and indeterminate questions is bound, I cannot but deeply believe, to bring the Court in conflict with political forces and exacerbate political feelings widely throughout the nation."

Stewart also heard dire warnings from Harlan. "Unless I am very much mistaken," Harlan wrote Stewart, "your vote will be determinative. . . . From the standpoint of the future of the Court, the case involves implications whose importance is unmatched by those of any other case coming here in my time." Despite Frankfurter and Harlan's intense lobbying, Stewart continued to keep his own counsel.

The second argument in *Baker v. Carr* took place on October 9, 1961. It was mostly a reprise of the original and did not impress any of the members of the Court. Following the argument and even before the conference, Frankfurter produced a sixty-page memorandum stating his beliefs in the strongest possible language.

Seven of the remaining eight justices, including Black, were muted by Frankfurter's barrage. Only Brennan chose to answer with a lengthy document of his own, outlining the injustice of malapportionment in politics. Brennan's rejoinder lacked all of Frankfurter's passion. All he asked was that the state of Tennessee be forced to appear in federal court to defend its apportionment system. He wasn't asking that it automatically be declared unconstitutional, as Black wanted. "I just think," Brennan told his brethren, "that Tennessee should be required to justify it."

The important thing, Brennan said, was that the Court not permit apportionment that "defied rational explanation." As had become his custom, much like the chief justice, Brennan believed a case should be thought through from back to front. Then a rationale could be created to justify the result. The trick in the apportionment case was to find a rationale with which Justice Stewart could live. Potter was a man Brennan felt he understood. Brennan shared much of the same values as Stewart, with whom he played golf at the country club. Stewart was much more inclined to join the chief justice and Brennan at a ball game. And although his instincts were to be more restrained, he was less inclined to enjoy Frankfurter's intellectual games and parlor-room life-style. He was more impressed with Brennan's diligence. Brennan was a man very much like himself.

As Warren went down the line of justices, just as he had done the previous April, the votes lined up the same way. Harlan insisted that a disparity between urban and rural representation simply didn't "offend" the Constitution. Clark clung to his position, arguing that the plaintiffs in the case hadn't exhausted all their avenues of relief. A ruling by the Supreme Court in such a matter, he said, should be a matter of last resort. There were surely other things the plaintiffs could do, such as amend the state constitution. Whittaker, who had been the subject of intense harangues by Frankfurter, also voted to uphold the *Colegrove* precedent. He seemed the weakest of the bloc, saying he wasn't sure of his position, but he would hold to it.

Once again the discussion came to Stewart and once again it was tied, four votes to four. Immediately Stewart admitted that it was Brennan's argument that had convinced him. Stewart was prepared to rule that, like *Gomillion*, the apportionment in Tennessee was so distorted it had to be rectified. But it should be fixed, he said, on the narrowest possible grounds. With that understanding, he was prepared to be the fifth vote to rule in favor of the Tennessee plaintiffs.

Although Black was thirsting to write the majority ruling in *Baker* v. *Carr*, the chief justice realized that Black's views could not hold the majority. Nor could Justice Douglas's. Either of those justices would lose Stewart's vote for sure. If either was assigned to write the opinion, he was almost certain to impose a remedy on the state of Tennessee. That left Warren only two possibilities. The safest move would be to assign the opinion to Stewart himself. That, in fact, was Black's advice, who did not believe that even Brennan had the ability to write an opinion that could withstand Frankfurter's withering assaults. In the end, Black told the chief, Stewart would possibly defect.

But Warren had more faith. He went to see Brennan, who was confident he could hold on to Stewart. So once again, it was to Brennan that Warren turned. Only Brennan, Warren believed, had the skill to craft an opinion that would overturn *Colegrove*, give the federal courts the powers they had long been denied, and hold Potter Stewart.

Brennan finished his draft in mid-January and sent the first copy to Stewart. As Stewart had suggested, Brennan had limited his opinion to a statement of the federal court's jurisdiction. He did not order the courts of Tennessee to do anything. Stewart sent a memo back to Brennan saying he agreed with the opinion. On January 27, 1962, Brennan sent it to Warren, Black, and Douglas, telling them that he had Stewart's vote solid.

But the battle was not over. Frankfurter and Harlan still hoped that somehow they could persuade Stewart to change his mind again. On February 8, Harlan wrote Stewart, "Feeling as strongly as I do about the shortsightedness and unwisdom of what is proposed to us, I hope you will not think it presumptuous of me to ask you to await (if your mind is still open) what I am writing (which will not be long) before casting what will be the decisive and if I may say so, fateful vote in this case."

On February 14, Frankfurter circulated yet another memo to the conference, taking Brennan's draft of the majority opinion to task:

> Considering the gross inequality among legislative electoral units within almost every state, the Court naturally shrinks from asserting that in districting even substantial equality is a constitutional requirement. Room is allowed for weighting. This of course implies that geography, economics, country versus city, and all the other factors which have throughout our history entered into political districting are to some extent not to be ruled out in future reapportionment litigation. To some extent—there's the rub. In effect today's decision empowers the courts of this country to comprise what should constitute the proper composition of the legislatures of the 50 states; if State courts should for one reason or another find themselves unable to discharge this task; the duty of doing so is put on the Federal courts or on this

Court if State decisions do not satisfy this Court's notion of proper dis-
tricting.

Frankfurter was totally fearful that this would constitute such a
usurpation of court prerogatives, that it would undermine the authority of the Court itself.

But rather than make headway, Harlan and Frankfurter actually lost
ground. They had expected to be joined in the dissent by Harlan,
Whittaker, and Clark. In that regard, Frankfurter had asked Clark to
research a portion of the dissent, specifically the section dealing with
other remedies that ill-represented citizens of Tennessee might seek.
Clark was surprised to find that Tennessee's constitution provided no
opportunity for amendment by the public at large. Any change in Tennessee's apportionment policy would have to come from the very legislature that was at issue. On March 7, Clark regretfully notified
Frankfurter that he too, like Stewart, was joining Brennan.

"Preparatory to writing my dissent in this case, along the lines you
suggested of pointing out the avenues that were open for the voters of
Tennessee to bring about reapportionment despite its assembly, I have
carefully checked into the record," Clark wrote Frankfurter. "I am
sorry to say that I cannot find any practical course that the people
could take in bringing this about except through the federal courts."

Gingerly Clark continued: "Having come to this conclusion, I decided I would reconsider the whole case and I am sorry to say that I
shall have to ask you to permit me to withdraw from your dissent. I regret this . . . but the voters of Tennessee have no other recourse."

Incredibly, as Clark began to shift toward Brennan, Stewart, under
unrelenting pressure from Harlan, began to waver. Harlan was urging
Stewart to join his dissent from Brennan's opinion, specifically stating
that while in this particular case the matter was being sent back for a
new hearing, the rights asserted by the plaintiffs "are not assured by
the federal constitution." Harlan's efforts pleased Frankfurter. "Send
your own hot shot into *Baker* v. *Carr*," he urged Harlan.

Meanwhile, Justice Douglas began preparing a separate opinion of
his own. Worse, from Brennan's point of view, Douglas sent a memo
urging the justices to rush the opinion, because it was an election
year—a notion that the others felt was highly improper. It fell on
Brennan to scurry from chamber to chamber trying to calm down the

situation. Douglas's statements were giving new concerns to Stewart. Clark now wanted to join Brennan's opinion. Under the maxim that there's no zealot like a convert, Clark became as adamant as Douglas that Brennan wasn't going far enough. He wanted to strike down the entire law.

With Clark's vote in hand, it suddenly didn't matter whether Stewart's vote held or not. Black and Douglas inquired as to whether the opinion shouldn't be rewritten and made stronger. But Brennan had given his word to Stewart. He had massaged his colleague masterfully. Now, at the last minute, he was being called upon to abandon Stewart. Brennan refused to go along. He would stay with Stewart and the opinion would have to come down as he had written it.

On March 26, Brennan announced the dramatic decision of the Court. It would forever change the nature of politics in the United States, almost instantly giving more power to the residents of the big cities and stripping the more conservative rural Americans, the landowners, of power they had enjoyed for nearly two hundred years.

"What the Court is doing," Harlan declared, "reflects more an adventure in judicial experimentation than a solid piece of constitutional adjudication."

Frankfurter added: "There is not under our Constitution a judicial remedy for every political mischief, for every undesirable exercise of legislative power. The Framers carefully and with deliberate forethought refused to enthrone the judiciary. In this situation, as in others of like nature, appeal for relief does not belong here. Appeal must be to an informed, civically militant electorate." Just as he had done in his *Cooper* v. *Aaron* opinion, Frankfurter's eloquent words swamped Brennan's clunkily written majority opinion.

As even *The Washington Post* described: "On the basis of legal scholarship and forensic ability a jury would award victory to the minority. In contrast to Mr. Frankfurter's tour de force, the opinion of the Court, written by Mr. Brennan, was pallid and technical." Adding to the insult, the *Post* continued: "Perhaps it was necessary to water it down and make it largely a review of what the Court had decided in previous cases in order to obtain substantial majority support. In any event, one turns largely to the concurring opinions of Justices Stewart, Clark, and Douglas for the rationale of what the Court has done."

Writing in *The Washington Star*, columnist William S. White mourned the obvious. "Men who have long tried to hold the Supreme Court in special veneration cannot now deny that it is rewriting the Constitution and meddling in politics to suit the wishes of some—but only some—of nine unelected men.

"This is the new central, the true and tragic meaning of the new divided Court decision claiming for the federal judiciary the unexampled power to make its own determination as to whether state legislatures are rationally apportioned," White wrote.

On the floor of the Senate, the powerful chairman of the Judiciary Committee rose slowly from his seat. Mississippi senator James Eastland had rarely been more enraged. The Baker v. Carr ruling, he predicted, will make it impossible for the Court "to ever be restored to the point of dignity." He said that Brennan's ruling had reduced the sovereign states "to the status of automatons, who must blindly follow the voice and direction of the federal judges." Eastland then introduced records showing that since his arrival on the Court, Brennan had participated in fifty-one cases involving national security and had voted favorable "to the position urged by the Communists," forty-nine times.

Though Frankfurter had won the raves of the critics, Brennan had carried the day. This defeat, this reversal of his carefully thought out decision in Colegrove in 1946, was more than Frankfurter could bear. Meanwhile Justice Charles Whittaker had found the tension and arm twisting so bad that it had driven him to the hospital for exhaustion. He ended up not participating in the ruling. One week later Whittaker quit the Court and took a job with General Motors.

A few weeks later, on April 6, 1962, the exhausted and bitter Frankfurter suffered a disabling stroke. He became a virtual recluse from the Court and on August 28 handed in his resignation to President John F. Kennedy. The aftermath of Baker v. Carr had been to create two new Court vacancies for the president to fill.

It had been widely assumed in Cambridge that the accession of a Harvard Law School graduate to the presidency would grease the wheel for Justice-in-Waiting Paul Freund. But Kennedy's first inclination on hearing of the resignation of Charles Whittaker was to appoint a different Harvard Law graduate, a black judge named William H. Hastie. But according to written recollections by Robert Kennedy, Warren argued that Hastie was a Frankfurter disciple. "He's not a liberal," Warren informed Bobby. The attorney general apparently got the same message from William O. Douglas. Douglas told Kennedy that Hastie would be "just one more vote for Frankfurter." The same reasoning that blocked Hastie applied to Paul Freund. Kennedy skipped both men and instead named Byron R. White, an assistant attorney general who had been a Kennedy friend since his PT-109 days.

When Frankfurter himself resigned, Freund was again passed up. Kennedy did more than merely appoint someone who did not share the same philosophy of judicial restraint as Frankfurter, the new president selected one of the most liberal activist lawyers in the country: Arthur Goldberg, a former general counsel of the Congress of Industrial Organizations and at the time Kennedy's secretary of labor.

According to a student at Harvard, Freund was so angry at Goldberg's selection, he chucked a typewriter through an office window. A Freund appointment would have put the Court right back where it had been with Frankfurter. He would have been a strong conservative voice and with the surprisingly conservative White would have formed the foundation for a new 5 to 4 majority with Harlan, Clark, and Stewart.

Instead Brennan and Warren received one of the most enthusiastic advocates of judicial activism that could be found. Arthur Goldberg would never harbor doubts about "going too far." For the Court's four-member liberal bloc, he became the automatic fifth vote.

In no issue did that become more important than in apportionment. Within three years of the *Baker* v. *Carr* decision, Stewart's misgivings became no more than minor footnotes. The federal courts would soon order exactly what parameters states had to follow. It was one man, one vote. States would not even be allowed to have a senatelike chamber, where the election of members was not related to population. Brennan's ruling had done what he and Black had predicted it would: open the door to what they wanted in the first place. For the next seven years Brennan's skills as a playmaker and conciliator would hardly be needed.

CHANGING THE FACE
OF THE LAW

"WITH FIVE VOTES AROUND HERE you can do anything," Brennan would tell his clerks. And for the seven years between 1962 and 1969, Brennan, Black, Warren, Douglas, Goldberg, and later Thurgood Marshall and Abe Fortas, did exactly what they wanted. In the entire history of the Court, there was neither a coalition nor a period of activism that could even moderately compare with what was to happen.

The departure of Frankfurter from the Court had been greeted by Brennan like a breeze of cool air. The presence of his old professor had been so stifling that sometimes Brennan found it unpleasant even to come to the Court. With Felix gone, Brennan was relieved to give himself completely to the main goal of Justice Black. For nearly two centuries of the nation's history, the Bill of Rights had merely been words on parchment. As they long as they were not applied to tyrannical acts of the state legislatures, the first ten amendments had little real meaning. Black had written many opinions making the Bill of Rights binding on state laws, but, as in *Colegrove* v. *Green*, they mostly came in losing causes. Whatever victories had come for the Alabamian had been sporadic and without pattern. An occasional shift by Justice

Clark or Justice Burton might have caused an aberrant ruling to go Black's way, but those decisions had created few precedents on which the Court could build.

The arrival of Arthur Goldberg in 1962 changed everything, drastically and immediately. An unabashed liberal, Goldberg was the first justice in many years to come to the Court fully molded in the Black philosophy. He was one man who needed no persuasion when a case was presented.

Black and Brennan had already formulated the outline for what they wanted to achieve in their NYU speeches. Now, with the full endorsement and support of the chief justice, and with Goldberg's fifth vote a certainty, they set about to accomplish their aims. As Brennan himself observed several years later: "It was in the years from 1962 to 1969 that the face of the law changed."

In no area did things change more than in the field of criminal law. Few constitutional provisions relating to the rights of criminal defendants had been made applicable to the states. But in 1962 Brennan and Black led the Court in ruling that the Eighth Amendment barred cruel and unusual punishment by the states for the first time. In *Robinson v. California*, Brennan wrote that the state of California had no constitutional right to imprison a citizen of the United States for being addicted to narcotics. Brennan's ruling, equating constitutional law with a subjective sense of human dignity, would lead ten years later to the famous and lengthy opinion that would strike down the death penalty. His passion for protecting the rights of individuals against the police and the state was by now his most well established pattern. It had been the cornerstone of Brennan's liberal leanings all the way back to his decision in the *Tune* case.

So it was no surprise when Brennan gave his blessing to Black's opinion in the 1963 criminal justice landmark decision *Gideon v. Wainright*, which held that a state could not deny a criminal defendant the right to counsel. The honor of writing the opinion in *Gideon*, the earliest of the series of cases that would change America more drastically than all the bills of Congress in that year, went to Justice Black. After nearly thirty years on the Court, Black finally created a reality out of his most deeply treasured belief: that due process of law required that a defendant accused of a crime at least be represented by counsel.

Brennan played a more direct role in the 1964 case of *Malloy v.*

Hogan, which applied the Fifth Amendment guarantee against self-incrimination to the states for the first time. Hogan had been arrested in 1959 during a Hartford, Connecticut, gambling raid. He was sentenced to a year in jail and fined $500. Sixteen months later, on January 15, 1961, Hogan was called before a state investigating committee to testify about his gambling activities. Hogan refused and was sent back to jail for contempt of court. As was the pattern of the day, the Connecticut Supreme Court ruled that although American citizens had rights against self-incrimination, residents of Connecticut did not. Hogan was ordered to testify.

Brennan overturned the Connecticut judges and freed Hogan from a second jail term. Admitting that his ruling was a departure from precedent, Brennan clearly explained that the movement that started with *Robinson* v. *California* and *Gideon* v. *Wainright* would not stop. The state of Connecticut would have to live by the same rules as the U.S. government. No longer could defendants in state actions be forced to testify against themselves. Hogan had already served his time, he couldn't be compelled to serve it twice. The Black-Brennan doctrine of incorporation as enunciated in their NYU speeches, rolled on. With Frankfurter gone, there was no one on the Court to halt the trend.

The strand of *Malloy* was followed by *Pointer* v. *Texas*, which concluded that a defendant had a right to be confronted by the witnesses against him. Pointer was a Texan who had stolen $375 at gunpoint from a man named Kenneth W. Phillips. Before Pointer's trial, Phillips answered a number of questions from the police and described the robbery. But before the trial the victim moved to California.

Pointer was a bad man, that was for sure. But he had what was then considered the odd idea that at his trial his lawyer should be able to cross-examine his accuser. The supreme court of Texas couldn't understand why that was necessary. So Brennan and Black, who worked together on the decision, wrote their opinion in a most condescending fashion. "The Sixth Amendment is part of what we called our Bill of Rights," they began. "There are few subjects, perhaps, upon which this Court and other courts have been more unanimous than in their expressions of belief that the right of confrontation and cross-examination is an essential and fundamental requirement for the kind of fair trial which is this country's constitutional goal." The five-man majority now had a head of steam.

Although it never became a widely recognized case, few of the Brennan decisions were more controversial than the one written in *United States v. Wade*. Wade was a bank robber from Texas who had been plucked out of a police lineup by the teller he had victimized. The police, however, had never bothered to inform Wade of his right to counsel. The notion that a criminal defendant was entitled to counsel during the police lineup struck many "law and order" judges as absurd. After all, Wade had not yet even been charged with a crime. A federal judge named Warren E. Burger at the federal court of appeals in Washington described the concept of representation by counsel at a lineup as a "Disneyland contention." Burger even ridiculed the lawyer who had brought up the idea, saying: "Some court-appointed counsels find it expedient to protect themselves by raising every point, however absurd, which indigent appellants suggest."

After studying the specific nature of the Wade prosecution, however, Brennan concluded differently: "The lineup was a critical stage of the prosecution at which Wade was as much entitled to the aid of counsel as at the trial itself." In this case, as in many others, Brennan was far ahead of Chief Justice Warren, who fretted repeatedly during conference that an unscrupulous lawyer could cause the identification to be lost by delaying a lineup. A victim's memory might only last so long. But with Black, Douglas, and Goldberg behind him, Brennan felt confident in moving beyond Warren's narrower agenda. Warren's reservations were not strong enough to cause him to desert the alliance. The *Wade* case provided ample evidence that Warren was following Brennan's lead, not directing the Court himself.

"The government characterized the lineup as a mere preparatory step in the gathering of evidence," Brennan said. "But the confrontation compelled by the state between the accused and the victim or witnesses to a crime, to elicit identification information, is peculiarly riddled with innumerable dangers."

Burger might call it "Disneyland," but the extension of constitutional rights to criminal defendants was hardly a fantasy for Brennan. Unlike Burger and Harlan, who had grown up in idyllic circumstances and been educated in ivory-tower environments, Brennan had seen police and governmental abuse since the age of ten. And in this string of criminal-rights cases he did more than his share to fix it. In a way, these cases were easy for Brennan.

Brennan's most personally difficult case arose in March of 1963 when he was forced to take an active and public position in the Court's leading school-prayer case of the era, *Abington School District v. Schempp*. The Schempps were a family of Unitarians living in Abington Township, just outside of Germantown, Pennsylvania. Each morning at Abington High School, where the Schempp children attended school, prayers were piped through the intercom. Such practices were mandated by a Pennsylvania law declaring: "At least ten verses from the Holy Bible shall be read without comment at the opening of each public school on each school day. Any child shall be excused from such Bible reading upon the written request of his parent or guardian." In this case the federal appeals court ruled that the Pennsylvania requirement was unconstitutional, so Brennan was privately hoping the Supreme Court would not even hear the case. But those hopes were not to be realized. In a similar case in Maryland, a court of appeals had ruled by a 4 to 3 vote the opposite way, saying prayers in the schoolroom were not in violation of the Constitution. Warren felt the Court had no alternative but to settle the matter definitively. Black, who also agreed, had long been certain that any prayer in public schools violated the constitutional proviso against the establishment of religion.

Only Justice Potter Stewart could not bring himself to strike down the practice of prayer in the public schools. Even Harlan could not defend it. Chief Justice Warren asked one of the Court's most conservative members, Justice Clark, to write the opinion, a move he hoped would deflect some of the partisan criticism he knew would come.

For the rest of his life, Brennan would point to *Abington v. Schempp* as the most wrenching personal decision of his career. He had come from a religious family. In his early years, Brennan had prayed extensively in parochial school. And throughout his adult life, Brennan made it a rule to attend Mass every week. There was hardly an interest group more opposed to the banning of prayer in the public schools than Irish Catholics. And he was still the only Catholic justice, chosen in part because he was a Catholic, about to rule in a case in which the church had deeply held beliefs.

Rarely did Brennan perceive himself as the "Catholic justice." At his confirmation hearing when he had been asked about possible conflicts between the church and the Constitution, Brennan had answered that it was the Constitution he was swearing to uphold. But now, in a reverse way, Brennan felt obliged to explain himself. Even Justice Douglas had restrained his concurring opinion to just a few pages.

As the only Catholic on the Court, Brennan felt he had to set out his position carefully. Clark's opinion for the Court ran a mere twenty-three pages. Brennan's astonishing separate concurrence ran more than seventy pages and summed up not only his own views but superseded Clark's opinion in importance by stating more clearly than Clark exactly what it was the Court was holding.

Although most justices relied exclusively on their clerks for research, Brennan was in the habit of spending evening after evening at home, reading history and philosophy. In the living room of his rented Georgetown home, Brennan's wobbly green card table was covered with books and legal briefs. From the end of dinner until just after 10 P.M., Brennan would sit quietly and read and study. Even more than she had in New Jersey, Marjorie hated stuffy lawyer parties, so there was no great urge to go out in the evenings. Night after night, Brennan curled up with the complete works of the liberal thirteenth-century Catholic theologian Saint Thomas Aquinas.

So when the oral argument took place on February 27, 1963, Brennan felt mentally ready to tackle the assignment. Could it be, he asked, that the Founding Fathers had banned religious ceremonies in many official government functions while they meant to condone them in others? On the Monday after the argument, Brennan told the brethren he felt the uncustomary need to work alone on the opinion. It was the first sign that he felt a special pull on the school-prayer issue. This would be his own opinion, Brennan said. He was a religious man, but on the Court, the Constitution was the Bible.

"This Court's historic duty to expound the meaning of the Constitution has encountered few issues more delicate or more demanding than that of the relationship between religion and public schools," he began. But just as the Established Church of England could not impose its Protestantism on the people of Ireland, state governments and school boards had no business mandating prayer in schools. "It should not be necessary to observe that our holding does not declare that the First Amendment manifests hostility to the practice or teaching of religion, but only announces an application of prohibitions embedded in the Bill of Rights."

It was already becoming commonplace that regardless of which justice wrote an opinion, Brennan would, at some point, have to explain it. Foreshadowing what would later become a fierce public debate over the original intent of the Founders, Brennan said the opinions of the Founders had little relevance in the modern world. For one thing, he pointed out, the public school system wasn't even established on any widespread scale until the presidency of Andrew Jackson. Said Brennan: "A too literal quest for the advice of the Founding Fathers upon the issues of these cases seems to me futile and misdirected." Regardless of what Jefferson may or may not have thought, Brennan had concluded, it was up to modern man to decide what was right in the modern world. "Our interpretation," he said, "must necessarily be sensitive to the much more highly charged nature of religious questions in contemporary society."

In what would become a hallmark of Brennan opinions, he ranged through the ages and the centuries in search of truth. He didn't just write an opinion, he wrote a history, a volume about school prayer. His conclusion was guided by what he had learned. Just as Aquinas had written that knowledge arises from reason, it was reason and fairness, not precedent and law, that would dictate Brennan's jurisprudence. "The panorama of history," he decided, "permits no other conclusion than that daily prayers and Bible readings have been designed to be religious exercises." History, not law, was his model. Yet it was his complete knowledge and mastery of the law and precedents that enabled him to persuade his brethren. He had learned his lessons of the first five years. Now Brennan considered and answered every possible rejoinder, every potential argument that might be used to shred his and the Court's conclusions. In each matter he showed the flaws in the opponents' logic.

Finally, he returned again to what he knew would come: the claim that the Court was hostile to religion. It was not, he said. The Court only commands government to be neutral in matters of religion. And point by point, Brennan went back over each case in which it was fine for the government to countenance religion. Sunday blue laws were fine. It was permissible to have a chaplain in the armed services and in federal prisons. "Such activities," he declared, "are a far cry from the sponsorship of daily Bible reading and prayer recital."

His *Schempp* opinion was a tour de force. What emerged strongly was Brennan's now full-grown conviction that the Constitution was a living, breathing document and that the Supreme Court had no intention of considering the original intent of the Founders in its decision making.

In *Schempp*, Brennan had worked mostly alone, with his own conscience as his guide. But that was not the typical Brennan approach. Although the new majority on the Court made his skills as a middleman less important than they had been when the ideological split was more even, often they still came into play. And in no case was that more apparent than in Brennan's work in *New York Times* v. *Sullivan*, a landmark free-speech case. Like *Baker* v. *Carr*, *New York Times* v. *Sullivan* changed American law and culture in a profound way. And just as in *Baker* v. *Carr*, Brennan proved to be the only justice who could write an opinion that would bring most of the justices together in a firm majority.

Oddly, the *Times* case involved not an article but an advertisement. L. B. Sullivan was an elected commissioner of Montgomery, Alabama. On March 29, 1960, *The New York Times* carried a full-page political advertisement about the struggle for civil rights in the South. The advertisement never mentioned Sullivan, but it did say that truckloads of police "armed with shotguns and tear-gas ringed the Alabama State College campus." Sullivan, who was apparently a man of thin skin, claimed that since he was the city commissioner in charge of the police the paragraph libeled him. His lawyers found seven citizens of Montgomery to testify that when they read *The New York Times* they immediately assumed the ad was talking about L. B. Sullivan. Though the circulation of *The New York Times* in Montgomery in 1960 was about five papers, the circuit court of Montgomery awarded Sullivan $500,000 in damages. On August 30, 1962, the supreme court of Alabama upheld the judgment against the *Times*, stating that it was irresponsible for the paper to print an ad so misleading when the paper's news department had information proving the falsity of the claims in the ad.

The *Times* acknowledged that the advertisement had been riddled with errors. It said, for example, that nine students from the college had been expelled for leading a demonstration at the state capitol, while they had really been punished for demanding service at a lunch counter. In addition, their attorney admitted that police had never "ringed" the campus. They had been "deployed" nearby.

To accept a case on appeal from a state supreme court, lawyers for the appellants had to show that a constitutional issue was involved. And prior to *New York Times* v. *Sullivan* libel had always been a matter of state, not federal law. *The New York Times* asked the Supreme Court to accept the case on what is called a writ of certiorari. It was submitted to the Court on November 21, 1962. The state of Alabama responded with its petition on December 15, 1962. They argued that the federal courts had no power over libel. That power, the brief said, resides in the legislatures. On January 7, 1963, a notice was posted that the Supreme Court had agreed to hear the case. Libel law would never be the same again.

The oral argument in the case had taken place on January 6, 1964. As was his custom, Brennan asked relatively few questions and none of them provided much insight into what he was thinking. To outsiders and those watching the proceedings, Brennan gave away little. But when the conference convened on the following Friday morning, Brennan had a perspective on the case totally different from that of any other justice. The prevailing view was that the libel verdict be dismissed on the narrowest grounds possible: that the advertisement had not defamed Sullivan because it had not specifically named him, and that it certainly hadn't damaged his reputation. In Alabama, if anything, Justice Black observed, it probably helped Sullivan's career.

Such a ruling would have left the basic law of libel intact. Traditionally the plaintiff in a libel case is required to show how statements have caused injury. The ruling suggested by a majority of the Court would simply amplify that point by saying Sullivan had failed to meet that burden.

It was Brennan who first suggested that the mere fact of an error is not necessarily a cause of action. The plaintiff in a libel action, Brennan suggested, should not just show that there was a mistake but that the error was intentional and motivated by ill-will or "actual malice." Making the test to win a libel suit more difficult, Brennan told the conference, would go further toward preserving the constitutional ideals of free speech.

Had Brennan not been asked to write the opinion in *Times* v. *Sullivan*, his beliefs probably would have been submerged to the will of the majority. But Chief Justice Warren by now had total confidence in

Brennan's abilities to write an opinion that would hold the Court. As always, any opinion assigned to Black or Douglas ran the risk of losing several justices. Warren always wanted as many justices to speak together as possible. So, as he did in *Baker* v. *Carr*, Warren gave Brennan the assignment.

By the end of January, Brennan had finished his first draft, which contained three distinct sections. The first dealt with the facts of the case, the second discussed the meaning of the First Amendment, and the third compared the actual evidence against what the Constitution required. He had composed this first draft himself. Only after it was completed did he show it to his law clerks and seek their comments and correction. On February 6, with minor changes, the second draft was sent out to the brethren for their comments. Brennan would then wait patiently for the answers to come back.

The first note came from Justice Warren, who was happy to join Brennan's opinion. A few days later, Justice White reported that he found Brennan's views to his liking. But then came the bad news. The three most liberal justices, Douglas, Black, and Goldberg, found Brennan's formula too conservative. If the Court was going to go beyond the narrow ruling discussed in conference, the ruling that would have left things as they were, they didn't want an opinion that to them seemed to restrict free speech. It was the view of Douglas, Black, and Goldberg that the constitutional right of free speech was absolute when it applied to public discourse. There should be no "actual malice" standard.

Brennan's formulation was remarkably similar in its concept to what he had done in the *Roth* obscenity case. In that case Brennan had tried to save true literature by allowing states to outlaw hard-core porn. Here Brennan seemed to be following the same line of thought. The three most liberal justices did not have the votes to rule a total exception to libel. But by making the test harder, Brennan hoped to accomplish the same thing while convincing the middle-of-the-road justices to come along with him. The only problem now was that the liberals were off on a different track. He still needed two more votes, and they had to come from Stewart, Harlan, or Clark.

Things did not look promising. Harlan was concerned about the definition of a public official. "I would not want to foreclose a cop, a clerk, or some other minor public official from ordinary libel suits without a great deal more thought," he wrote Brennan. Furthermore, Harlan disagreed with the final resolution of the case. Brennan wanted to overturn the Alabama verdict and not have a new trial. Harlan agreed but felt Brennan had failed to explain fully why no new trial was necessary. As a conservative and an advocate of states' rights, Harlan wanted to make sure this point was made before he agreed to it.

Since Harlan had succeeded Frankfurter as the leader of the conservative faction, Brennan was anxious to please him. For one thing, Harlan could probably deliver the vote of Justice Clark. But more important, when a decision was supported by justices from both Court factions, its level of acceptance by the public was greater.

Thus, Harlan's memo caused Brennan to generate a fourth draft. In it, Brennan did all that Harlan asked. He explained in detail that there was nothing to be gained from a new trial in the the *Times* case. But after reflection, Brennan found his revisions inadequate. On the advice of Justice Black, Brennan decided it might be better to go ahead and let Alabama have a new trial. Did the Court want to be flooded with motions for dismissal in similar cases? It might be better for the federal courts to send those disputes back to the state courts.

So Brennan began a fifth draft, already four more than any other justice would attempt. This time he ended the opinion by sending the case back to Alabama "for further proceedings not inconsistent with this opinion." He accompanied draft five with a memo to the other justices explaining the change and the reasons for it. The following morning Brennan had a memo from Harlan, who could no longer agree to part three of the opinion. But while Harlan was recalcitrant, Justice Stewart had decided that the fifth draft was good enough for him. Brennan now had four votes, but he still needed Justice Clark.

Ordinarily the justices communicated with one another by memo, usually written in stilted lawyer language. Occasionally there would be a discussion about a case over lunch, and Warren and Brennan regularly discussed cases in person before the conference. Brennan himself gained most of his intelligence about the thinking of the other justices from his clerks, who met often with the clerks of the other justices to gossip about what their justices were thinking. Brennan encouraged these encounters. On their hiring, the clerks were specifically told to discuss the cases with their colleagues. Brennan frequently told his clerks: "I take help from wherever and from whomever I can get it."

Brennan's clerks were like honeybees in a field of clover. They sent out feelers and brought back ideas. In many ways they were Brennan's personal trademark. Brennan was a politician, an operator who conceived of his role in a completely different fashion from that of most judges. He worked the justices the way Lyndon Johnson worked the floor of the Senate. Nothing illustrated his mastery of this technique more than his work in *New York Times v. Sullivan.*

Brennan needed to know what Clark was thinking. He sent out his clerks and they returned with disturbing news. Clark had originally been inclined to join Brennan's opinion, but now he was changing his position. He wanted to stay close to his fellow conservative, Justice Harlan. Brennan then did what was for him a rare thing. He ventured down the hall of the courtroom to Justice Clark's chambers, slipped in, and shut the door. Before Brennan could speak, Clark handed him a printed memorandum. The visit had come too late. Clark's memo echoed Harlan's feelings. Brennan left the meeting with only four votes for his opinion.

The usually cheery Brennan came back to his chambers in an extremely foul mood. He had labored over five separate drafts and now it appeared that all the work was for naught. There was no choice but to go back to the liberal side and try to persuade Douglas and Goldberg. Sensing Brennan's frustration, both men were willing to help. Goldberg wrote a memo stating: "You know my view that your evidence warrants the rule of an absolute privilege for comment on official conduct . . . but I am certainly agreeable to joining your excellent opinion and then writing very briefly that I would go beyond to the extent I have indicated. You can count on my vote." Only Brennan's mentor, Justice Black, refused to compromise. While Brennan was contemplating what changes to make to satisfy Goldberg and Douglas, his clerks reappeared with news that Clark was having second thoughts after Brennan's visit, while Black was urging Douglas and Goldberg not to back down.

By March 5, Brennan was working on yet a seventh draft, still wrestling with the issue of whether Sullivan should get a new trial. And by the time the conference met to take up the case on March 6, Brennan had circulated an eighth draft, with more changes designed to satisfy Clark. The vote was taken and Brennan had his majority. On Sunday evening, March 8, Brennan received a call from Harlan at home. Exactly what was said is not a matter of public record, but the gist of the call was that Harlan, out of respect for all the work Brennan had put into the opinion, had decided to go along. He would vote with the majority after all. The following morning Harlan sent a note to his colleagues announcing: "I am withdrawing my separate memorandum in this case and am unreservedly joining the majority opinion."

Many of the issues with which the justices argued involved legal and technical questions, such as whether the case should be sent back for trial or reversed without a trial. For the public at large the result was much more tangible. Public discourse was protected from the threat of libel actions. Unless it could be proven that an error was malicious in its intent, mistakes could be made.

Wrote Brennan in the final version:

> Erroneous statement is inevitable in free debate . . . it must be protected if the freedoms of expression are to have the breathing space that they need to survive. . . .
>
> A rule compelling the critic of official conduct to guarantee the truth of all his factual assertions . . . leads to a comparable self-censorship. Under such a rule, would-be critics of official conduct may be deterred from voicing their criticism, even though it is believed to be true, and even though it is in fact true, because of doubt whether it can be proved in court or fear of the expense of having to do so.
>
> The constitutional guarantees require, we think, a federal rule that prohibits a public official from recovering damages for a defamatory falsehood relating to his official conduct unless he proves that the statement was made with 'actual malice'—that is, with knowledge that it was false or with reckless disregard of whether it was false or not.

The words *actual malice* would become, in effect, the law of the United States. For those who argued that the Supreme Court had become a legislative body, *New York Times* v. *Sullivan* certainly proved the point. No Congress, no state legislature, had enacted a criminal code specifying a standard of malice. Like the one-man, one-vote requirements that followed *Baker* v. *Carr*, actual malice became an accepted and virtually unquestioned part of American legal tradition.

Black wasn't satisfied. Yet the votes hadn't been there for his position. Wrote Black:

> Malice, even as defined by the Court, provides at best an evanescent protection for the right critically to discuss public affairs and certainly does not measure up to the sturdy safeguard of the First Amendment.
>
> To punish the exercise of this right to discuss public affairs or to penalize it through libel judgments is to abridge or shut off discussion of the very kind most needed. This nation can live in peace without libel suits based on public discussions of public affairs and public officials. But I doubt that a country can live in freedom where its people can be made to suffer physically or financially for criticizing the government, its actions, or its officials. . . . An unconditional right to say what one pleases about public affairs is what I consider to be the minimum guarantee of the First Amendment.

No other case had demonstrated so clearly the distinction between Brennan and Black. Black's formulation could have never carried a majority. He would have gone down in flames rather than compromise. Brennan had sought and found a middle ground, and in doing so made law in a way few courts ever had.

GRISWOLD V. CONNECTICUT

O N O C T O B E R 1 2 , 1 9 6 4 , B R E N N A N received the news from home that his beloved mother, Agnes, had died. In a note to the chief justice, Brennan wrote; "While we all knew it would come to pass, Mother's passing is hard to accept." In a similar note to Harlan, Brennan added: "We were blessed to have Mother with us for so long."

It seemed to be a season of death. Former justice Burton died on October 29, 1964. The following winter, on February 22, 1965, Frankfurter, who had become almost an invalid since leaving the Court, also passed away. Shortly before he did, Frankfurter only half jokingly blamed his physical condition on the decisions of Warren and Brennan, writing in a letter: "They aren't doing much for my recovery."

Two months after Frankfurter's funeral service, the Court met for its hearing on what was to become part and parcel of its most controversial issue—abortion.

In 1965, of course, abortion was not the issue it would become seven years later. The problem faced by the Supreme Court in that year seemed a little simpler—birth control. The state of Connecticut had passed legislation that not only prohibited birth control pills, it prohibited doctors from talking about them to patients. In *Griswold* v. *Connecticut*, Estelle Griswold was actually arrested for giving advice to married couples about how to avoid conception. She had exacerbated her crime by prescribing contraceptive devices for her patient.

The justices were fairly united in their belief that the law had to go, but as usual they couldn't agree on why or how. The defense lawyers, who had argued the case before the high court, had rested their reasoning on a husband and wife's First Amendment freedom of association. That didn't sound right to Black. "The right of a husband and wife to assemble in bed is a new right to me," he chuckled during a conference on the case. Douglas, who wasn't chained to Black's literal sensibilities, saw no problem with extending the freedom of association to the marital relationship. Goldberg agreed, but Warren and Brennan weren't so sure.

Despite his lack of confidence that Douglas was on the right path, Warren felt Douglas had the most passion for the case and assigned him the opinion. His finished draft on April 23, 1965, stated: "Marriage does not fit precisely into any of the categories of First Amendment rights. But it is a form of association as vital in the life of a man or woman as any other, perhaps more so." (Douglas would know, of course. He would be married four times.)

"We would indeed have difficulty protecting the intimacies of one's relations to the NAACP and not the intimacies of one's marriage. Marriage is the essence of one's form of expression of love, admiration and loyalty. To protect other forms of expression and not this one, this central one, would seem to us to be a travesty."

Douglas's draft did little to coalesce even the liberals on the Court. There was always the danger that if the majority opinion writer wrote a poor opinion, the case could turn the other way.

Justices Harlan and White concurred only on the result, citing their belief that the Connecticut law should be overturned on the basis of the due process clause of the Fourteenth Amendment. They were sure that freedom of association had nothing to do with birth control in Connecticut. Neither had inclination to join Douglas's opinion and thus create a strong right to freedom of association that could be extended into other areas such as homosexual rights.

On April 24, 1965, Brennan interceded in an effort to save the decision. "I agree that the association of a husband and wife is not mentioned in the Bill of Rights," he told Douglas. "That is the obstacle we must hurdle to effect a reversal in this case." He asked Douglas to change the emphasis of his opinion and urged him to drop the freedom of association argument and instead concentrate on the rarely used Ninth Amendment, which proclaimed that the other rights enumerated in the Constitution were not exhaustive. Those actually listed in the Constitution, Brennan said, were just "examples" which "do not preclude applications or extensions of those rights to situations unanticipated by the Framers."

It was a remarkable judicial holding. Although totally consistent with what he had written in the *Schempp* school-prayer case in Pennsylvania, it was totally inconsistent with two hundred years of previous constitutional law. Brennan told Douglas; "The guarantees of the Bill of Rights do not necessarily resist expansion to fill in the edges where the same fundamental interests are at stake. . . . All that is necessary for the decision of this case is the recognition that there is a constitutional right to privacy. . . . For it is plain that in our civilization, the marital relationship above all else is endowed with privacy.

"With this change of emphasis," Brennan concluded, "there is a better chance it will command a court."

But more than merely commanding a court in the one Connecticut case, the little change of emphasis would later alter the political landscape in a way no one could predict. Brennnan's arguments persuaded Douglas to change his rationale. As a result, the Court stated for the first time that the American citizen had a "right to privacy." And it was that Brennan-formulated principle which would ultimately flower into an even more controversial and contentious issue—a woman's right to an abortion.

On March 18, 1965, in a reflection of the accelerated concern felt in conservative America over the activism of the Warren Court, the House of Representatives, in a punitive action, denied a bill that would have raised Supreme Court pay by a vote of 203 to 177. Brennan's salary of $39,500 per year put the justices on an equal pay footing with the most junior of lawyers in Washington. It was a pittance compared to the fees garnered by the heavy-hitting solicitors who came to argue at the Court. Many could make that much money trying one case before the Court. To try to make up the difference, the various justices took on outside work. Brennan, for example, was listed as a part-time lecturer at New York University.

A month later, President Lyndon Johnson summoned Arthur Goldberg to the White House. Johnson had long owed a big favor to his friend Abe Fortas and he didn't want to waste any time getting Fortas on his Court. Within the week, LBJ had talked Goldberg into quitting the Supreme Court to become ambassador to the United Nations. Fortas, who was named as Goldberg's replacement, had little interest in taking such a pay cut. But Johnson appealed to Fortas on patriotic grounds, citing the soldiers he was sending to Vietnam. "How can I send them into battle and not appoint you to the Court," he told his friend. He then marched Fortas into the White House pressroom and announced the appointment.

Fortas's arrival on the Court was welcome news to Brennan and Douglas. A Georgetown neighbor of Brennan's, Fortas had hired Brennan's son William J. Brennan III while a partner at Washington's prestigious Arnold, Fortas & Porter. Even more gleeful was the Court's most doctrinaire liberal, William O. Douglas. Fortas was in every real sense a Douglas protégé, and Goldberg's departure would mean little in terms of the Court's ideological drift.

In 1966, the Warren Court, with Fortas in place of Goldberg, continued its march toward the defense of criminal rights with the landmark ruling in *Miranda v. Arizona* requiring that police apprise criminal defendants of their constitutional rights. Like other decisions of the Warren Court, *Miranda* allowed no flexibility for the states and became, as Brennan predicted, the *Jencks* of its time—the most visible target at which opponents of the Court could aim.

Mindful of the storm his decision in *Jencks* had stirred up, Brennan urged Chief Justice Warren to allow some room for state legislatures to maneuver. He piously wrote Warren: "We cannot prescribe rigid rules. We are justified in policing interrogation practices only to the extent required to prevent denial of the right of self-incrimination. But should we not leave Congress and the States latitude to devise other means which might create an interrogation climate which has the similar effect of preventing the fettering of a person's own will."

Determined not to let Warren fall into the trap of *Jencks*, Brennan informed the chief that he could not agree to the chief's formulation. But Warren, annoyed at this open show of independence, urged Brennan to withdraw a threatened separate opinion. It was one of the rare times that the two quarreled. Brennan retreated from his position and the matter was forgotten.

For twelve years no justice had ever worked harder than Brennan. He had not come to the Court as a constitutional scholar (as Paul Freund had noted wryly, Brennan had not even taken constitutional law at Harvard), but he had become an expert and he had found a way to bring the Bill of Rights at last to the American people. Black was so sure that the Bill of Rights applied directly to the states, he couldn't be persuaded otherwise. But Brennan knew that the Founding Fathers had rejected that contention specifically. So Brennan had turned repeatedly in his cases of the 1960s to the Fourteenth Amendment, which declared no state could deny a citizen of due process. And what was due process if not the guarantees of the Bill of Rights themselves? Thus without becoming dogmatic or extremist, Brennan had found the vehicle that could bring Tom Clark or Potter Stewart over to his side when their vote was required.

In a speech in 1968, Brennan expounded on what he had learned during his miraculous twelve-year education on the Court:

> This approach has made the Fourteenth Amendment a potent tool in the attack upon the central problem of the twentieth century in our country. Society's overriding concern today is with providing freedom and equality, in a realistic and not merely formal sense, to all the people of this nation.
>
> We know that social realities do not yet fully correspond to the law of the Fourteenth Amendment. We do not yet have justice, equal and practical, for the poor, for the members of minority groups, for the criminally accused, for the displaced persons of the technological revolution, for alienated youth, for the urban masses, for the unrepresented consumer—for all, in short, who do not partake of the abundance of American life.
>
> Congress and the federal judiciary have done much in recent years to close the gap between promise and fulfillment, but who will deny that despite this great progress the goal of universal equality, freedom

and prosperity is far from won and that ugly inequities continue to mar the face of our nation? We are surely nearer the beginning than the end of the struggle.

In its service of that dream, the Fourteenth Amendment, though a hundred years old, can never be old. Like the poor old woman in Yeats's play, "Did you see an old woman going down the path?" asked Bridget. "I did not," replied Patrick, who had come into the house after the old woman left it, "But I saw a young girl and she had the walk of a queen."

But in identifying his struggle as just a beginning, Brennan was prophetic. The final years of the Warren Court would be marked by scandal, acrimony, illness, death, and even fighting among the liberals themselves. The glory years of the Warren-Brennan Court were over. Only difficulties lay ahead.

THE JUSTICES
UNDER ATTACK

ALTHOUGH BRENNAN HAD HAD DIS-
agreements with Douglas over the years, nothing so tested his mettle
as what became known as the "Tigar affair," a vicious intercourt battle
over the hiring of a controversial law clerk.

Brennan had long since decided to get his clerks from someone
other than Harvard's Paul Freund. The final break in his relationship
with his alma mater had come when Harvard Law School refused to
admit William J. Brennan III to its class. Not even the intercession of
Harvard Law's dean, Erwin Griswold, could convince the rabid anti-
Brennan admissions committee to admit the younger Brennan, who
had gone into the marines after college. Following the succession of
critical *Law Review* articles and a refusal to hang a portrait of Brennan
in the law school, it had been the final indignity perpetrated on Brennan by Harvard. His son went to Yale instead, and Brennan decided to
get his clerks elsewhere.

His decision was made easier by the knowledge that many of his former clerks had gone into teaching and could recommend their students. Among those former clerks turned teacher was Robert O'Neill
at the University of California Law School, known as Boalt Hall.

O'Neill selected Michael Tigar, a second-year student who had been at the top of his Boalt class as well as being editor of the *California Law Review*. There was a potential problem with Tigar, O'Neill told Brennan. In his undergraduate days Michael had been involved in numerous left-wing student activities and he had openly demonstrated against the House Un-American Activities Committee. None of this, Brennan initially professed, concerned him in the least.

After the announcement of his hiring was made, Tigar and Brennan were attacked by a variety of right-wing hate groups. A barrage of mail arrived at the Supreme Court, alarming even Chief Justice Warren, who was accustomed to political attack. The American Legion issued a statement citing Tigar's appointment with the comment: "Do not be surprised if another stream of decisions emerge from the Supreme Court loosening more shackles from the reds."

One letter came from Chief Justice Thomas Kavanaugh of the Michigan Supreme Court. He enclosed a clip of an editorial from a paper in Pontiac, Michigan. It read: "Our 'supreme' Court still 'carries on.' For a time, Americans fervently hoped each decision that was greeted with cheers by the crooks, lawbreakers and the Communists might be the last. Perish the thought."

The column went on to identify Tigar as an "ardent exponent of Communist activities" and concluded: "He leaves with a diploma to take up work for our 'supreme' court. Draw your own conclusions." Kavanaugh wanted Warren to know that he had written a letter to the editor in response to the editorial. "I wanted to correct the impression which some readers apparently have that he [the editorial writer] was referring to the Michigan Supreme Court."

In California *The San Diego Union* editorialized that the Tigar's appointment "raises questions of national security." The paper said Tigar's Communist activity "leaves little doubt of the kind of influence he will try to exert on the highest court in the land."

Warren clipped and saved all the letters, no matter how kooky, and sent copies to Brennan. After a discussion with Warren, Brennan called O'Neill and another former clerk turned professor, Robert Cole, and voiced his anxiety over the opposition. The professors asked Tigar to meet with Brennan in Washington. Brennan asked Tigar to provide him with a summary of his political activities. Tigar returned to Berkeley and complied, writing a detailed memo of all he had done during his active undergraduate career. Tigar called Brennan to discuss the contents of the memo. But before Tigar would show it to Brennan, he wanted a promise that it would remain confidential between the two of them. He asked that Brennan not even share it with the chief.

Brennan replied that it could not be done that way. The entire Court was being tarred by the violent reaction to Tigar's appointment, and Brennan felt it important that they be reassured. Most of all, he could not keep secrets from the chief justice.

Tigar was adamant. No confidentiality, no statement. His unyielding position gave Justice Brennan suspicion that Tigar was holding something back. Tigar went on a vacation while Brennan was left to ponder what to do.

On July 10, Tigar was summoned from a camping trip back to Washington. Brennan said that he had to be able to show the statement to other people. Tigar repeated that he would not testify formally or informally about his political beliefs or activities. Nor would he let Brennan do it by proxy.

At first Tigar had a few days to think it over. But before he could, Brennan called to tell him that the job offer had been revoked. He later admitted he had yielded to pressure from Justice Fortas, who had been visited by FBI director J. Edgar Hoover's top assistant, Clyde Tolson. When Fortas raised the possibility of a congressional inquiry, Brennan decide to cave. According to an account by author Laura Kalman in a biography of Fortas, Brennan told her: "The right wing deliberately set up a program—a system of pressure—that involved Abe Fortas, who was on the Court then; J. Edgar Hoover; and more particularly Hoover's right-hand man, Clyde Tolson.

"Tolson came over to see Fortas and Fortas came in to see me to tell me that if I went through with this there might be an inquiry which could prove embarrassing to Tigar and to me and the Court," Brennan told Kalman.

Fortas's pressure was supported by Warren, who casually reminded Brennan how close the Senate had come to passing the Jenner bill, which would have stripped the Court of jurisdiction over cases involving the powers of congressional investigations, loyalty rules for teachers and federal employees, and state regulations for admission to the bar. It had failed, but only by eight votes. To the always uncompromising Justice Douglas, who at that very moment was incurring public

wrath by marrying a nineteen-year-old woman, it was a shocking lapse
of character on Brennan's part. At that very moment, congressmen
were giving speeches demanding that Douglas resign, but he wasn't
backing down an inch. Douglas stormed angrily into Brennan's office
snarling, "You've got to stand up to those people." The usually talk-
ative Brennan had no reply.

Liberal columnist Andrew Kopkind, writing in *The New Republic*,
accused Brennan of hypocrisy, much as Murray Kempton had charged
after the McCarthy questioning at Brennan's confirmation. Wrote
Kopkind: "Brennan fired a law clerk because of his politics. That is the
simplest way to put it." Brennan salved his conscience by asking a personal favor of his friend Washington, D.C., attorney Edward Bennett
Williams. Would Williams be willing to give Tigar a job at his law firm?
Williams, who had several clients with cases at the Supreme Court,
was more than happy to oblige. Tigar was hired and became one of
Williams's best young litigators. Ultimately Tigar left private practice
and became a law professor at the University of Texas, where he is regarded as one of the outstanding law teachers in the land.

Although the Court's liberal majority increased to six (Douglas, Black,
Brennan, Warren, Fortas, and Marshall) with the replacement of Tom
Clark by Solicitor General Thurgood Marshall in October 1967, the
lights were dimming on a remarkable period in judicial history. That
same fall, after fourteen years as the focus of criticism, Chief Justice
Warren announced his intention to retire on June 13, 1968. He told
Brennan that his loyal deputy chief would be his first choice as a suc-
cessor. But there was no point in making a pitch to President Johnson.
There was no way LBJ was going to pass up the opportunity to make
his old friend and adviser Abe Fortas the chief justice.

Warren's departure had been carefully timed to make sure that
Johnson, and not Warren's longtime California adversary Richard
Nixon, appointed his successor. But Johnson's grand plan fell apart
amid revelations that Fortas had indirectly accepted $15,000 from his
law firm while sitting on the bench. Fortas's partner, Paul Porter, had
set up a special lecture at American University, then had given American the money with which to pay Fortas.

The arrangement, once publicly revealed, served as a lightning rod
for conservative critics. On October 4, 1968, Johnson withdrew the

Fortas appointment, although Fortas remained on the Court as an associate justice. Johnson then considered a number of possibilities, including sitting justices Brennan and Stewart. He seriously mulled over the possibility of returning Goldberg to the Court. Senator Phil Hart of Michigan was considered. But Johnson had no political strength left to make any appointment that could win approval. A consensus had developed on Capitol Hill that the new chief would have to be selected by Johnson's successor, either Nixon or his Democratic opponent, Hubert Humphrey.

Six days later, on October 10, the tired Johnson asked Warren to stay on as chief justice. The only hope now was that Humphrey could somehow pull out the election and keep Warren from being replaced by a nominee of his archenemy, Richard Nixon. But it was not to be. On inauguration day, January 20, 1969, Warren had the ironic duty of swearing in Nixon as president of the United States.

It was President Nixon who would eventually replace Warren with the chief justice of his choosing, Warren E. Burger. But that was only the beginning of the plans Nixon and his aides had for the Supreme Court. They were determined to reverse the direction of the Court, even if it meant destroying the careers and reputations of Warren's three most influential brethren, Fortas, Douglas, and Brennan.

If nothing else, Brennan's friendship with Judge David Bazelon, the judge whom he had met and befriended on his first day on the Court back in October 1956, made him extremely suspect to the new chief justice. Bazelon and Burger served on the same U.S. Court of Appeals for the District of Columbia for more than a decade. They were more than just professional rivals. They were bitter personal enemies as well.

To conservative thinkers, Bazelon was one of the most dangerous men in America. Almost invariably ruling in favor of the dispossessed, the mentally ill, and the accused, Bazelon had authored a compendium of far-reaching decisions on such topics as the insanity defense, environmental problems, the right of eighteen-year-olds to vote, and tax benefits to organizations that discriminate. Unlike Black, Bazelon felt the Constitution was a document without limits. His favorite maxim was a statement made in 1932 by Justice Brandeis: "If we would guide by the light of reason, we must let our minds be bold."

Bazelon was never nominated to the U.S. Supreme Court, but his opinions often became the law of the land. Cynics claimed that it was his personal friendships with the justices that led to so many of his radical rulings being upheld by the Court. In a 1981 article in *The Washington Post*, it was noted that "during the Warren Court era, it was a good idea for lawyers who wanted a Bazelon opinion upheld to mention Bazelon's name in the brief as many times as possible. . . . One mention of this name was worth 100 pages of legal research. It would remind the liberal majority that Bazelon did it—and if Bazelon did it, it must be all right." By the mid-1960s, Brennan was bringing many of the clerks Bazelon had trained over to the Marble Palace to serve him. They turned the clerk's office into an open bastion of Bazelon-type liberal thinking. Antiwar posters dotted the walls outside Brennan's chambers. Despite the public furor over Michael Tigar, Brennan didn't seem to mind. He was still the most easygoing of the justices and he never tried to dictate the personal thoughts or lives of his clerks.

Bazelon was well connected to Washington's power structure. His friends included leading developer Charles Smith and wealthy liquor dealer Milton Kronheim, Sr. He often shared a box at the Washington Redskins games with President Johnson and then–Redskins owner Edward Bennett Williams. Bazelon was not above ensuring the success of his opinions on appeal by befriending new justices on the Court, and that is exactly what happened with Bill Brennan. Although Marjorie did not, Brennan enjoyed the excitement of sitting with the president at the football games. He accepted Bazelon's invitation to become a partner in several business deals. Eventually he found himself joining Bazelon for lunch at least twice a week at an obscure private dining room known as Mr. K's, which was, in reality, the cafeteria for Kronheim's liquor company employees. Bazelon would often send for Brennan in a chauffeured Mercedes limousine. Frequently Douglas, the liberals' most beloved icon, would join them.

On the walls of the dining room were rows of pictures of the regulars who ate there—Brennan, Douglas, Americans for Democratic Action founder Joseph Rauh, New York senator Jacob Javits, and other unabashed members of Washington's liberal community.

Brennan had come to enjoy the company of Bazelon and his other friends. Every Sunday morning, for example, Brennan and Bazelon jogged, though witnesses said it was more like a fast walk, around the Kennedy Center. As Brennan described the sessions, Bazelon took the opportunity to agonize about the awesome responsibility of judging. There was no doubt that Bazelon's commitment to a liberal judicial agenda moved Brennan beyond a place that even Black had imagined. In reflecting later on those jogs with Bazelon, Brennan said, "It is not happenstance that his worries focus primarily upon the fate of the indigent or member of a deprived minority, for each is the primary victim of the legal system. His work above any other's has pointed the way to the cure."

But the relationship was not without risks. Bazelon had talked Brennan into investing in some real estate partnerships. When Johnson was in power, the arrangement had seemed harmless. But now that the Court was facing a hostile White House and Justice Department, some began questioning the legitimacy of a Supreme Court justice having a business relationship with a lower-court judge whose opinions he would consider. Thus when Nixon and his new chief justice took over, the anxiety level in the Brennan and Douglas chambers rose dramatically.

On March 10, 1969, the high court had issued a ruling in a case called *Alderman v. United States*. It was one of some twenty cases in which the defendants were hoping to void government prosecution with claims that the Justice Department had taped their conversations. Several of the *Alderman* cases involved espionage. Despite that, Justice Byron White ruled that the government had to turn over any transcripts of tape-recorded conversations.

On Wednesday, March 12, Brennan's secretary, Mary Fowler, received a call from a Justice Department officer stating that Jack Landau, of the Information Office of the Department of Justice, would like to speak with Brennan. Brennan had known Landau since 1966 when as a correspondent for Newhouse newspapers he had interviewed Brennan for the justice's tenth anniversary on the Court. His article, entitled "The Law: Justice Brennan's Decade," was one of the few that even came close to recognizing the role Brennan had played in the Warren Court revolution.

They apparently hit it off on a personal level as well. For in the spring of 1967, Landau, unaware of Brennan's black-sheep status at his alma mater, asked Brennan to write him a letter of recommendation for a Nieman Fellowship at Harvard, the most prized university fellowship a journalist can win. Brennan was luckier for Landau than he was at getting his own son into Harvard. Landau felt close enough to Brennan to write him a personal note on April 20, 1968, telling the justice that he was finished at Harvard and was returning to Washington.

When Landau came on the telephone, Fowler knew immediately who he was. "Is Justice Brennan in his office and would it be possible for me to see him for a few minutes?" Landau asked. Brennan told Fowler to "tell him to come over." Landau said he would be there in ten minutes.

Despite their warm friendship, Brennan claims he didn't know that Landau had been hired by Attorney General John Mitchell as director of public information. Nonetheless, Landau arrived at Brennan's chambers at 3 P.M. and was greeted warmly. Brennan asked when he had gone to work for Justice. It had happened some weeks before, Landau said. He told Brennan he was on a leave of absence from Newhouse, though he wasn't sure about returning.

Edgy, Landau began his conversation in what Brennan perceived to be a circuitous manner. He reminded Brennan that when he had been a reporter and had asked about a pending case, Brennan had slammed his fist down on the desk telling him he should know what an improper question that was to ask. Brennan listened to the recollection. Despite his excellent memory, he couldn't recall anything like that ever happening. Brennan was puzzled by the direction of the conversation. Landau then said he hoped Brennan wouldn't react that way again, because this time he was on an "urgent" and "important mission" from the attorney general.

Rather than bring the conversation to an immediate end, as he later admitted would have been proper, Brennan bade Landau to continue. The Justice Department was "very much upset," Landau began. He said that the opinion in *Alderman* had been read and studied by the attorney general, the solicitor general, and others in the department. They interpreted the ruling to mean that the transcript of any conversation, whatever its content, which had been obtained by illegal surveillance would have to be turned over to criminal defendants. Based on this interpretation, he continued, the CIA, the FBI, and the State Department had voiced alarm that this would require a decision to discontinue any criminal prosecution involving the turning over of the transcript of electronic surveillance on any embassy located in Washington.

So what was the problem? Brennan asked. He was growing impatient. The problem, Landau replied, was that the U.S. government was spying on virtually every embassy in Washington. Were that piece of information to become public, foreign relations would be destroyed. Landau explained that the Justice Department had not made the Court aware of this prior to its hearing, hoping that Justices Fortas or White—Fortas through his friendship with President Johnson, or White as a former assistant attorney general—would have known about the bugging and notified the brethren of the security threat.

Now, Landau said, Attorney General John Mitchell couldn't figure out how to get this information to the Court. Landau stated that "it would be most embarrassing" to foreign relations to have to admit that the U.S. government was bugging every embassy in the city. It had been decided that since Landau knew Brennan personally, he should be sent to convey the message.

Still Brennan did not ask Landau to leave. Instead he asked: "What does the attorney general want us to do?" Almost too nervous to speak, Landau uttered something Brennan interpreted to mean that if the Court did not undo what it had done in *Alderman*, the Justice Department might support congressional legislation to curtail the jurisdiction of the Supreme Court.

At that, Brennan suggested moving the conversation to the chief justice's office. At 3:30, Brennan brought the by now terrified public information officer into the chambers of Chief Justice Warren. The chief justice offered Landau a seat, but the messenger was too tense to sit. Brennan took a chair and related the conversation to Warren. Tersely Warren told Landau that the case had been decided on the merits and that any petitions for a rehearing would have to be determined in legal papers. At 4:15, Landau and Brennan walked back to the justice's chambers. Several weeks later the Justice Department made a motion for a rehearing, but it was denied.

Later Justice Douglas was to characterize the approach as "the first instance in the memory of anyone connected with the court in which the executive branch has made actual threats to the Court." In comments that proved to be prophetic, Douglas recognized the Justice Department approach as "the opening salvo of a long and intense barrage." Wrote Douglas, "It seems apparent that [Assistant Attorney General Richard] Kleindienst and perhaps Mitchell himself has a

cause, and the cause is to give the Court as much trouble as possible."
Although ridiculed in the press and by several of his brethren as paranoid at the time, Douglas was proved to be right. It was, indeed, the
beginning of a long and partially successful campaign to destroy the
independence of the Court.

Although Fortas had been determined to remain on the Court, despite
his rebuff as chief justice, the Nixon administration had other ideas.
On May 4, 1969, in a story that had almost certainly been leaked by
the administration, *Life* magazine published an article detailing Justice
Fortas's financial arrangement with an organization called the Wolfson
Foundation. Louis Wolfson had been a friend and former client of For-
tas's who had previously been under investigation by the Securities and
Exchange Commission. It was revealed that Fortas had agreed to serve
as a "consultant" to the foundation and accepted a fee of $20,000 in
January 1966.

Following publication of the article, Attorney General John
Mitchell himself paid a visit to the office of Earl Warren to give firsthand confirmation that the *Life* article was correct. By Saturday, May
10, Fortas was distraught over the situation. But it was a sign of the
times that when he called Black at eight o'clock in the morning, the
senior justice told Fortas it was too dangerous to talk over the telephone. Black's advice was not soothing. He told Fortas that he had to
resign for the good of the Court.

The Monday papers brought revelations of more questionable financial dealings by Fortas. By Wednesday, May 15, after a series of tense
conferences among the brethren, Fortas announced his resignation.
The hope among the remaining justices was that the heat was off.

Justice Brennan had been strangely silent and remote during the
sessions on Fortas. His wife, Marjorie, had been diagnosed with throat
cancer. Since he had gotten the word, it had been difficult for Brennan
to be his usual jovial self. And unbeknownst to the others, Brennan
was more than just a court brother of the now tainted Fortas; he was
his partner in several business deals. It didn't take long, less than an afternoon, for conservative opponents of the Court to redirect their aim
from the fallen Fortas to Brennan.

On the floor of the House, Louisiana congressman John Rarick took
the floor. "It is with mixed emotions that I receive the announcement

that Justice Fortas has resigned," he declared. "I say mixed emotions because we have only one out—that others should resign for similar reasons. . . . Apparently members of the high court have entangled themselves into holding partnerships in land companies for tax loop-hole benefits and for identity concealing fronts. A form of judicial investment conglomerate. . . . Little wonder urban renewal and model cities programs find favor under color of the law, in the eyes of some members of the judiciary . . . some judges are not entirely disinterested."

Such comments could be dismissed if they had only come from extremists like Rarick. But even mainstream papers like the *Minneapolis Tribune* were singing the same song: "The issue is what Fortas did, all right, but several of his brethren could well afford to spend a few sleepless nights wondering if what they have been doing equally offends the principle of detached noninvolvement."

Then Rarick inserted into the *Congressional Record* the public documents showing a potentially embarrassing web of Brennan real estate partnerships, held with several lower-court judges and some major Washington real estate developers. Declared Rarick: "Is it not conceivable that the Fortas resignation is intended only to frustrate further inquiry? We have the responsibility to our people not to permit ourselves to be pacified by the departure of one—Abe Fortas—when there remain on the federal judiciary others whose similar interests damage the solemnity of the judiciary.

"If corruption in the federal judiciary exceeds one member, it is no less corrupt by losing one of several corrupting influences."

Making matters worse, at virtually the same time, a Catholic University law professor, William Roberts, had filed a petition in the Supreme Court asking that Brennan be disqualified from hearing any case in which his friend and business partner David Bazelon had ruled as a member of the District of Columbia Court of Appeals.

Roberts, who had filed a motion in the appeals court to block dissolution of an institute that he directed at Catholic University, argued that as a partner with Bazelon in a Virginia apartment complex, Brennan should not be sitting in judgment of opinions written by Bazelon or another real estate partner, J. Skelley Wright, also a federal judge. It was exactly the type of attack Brennan most feared, for it was the one on which he was most vulnerable. He had suffered a lapse in judgment by agreeing to the deal and the situation now had the potential for plenty of embarrassment. Roberts's motion was quickly dismissed by the judge in the case, but Brennan worried that it could be the start of a wave of disqualification motions, each one serving to embarrass him, to peck at him until he too had to resign.

Douglas was under fire as usual, this time for a financial arrangement with the Parvin Foundation. By nature Douglas was the most combative member of the Court, while Brennan tended to tactical retreat. Douglas had hired one of the nation's top lawyers, Simon Rifkind, to take his case. On May 24, he wrote his sister: "The word here went out from the High Command that the first three to go would be Abe Fortas, the second myself and the third Brennan. I am sorry that Abe resigned. But I don't lie awake nights as there is nothing to worry about. There is nothing I have done of which I am ashamed, which I would not do again, or which is illegal or unethical." Douglas and Rifkind beat the charges of financial impropriety. But the attempts to undermine the integrity of the Court and make it vulnerable to ethical assaults from the Right continued.

Almost from the day in 1957 when Brennan was confirmed on the Court, the federal government had been engaged in a long-running battle with El Paso Natural Gas Company, one of the West's largest suppliers of natural gas. The federal complaint against El Paso was spurred by the company's purchase of its own competitor in the California market, the Pacific Northwest Pipeline Corporation. Indeed, lawyers for El Paso had looked on with horror at Justice Brennan's rulings in the Du Pont–General Motors cases. A determination by El Paso officials was made that the case would be won not by legal but by political means. That was possible because El Paso had hired Richard Nixon's and John Mitchell's former law firm, Mudge, Rose, Guthrie & Alexander, as its counsel.

In 1964, when the Democrats still controlled the White House, the Supreme Court ordered a partial breakup of El Paso, as well as the creation of at least one other company that would put competition back into the California market. As the Court itself described the action: "That mandate in the context of the opinion plainly meant that Pacific Northwest or a new company be at once restored to a position where it could compete."

By 1968 the parties were still haggling over how the Supreme Court's mandate could be accomplished, particularly the complicated details of how the new company would be formed from the old. But the election of Richard Nixon as president suddenly changed the equations. Three days after Nixon's former law partner took over the Justice Department, Mitchell announced the federal Clayton Act complaint was being dropped. El Paso then filed a petition with the Supreme Court saying that at the agreement of the parties the case was being dismissed. A Jack Anderson column on April 23, 1969, noted that Nixon and Mitchell's law firm had already received $771,000 from El Paso. It now seemed that this was a fee well earned.

Anything that made Richard Nixon happy made Earl Warren squirm. At a conference of the justices on May 2, 1969, Warren suggested that the Court deny the motion to dismiss and keep the pressure on El Paso even without the Justice Department. Normally an agreement between parties to dismiss a suit would be automatically approved by the Court. But not always. If the justices felt that their previous "mandate" had not been complied with, they could legally continue to administer the case from the bench. That was exactly what Warren, Brennan, Black, and Douglas wanted to do, although Douglas's notes of their May 2, 1969, conference reflect some concern: "The Chief Justice knows little about financing of this kind."

The only question, Douglas said, is "have they complied with our mandate? It is clear they have not done so." In an opinion drafted but never published, Douglas wrote: "Dismissal of the appeal at this time may indeed be a magnificent award to El Paso for its unlawful activities and demonstrate that corporate misconduct and corporate wrongdoing do pay."

Brennan agreed with Warren, though not in Douglas's strong terms, but felt there had to some equitable way to get the new company into California despite the Justice Department's withdrawal of its complaint. Since two justices, White and the newest justice, Thurgood Marshall, did not participate, and since Fortas was now gone from the Court, Warren had a four-man majority to flout Nixon and Mitchell.

Probusiness justices John Marshall Harlan and Potter Stewart were incredulous that the Court was refusing to yield to the government's wishes. Douglas wrote of Harlan: "What's happening is so exotic, he can't be rational."

Six weeks later, Warren announced the decision of the Court demanding that its order for the divestiture of El Paso be complied with. The original order had been written by Douglas, but he had written two previous *El Paso* opinions and didn't want his name on the third. So it was rewritten by Brennan, and it was Brennan who arbitrarily changed it from a per curiam, or unsigned, opinion of the four-member majority. Instead, he put Warren's name on it.

Stripped of Douglas's inflammatory language, the latest *El Paso* ruling emphasized that the Court could not agree to a settlement that flouted the previous mandate of the Court intended to ensure competition in the California gas market.

More striking than the Douglas-Brennan-Warren opinion was the strong dissent by Harlan. Douglas was right about one thing. Harlan, who had thought Brennan incompetent during the Du Pont divestiture, simply wasn't rational when it came to monopolies. The former Wall Street lawyer wrote: "The action taken by the Court today will be dismaying to all who are accustomed to regard this institution as a court of law. All semblance of judicial procedure has been discarded in this head-strong effort to reach a result that four members of this court find desirable. In violation of the Court's rules, the majority asserts the power to dispose of this case according to its own notions, despite the fact that all parties participating in the lower court decisions are satisfied. . . .

"The Court's conclusion that its mandate has been disobeyed is, in short, based upon completely factual premises born of a superficial acquaintance with the 14,000-page record. This is not surprising since the majority has seen fit to decide this important case without the benefit of significant oral or written argument. And yet it is upon this tenuous basis that the Court has chosen to shatter centuries of judicial tradition in order to reach a decision which does not even promise to further the interests of California's gas consumers."

The *El Paso* case marked the finale of Earl Warren's tenure as chief justice. But what had started so gloriously was ending in confusion and embarrassment. Fortas had been run from the Court. Instead of a Democrat naming his successor, Warren would be replaced by a Nixon appointee. Douglas was under attack for accepting money for speeches. Even Brennan was receiving fire. In his final days, Warren decided to ask his colleagues to serve under a new code of ethics. Even though associate justices by this time made just $60,000 per year, Warren asked if they would be willing to eliminate outside income. With the exception of Douglas, all were.

At Warren's farewell party, Fortas didn't show up. A week later Brennan organized a second farewell party aboard the presidential yacht *Sequoia*. It was three days after the Senate confirmation of Warren's successor, Warren E. Burger. The choice of a gift for Warren was odd, a Winchester rifle.

With Nixon's first appointee headed to the Court, Brennan felt more vulnerable than ever. Warren had been like a father to him. And with the pressures building, it was no time to lose your best friend or mentor. Finally, on June 11, 1969, Brennan made a decision. He sold his AT&T stock, left to him by his mother, as well as his holdings in Public Service of New Jersey. In addition, Brennan announced he was canceling all speeches and public appearances. According to Yale professor Fred Rodell, he even refused to meet a group of students, something that had become an annual tradition. Brennan's annual summer teaching job at New York University was axed. His interests in all his real estate partnerships were sold back to the Washington developer who had organized them.

As was traditional in the summer, the justices retired to their vacation homes. Brennan and his beloved Marjorie went to Nantucket. But at the end of July, they stopped for a couple of nights at the Westport, Connecticut, home of Ethel and John Harlan. Much of the concern that evening was over Hugo Black. Three days earlier, his doctor had found a small blood clot in Hugo's brain. Black, then eighty-three, desperately wanted to stay on the Court for two more years, until he was eighty-five. But the small stroke he had suffered threatened that goal. When the Brennans arrived at Westport, Black called Harlan to talk about his physical problems and whether he could continue on the Court. After they had talked for some time, Harlan turned the phone over to Bill, Marjorie, and finally back to Harlan's wife, Ethel. The call had encouraged Hugo to try to stick it out.

But when the conversation turned away from Black's health, Harlan brought up the subject of the *El Paso* case. He reiterated to Brennan how wrong he felt the decision had been. And it wasn't just Harlan who felt that way. Burger had also taken an interest in doing what he could to get *El Paso* reversed. The papers were already speculating that Brennan would turn out to be Burger's right-hand man, just as he had been Warren's. It served to put Brennan in a fairly cooperative mood, because even before the 1969–70 term began in October, Brennan had written Black and Douglas about the possibility of granting an *El Paso* motion to rehear the controversial case.

Under Rule 58 in the Supreme Court rule book, the Court would take a case for rehearing only if one of the members of the voting majority requested it at conference. With Warren now off the court, that meant that either Brennan, Black, or Douglas would have to make such a request to the brethren.

There was a good chance that if the case was reheard El Paso would win. Replacing Warren with Burger made the case 3 to 3, but Nixon's newest appointee, expected to be conservative South Carolina judge Clement Haynsworth, would certainly make it 4 to 3.

Brennan's letter to Black and Douglas, dated September 25, 1969, asked for a meeting of the three "to discuss the Petition for Rehearing." Brennan said in the memo that since the ruling last spring he had searched some new documents that had "apparently by inadvertence" been omitted from the court record, and wanted to discuss whether "a case has been made for a rehearing."

But Brennan's memo was inconclusive. Even if El Paso knew about it, which was possible in view of the extensive electronic surveillance then in vogue in Washington, company officials didn't want to leave such an important issue to chance. The firm hired veteran Washington lobbyist Thomas ("the Cork") Corcoran to do whatever he could to get the case reopened. According to Bob Woodward and Scott Armstrong in their book *The Brethren*, the sixty-nine-year-old Corcoran first paid a visit to the aging Justice Black. According to Black's memoirs, he immediately pitched Corcoran out of his office, telling him that he would not recuse himself from the case, nor would he change his vote.

Undeterred by his first rejection, Corcoran next went to the chambers of Brennan, with whom he had occasionally sat at Saturday Mass.

Brennan claims that he too threw Corcoran out, telling him that he could not discuss a pending case. But he admitted to his clerks, as his letter of September 25 shows, that he had already been convinced by Harlan that the *El Paso* case had been wrongly decided.

After conferring with Black on Wednesday, October 8, Brennan decided that he would no longer participate in deliberations on the *El Paso* case. What El Paso had done by hiring Corcoran was ironic, because had they not interceded in such a clumsy way, they might have won.

Brennan suffered an ethical lapse in *El Paso* by allowing his conversation with Corcoran to go on longer than Black's. Friends of Brennan excused his pattern of odd behavior. His wife's illness seemed to have sapped him of his usual energy. Surgery for cancer had been scheduled for October 23.

Her illness cast a pall over the entire Court family. Elizabeth Black wrote in her diary: "Marjorie Brennan has been constantly on my mind and heart. Yesterday I wrote Bill a note to tell him that my prayers are with them. Marjorie has tried to quit smoking and just couldn't. Dear Marjorie, so pixie-like, quick, warm-hearted and humorous. I do pray God she recovers."

On October 23, doctors performed the surgery and it went reasonably well. Harlan wrote her: "I am pleased you are beginning to feel more comfortable and I have no doubt you will come through this ordeal with flying colors."

Wrote the justice back to Harlan about the effects of the chemotherapy: "Marjorie is the bravest imaginable—I'm sure I could not have taken it this long. It's difficult to stand by helplessly, but I'm ashamed of myself when I see how wonderfully she takes it."

The following summer Brennan wrote a personal note to Justice Douglas: "Marjorie's treatments have been extended once more and our hopes for getting away from Washington grow dimmer. The treatments cause her considerable distress, particularly a deep and exhausting fatigue. But we're hoping for the best."

On July 1, 1970, the Court held a birthday party for Marjorie. But it was a bittersweet occasion. Elizabeth Black wrote in her diary: "It's hard to write a birthday toast to somebody with only a 10 percent chance to live. He married Marjorie when she was 20 and she is now

63 and he loves her more now then he did then. It was all pure nostalgia and our laughter bordered on tears."

Marjorie defied the odds for some thirteen years, succumbing in 1982. It was during those years that Brennan went home at 3:30 P.M. every day and rarely left town. It was his "blue period," and he thought frequently about leaving the Supreme Court.

But while Nixon was in power, Brennan couldn't run away from the Court. He owed Earl Warren more than that. And yet, he had never felt as trapped as the *El Paso* case had made him feel. Even Harlan, with whom he had warm personal relations despite their political disagreements, was furious with Brennan for talking to Corcoran. Brennan told Harlan he had no choice now but to recuse himself from the deliberations. Now he could not be the justice to bring up the matter for a rehearing. Since neither Black nor Douglas had any intention of doing so, it seemed the case was closed.

But this was not so. Burger, anxious to reward his White House patrons, thought he had figured out a way to get around the problem. He would simply change Rule 58. Burger decided that a more equitable rule would be to allow any justice, whether that individual had been on the Court or not, to bring up a vote on a rehearing petition.

Despite Brennan's claim that he had recused himself from *El Paso*, he was willing to vote with the new chief on the rules change. On June 15, 1970, Brennan wrote a memo to Douglas asking what day he would be in the building, "so that he [Burger] can convene a conference on *El Paso*.

"If you are not coming in, I need some instructions," Brennan said. "The Chief Justice held an *El Paso* conference late Friday afternoon. Seven attended (all but you and Thurgood). Byron and I listened but took no formal part because we're out of *El Paso*. Without you, therefore, there was no quorum." Nevertheless, the five agreed that "a motion to grant rehearing may be made by any justice, whether by John or Potter who were in dissent, or by the Chief Justice and Harry [Blackmun, who had taken the other vacancy after the rejection of nominee Clement F. Haynsworth] as new appointees."

Brennan then asked Douglas: "If you dissent from the construction, will you write a dissenting opinion?"

The process sickened Douglas. "I doubt the wisdom of the change in the rule irrespective of *El Paso*," Douglas told Brennan. "Second, I certainly think that the *El Paso* case would be the worst possible occasion for making the change. If the change is desired, let's put the proposed change in Rule 58 down for discussion for the first conference in October free from any impact of the *El Paso* case or from any association with it." Douglas added that he would most definitely be issuing a dissent.

Four days later, Douglas distributed a blistering dissent to his colleagues. Had it been released it would have revealed the most bitter internal dispute at the Court since the Jackson-Black feud twenty years earlier. After listing several good reasons why the rule should not be changed, Douglas wrote:

> "I am reluctant to state my fourth and final objection to today's action for it may be misunderstood as impugning the motives of the new majority of four. I have no such thought as my Brethren are above reproach. But *El Paso*, so unsavory in its total setting, is the least worthy of all cases to ride to victory on a strained and unheard of construction of Rule 58.
>
> This case has exerted a hydraulic pressure wholly out of proportion to its intrinsic importance. Perhaps before the final chapter is written we can make a public record showing what individuals have gained and what rewards they have received from this whole venture in high finance.

Douglas's whistle-blowing threat was not lost on his colleagues. Ten days later Burger decided to abandon his effort to change the rules on rehearings. The final nail was hammered into the *El Paso* case. Douglas's dissent never saw the light of day. Brennan was relieved the matter was over. It had been a most troubling affair at a most troubled time.

No one was more anxious to forget what had happened than Brennan. In 1980, a complaint was filed against Corcoran with the disciplinary committee of the District of Columbia Bar Association. Among those writing letters of support for Corcoran was none other than William J. Brennan. He, who was known for recalling cases and facts dating back decades, claimed to have "no independent recollection" of any contact with Corcoran. On the strength, or rather the weakness, of Brennan's memory, the committee dropped its inquiry. In 1986 Brennan wrote the foreword to the memoirs of Hugo and Elizabeth Black. On page 231 of those diaries, the Blacks confirm the basic details of Corcoran's approach to Brennan, as well as Brennan's report of the episode to his fellow justices.

ROE V. WADE

I<small>T WAS EARLY</small> J<small>UNE OF</small> 1972 <small>AND</small>
Bill Brennan and Potter Stewart were having one of their frequent
lunches at the Methodist Home cafeteria across the street from the
Supreme Court. The building housed many senior citizens, most of
them older women. The two justices had on one occasion been asked
to leave by a patron after offending nearby diners by repeatedly saying
the word "fuck." They were allowed to finish their meal only after
Brennan explained to the manager that they were just discussing an
obscenity case.

But on this day, obscenity cases were far from the minds of the two
justices. Instead they had come to commiserate over the sad changes at
the Court in the short time since Warren Burger had replaced Earl
Warren. While Warren had come to the Supreme Court determined
to make history, Burger, from the day of his arrival on June 9, 1969, had
seemed concerned only with the most trivial matters. He spent his
days worrying about the lights in the Court chambers, the shape of the
bench, the lack of a Xerox machine, an assistant for the library (in a
memo sent to all the justices marked confidential), and times of meet-

ings and conferences. If such attention to minutiae wasn't bad enough, he decided to appoint an entire commission to study reform of the Court. His choice to head the committee was none other than Frankfurter's old friend and ally Paul Freund. Freund's chief deputy was another confirmed Brennan foe, Yale professor Alexander Bickel.

Ultimately the Freund committee proposed the creation of a national court of appeals that would strip the Court of its most basic power, the right to determine which cases it would hear. Numerous bills were introduced in Congress to put the committee recommendations into law, but they failed to win widespread acceptance.

It wasn't that Burger didn't have an ideological agenda. He had a negative one—to undo everything Brennan and Warren done. It had partly been his constant criticism of the Brennan rulings that had first brought him to Richard Nixon's short list as a Supreme Court candidate. In a 1967 speech at Ripon College, Burger had blasted "legal technicalities," such as whether a defendant had been beaten or whether one accused of a crime was represented by a lawyer. In speech after speech, Burger had described such debates as clogging the court system with "minutiae." In particular Burger parted company with the Founding Fathers on the constitutional proscription against self-incrimination. In 1968, Burger had declared in a speech that criminal defendants might not have any such right. Skip all that stuff, Burger would say: "Go swiftly, efficiently and directly to the question of whether the accused is guilty."

Burger had never abandoned his belief that most such protections, many of them authored by Justice Brennan in the sixties, were nothing more than "Disneyland contentions," tricks by defense attorneys designed to set a guilty man free.

Reversing the direction of the Court seemed at first to be a fairly simple task. Justices Black and Harlan had been replaced by archconservative Nixon Justice Department lawyer William Rehnquist and by Lewis Powell, a proper Richmond lawyer and a former president of Burger's beloved American Bar Association, wrongly assumed by the new chief to be as interested as himself in undoing the Warren Court excesses.

The third new member, replacing Fortas, was Harry Blackmun, Burger's so-called Minnesota Twin, who had grown up just six blocks from him in St. Paul. In Burger's mind, Blackmun would be a certain vote for the conservative position. For a time Burger was right. In his first 119 votes, Blackmun voted with Burger 113 times.

As the *El Paso* case had illustrated, Burger was willing to change a rule to do the bidding of the White House. But his failure in that case was prophetic. Burger would preside over the Supreme Court as chief justice for some sixteen years, but his calculations on what he would be able to accomplish turned out to be totally wrong. Burger would certainly be the "chief" justice in the administrative sense, but on the matters that counted, the philosophy and direction of the Court, the views of Brennan repeatedly prevailed. As the chief justice de facto, Brennan not only protected his cherished Fourteenth Amendment decisions of the Warren Court years but extended and strengthened individual liberties against the often abusive power of the states.

It was assumed, of course, that the four new Nixon appointees, aided by the two largely conservative holdovers, Byron White and Potter Stewart, would join with Burger in reversing the rulings of the Warren Court. Justices Marshall and Douglas felt helpless against the coming onslaught. They were certain that the years of progress had come to a halt.

But not Brennan. Lunching with Stewart, his thick eyebrows arched in surprise at the stream of invective his colleague was willing to hurl at the new chief justice, Brennan was encouraged by Stewart's statements that not only was he appalled at the personality of the new chief but that as a result he would not support Burger's conservative agenda. In effect, Stewart was signing on to the liberal camp.

On his return to the office, Brennan handwrote a note and sent it over to Douglas: "I will be God-damned," Brennan scribbled in pencil on a small square white pad. "At lunch today, Potter expressed his outrage at the high-handed way things are going, particularly the assumption that a single Justice, the Chief Justice, can order things his own way and that he can hold up for the nine anything he chooses, even if the rest of us are ready to bring down 4 to 3. He also told me he will not vote to overrule *Miranda*, and resents CJ's confidence that he has Powell and Rehnquist in his pocket."

Stewart's growing antipathy toward Burger had an important side effect, for in 1971 the Court had begun to grapple with what would ultimately be its most controversial decision: whether a woman could legally be blocked by a state legislature from ending a pregnancy by abortion.

Although the Texas case of *Roe* v. *Wade* has become the dominantly known case, it was one of two cases that the Court had come to consider in 1971. The other, an appeal of a Georgia antiabortion law, was called *Doe* v. *Bolton*. In the minds of the justices, *Doe* v. *Bolton* originally seemed of equal importance to *Roe* v. *Wade*.

The Texas law was by far the more restrictive of the two state statutes under attack in the abortion cases. The Texas penal code mandated a punishment of not less than two years in prison for any doctor or layperson performing an abortion. Any abortion performed without the consent of the woman involved doubled the penalty. If during an abortion the mother died, the attending doctor could be charged with murder. The only exception in the Texas law was for the "purpose of saving the life of the mother."

The Georgia legislature had approached the matter in a more complicated fashion. Rather than banning abortions outright, the Georgia criminal code permitted a difficult and complicated process by which a woman could get an abortion provided it was performed in a licensed hospital by a licensed physician. Applicants for abortions had to be approved by the State Department of Public Health. In addition, the woman had to have letters from two doctors stating that the abortion was necessary. The Georgia law also allowed relatives of the woman to petition the superior courts to halt the abortion.

Neither Powell nor Rehnquist, assumed to be Burger's allies, had been seated on the Court in time for the original oral arguments on the case. Both were seated the week after the oral arguments. Initially Burger, who was opposed to the Court's becoming involved in abortion, figured to stymie any liberalization of abortion laws. Such an act, he believed, would be an unwarranted expansion of federal power.

In the initial seven-justice conference on abortion, Blackmun and Stewart had seemed to agree with the chief justice and White that the Supreme Court had no jurisdiction over the cases. Burger thought both state laws were constitutional, although he did term the Texas law "archaic and obsolete." But Brennan was outspoken in his belief that the laws of both states were definitely unconstitutional.

Following the first argument of the cases in December 1971, Burger found that only Justice White totally agreed with him. Stewart, although his final opinion was not set, was not opposed to hearing the cases on jurisdictional grounds.

Burger was disappointed to find that Blackmun, his usually reliable twin, was similarly very much torn. It was hardly that the conservative Blackmun had revealed strong beliefs in a woman's right to choose an abortion, or in the sanctity of a right to privacy. Nor did he originally have any particular interest in extending the scope of Brennan's declarations about "penumbras" of rights, such as had been stated in *Griswold*. Blackmun, however, had been a member of the board of the Mayo Clinic in Rochester, Minnesota, and had for years served as the clinic's chief lawyer. Now, prominent among those who had filed briefs with the Court urging it to strike down the restrictions against abortion had been David Decker, chairman of the Mayo Clinic's Department of Obstetrics and Gynecology; Joseph Pratt, Mayo's director of gynecological surgery; and twenty-two others who could be counted as the most prominent medical leaders in Blackmun's home state. The argument they had presented had nothing to do with the unfairness of it all for women. The doctors saw the laws as an unconstitutional interference with the right to practice their profession, and both states' antiabortion laws mandated tough prison sentences for doctors who performed illegal abortions.

The Mayo brief to the Court declared that the laws "unfairly discriminate against physicians and denies physicians equal protection of the laws." The doctors further argued that the Texas law, which allowed abortions only to save the life of the mother, was too vague because it failed to say how certain of death a physician must be. Childbirth was always a dangerous happening. What if a woman denied an abortion threatens suicide? Could a doctor then perform the abortion to save the life of the mother?

That issue—a doctor's right to practice—most concerned Blackmun. Striking a blow for the constitutional rights of women, as Brennan was urging his brethren to do, both at his lunches and in the conference, was the furthest thought from Blackmun's mind.

Following the postargument conference it was clear that Brennan had a four-man majority that would enable himself or Douglas to write the sweeping constitutional decision they wanted. Thurgood Marshall, jokingly referred to by his clerks as Mr. Justice Marshall-Brennan, could be counted on to support whatever Brennan asked; Stewart had come around to Brennan's opinion, as much out of annoyance at the chief as anything else. But his vote was the least firm of the four. It was then announced, to the shock of both the chief justice and Douglas, that Blackmun, because of his concerns for the doctors, would vote to invalidate the antiabortion laws. When Burger saw the direction his friend was taking, he declared that he too would join the majority to allow abortion in *Roe v. Wade*. Burger's move was strictly tactical. The long-standing tradition of the Supreme Court was that the chief justice could assign the writing of the opinion only if he was in the majority. Otherwise the senior justice in the majority, in this case Douglas, could assign the opinion.

Burger's last-minute switch enabled him to assign the writing of the opinion to Blackmun, the least convinced of the five-member majority, now six, ready to strike down the Texas abortion law. Not only was Blackmun the least convinced, he was preparing to rule on entirely different grounds from the other four. Blackmun, Burger felt sure, figured to write the law so narrowly that it might apply only to the archaic Texas statute. He was sure to ignore the right of privacy arguments and leave the states plenty of room to restrict abortions if they did it in a manner a little less vague and arbitrary than it had been done in Texas and Georgia.

As Blackmun disappeared into his chambers to write his opinion, Brennan and Douglas conferred. Douglas was livid. He had not heard Burger say one word about striking down the Texas law, in fact Burger had declared the law constitutional. He considered Burger's usurpation of the assignment right a gross violation of Supreme Court tradition. Douglas wrote an angry note to the chief. He still couldn't believe that either of the two Minnesotans really wanted to strike down the antiabortion laws. "My notes show there were four votes to hold parts of the law unconstitutional. There were three to sustain the law as written. One of the four, rather than one of the three, should write the opinion," he said.

Brennan urged his volatile friend, whose trust it had taken him so long to earn, to calm down. There were ways, he told Douglas, to get the opinion they wanted. Moreover, he said, there would be no rush because Blackmun was notorious for being the slowest member of the Court. Brennan, because of his devout Catholicism, was prepared to tread slowly. In the abortion cases, he was content to let Douglas take the public pressure. But as usual Brennan quietly controlled the outcome.

On December 30, 1971, Brennan outlined the more expansive constitutional issues, which over time would seep into the Court's final ruling. He wrote Douglas: "I appreciate that some time may pass before we hear from Harry and, like you, therefore write my comments down so that I won't forget them.

"First, there seem to be a number of threshold issues that are of varying difficulty. Some, I think, must be expressly addressed, while others perhaps require no discussion or should be simply finessed. None, in my opinion, forecloses the crucial questions here—the existence and nature of a right to an abortion."

Unlike Blackmun, Brennan was not troubled about the infringement of a doctor's rights; from the outset his concern was for the pregnant woman. He wrote: "I would identify three groups of fundamental freedoms that 'liberty' encompasses:

> First, freedom from bodily restraint or inspection, freedom to do with one's body as one likes, and freedom to care for one's health and person; second, freedom of choice in the basic decisions of life, such as marriage, divorce, procreation, contraception, and the education and upbringing of children; and third, autonomous control over the development and expression of one's intellect and personality.
>
> There is a sphere within which the individual may assert the supremacy of his own will and rightfully dispute the authority of any human government . . . to interfere with the exercise of that will—rather than the holding that compelling public necessity may justify intrusion into bodily freedom.
>
> I would peg the right to care for one's health and person to the right of privacy rather than directly to the First Amendment partly because it would seem to be broader than the right to consult with and act on the advice of the physician of one's choice and include, for example, access to nonprescriptive drugs; and it identifies the right squarely as that of the individual, not that of the individual with his doctor.

Brennan warned that despite the freedom of association guarantees of the First Amendment, a state might well be able to prove it had a compelling interest in restraining abortions. "The right of privacy approach, in contrast, merely states that there is a fundamental interest in the individual's safeguarding his health.

"The decision whether to abort a pregnancy obviously fits directly within each of the categories of fundamental freedoms I've identified and therefore should be held to involve a basic constitutional right."

As in most of his monumental decisions, Brennan reached the decision first, then worked on the best reasoning that could "capture a court." He told Douglas: "Again like you, I would next emphasize that this conclusion is only the beginning of the problem—that the crucial question is whether the state has a compelling interest in regulating abortion that is achieved without unnecessarily intruding upon the individual's right. But here, I would deal at length not only with the health concern for the well-being of the mother, but with the material interest in the life of the fetus and the moral interest in sanctifying life in general."

Brennan acknowledged that "this would perhaps be the most difficult part of the opinion. I would come out where Justice Clark does in his *Loyola University Law Review* article—that 'the law deals in reality, not obscurity—the known rather than the unknown. When sperm meets egg, life may eventually form, but quite often it does not. The law does not deal in speculation. The phenomenon of life takes time to develop and only after it is actually present, it cannot be destroyed.'

"The inconsistent position taken by Georgia in allowing destruction of the fetus in some, but not all cases might also be mentioned. Thus although I would, of course, find a compelling state interest in requiring abortions to be performed by doctors, I would deny any such interest in the life of the fetus in the early stages of pregnancy. On the other hand, I would leave open the question when life 'is actually present—whether there is some point in the term before birth at which the interest in the life of the fetus does become subordinating."

Noting that the Georgia law restricted abortions to hospitals, Brennan expressed his view that "statistics apparently indicate that abortions in the early part of the term are safe, even when performed in clinics rather than hospitals. Secondly, if there is a right to an abortion in the early part of the term, that right cannot be denied through cumbersome and dilatory administrative procedures or requirements."

And finally, Brennan wrote: "The right of privacy in the matter of abortions means that the decision is that of the woman and hers alone. The only restraint a State may constitutionally impose upon a woman's individual decision is that the abortion must be performed by a licensed physician."

In November of 1971, while the Court waited restlessly for Blackmun to produce something, Brennan did manage to get the writing assignment in *Eisenstadt v. Baird*, a case from Massachusetts that involved a state law prohibiting the distribution of contraceptive foam to unmarried women. After giving a lecture on population control to a Boston audience, Thomas Baird, a disciple of family planning, invited members of the audience up to the stage, where he handed out numerous contraceptive items, including a package of Emko vaginal foam. Baird was immediately arrested and charged with violating the law making it a crime for any person except a physician or a pharmacist to give away contraceptive items and then only to married couples.

On the surface *Eisenstadt* had nothing to do with abortion. Burger argued at the conference that a state had a right to regulate contraception as a matter of public health. His views failed even to influence Justice White, the most rabidly antiabortion justice on the Court. Brennan had a six-member majority and as the senior justice in the majority; Douglas assigned him to write the opinion. Douglas himself believed the case to be one of free speech. No one agreed with him, however, so he could not write the opinion himself. Brennan was prepared to write the ruling on Fourteenth Amendment grounds, that it was treating married and unmarried couples differently and thus violating the guarantees of equal protection.

Brennan found a way not only to connect the case to the abortion debate but to use it as another strong leg on which a future opinion legalizing abortions could stand. The Massachusetts argument was that its law was intended to keep hazardous medicines out of the hands of the public. Surely, no one could question the right of a state to regulate issues of public health. But Brennan did, if those regulations were unreasonable. "The goals of deterring premarital sex and regulating the distribution of potentially harmful articles cannot reasonably be regarded as legislative aims [of the law]. We hold that the statute, viewed as a prohibition on contraception per se, violated the rights of single persons under the Equal Protection Clause of the Fourteenth

Amendment." Looking through the fog of the law, Brennan had quickly realized that the true legislative intent of the Massachusetts legislature was not to protect health but to protect morals by regulating private sexual lives.

Brennan believed that since *Griswold* made it impermissible to ban the distribution of contraceptives to married persons, a prohibition of birth-control materials to unmarried persons, would be equally unconstitutional. "The marital couple is not an independent entity with a mind and heart of its own but an association of two individuals each with a separate intellectual and emotional makeup," he wrote. "If the right of privacy means anything, it is the right of the individual, married or single, to be free from unwarranted governmental intrusion into matters so fundamentally affecting a person as the decision whether or not to bear a child."

Coming as it did before Blackmun's first draft in *Roe v. Wade*, there was no way that anyone at the time could see what earthshaking significance Brennan's choice of words would ultimately have. But what he had quietly done was build the bridge that would connect the earlier *Griswold* decision with *Roe v. Wade*. In *Eisenstadt v. Baird*, Brennan almost surreptitiously convinced his brethren to approve the proposition that there are constitutional protections in matters of child bearing. On a Court that is also searching for precedent, it would prove to be important.

Thus, it was William Joseph Brennan, and not Blackmun, the opinion's author, who laid the framework for the most controversial decision in Supreme Court history.

On May 18, 1972, Blackmun finally circulated his first draft of *Roe v. Wade*. But it contained little of the sweeping constitutional protections Brennan wanted. Blackmun decided *Roe v. Wade* on the grounds that the Texas law was unconstitutionally vague. True to his original instinct, Blackmun wrote that the law improperly thwarted a doctor's professional obligations and duties. The exemption for saving the life of the mother, he wrote, "is insufficiently informative to the physician to whom it purports to afford a measure of constitutional protection but who must measure its indefinite meaning at the risk of his liberty."

Blackmun, whose ultimately radical opinion would fixate the nation for the next twenty years, started the process with cautious words:

"Our holding today does not imply that a State has no legitimate interest in the subject of abortions or that abortion procedures may not be
subjected to control by the State. We do not accept the argument that
a pregnant woman has an unlimited right to do with her body as she
pleases. The long acceptance of statutes regulating the possession of
certain drugs and other harmful substances, and making criminal in-
decent exposure in public, or an attempt at suicide clearly indicates
the contrary."

It is astounding in retrospect that Blackmun's initial conclusion was:
"There is no need in Roe's case to pass upon her contention that a pregnant woman has an absolute right to an abortion or even to consider
the opposing rights of the embryo or fetus during respective prenatal
trimesters. We are literally showered with briefs—with physicians and
paramedical and other knowledgeable people on both sides—but this
case, as it comes to us does not require the resolution of those issues."

Brennan was pleased to get anything from the overly deliberate
Blackmun, but he saw this draft of the opinion as only a start. According to one memo sent directly to Blackmun, Brennan warned the new
justice away from deciding the case on narrow technical grounds.
Such a ruling would only enable states to clarify their statutes and
then continue to keep women from getting abortions. As Brennan
wrote his memo, Blackmun was still working on the presumption that
the only problem in Roe v. Wade was that the Texas abortion law was
"too vague."

"A majority of us feel the Constitution required the invalidation of
abortion statutes save to the extent they required that an abortion be
performed by a licensed physician within some time limit after conception," Brennan told Blackmun. "Your circulation invalidates the Texas
statute only on the vagueness ground. This does not mean I disagree
with your conclusion as to the vagueness of the Texas statute. I only
feel there is no point in delaying any longer our confrontation with the
core issue."

Despite Brennan's persistence, Blackmun's second draft in the abortion cases revealed little change in thinking. In place of the exception
that an abortion could be performed to save the life of the mother,
Blackmun mandated language that would substitute "a doctor's best
clinical judgment." In other words, in a doctor's best judgment, an
abortion could be performed. It was hardly as much as Brennan and

Douglas wanted. They wanted the choice in the hands of the pregnant woman, not the doctor. But they acquiesced, figuring it was as good as they were going to get. At least it struck down the offensive Texas and Georgia laws and it had the practical effect of making the availability of abortions much easier. After reading it, Brennan told Blackmun he thought it was a fine opinion. "I'm happy to join it," Brennan said. He couldn't resist sending a few more suggestions for the next and "hope-fully final draft."

Chief Justice Burger was prepared to join Blackmun's opinion, but he still had hopes of undermining the process altogether. With the ar-rival of Rehnquist and Powell on the Court, he figured to have four strong votes against striking down the abortion statutes. As was clear from his reluctance to recognize a woman's right to privacy, Black-mun's vote might still be recaptured. All that Burger needed to do was find a way to get the new justices involved in the case. Burger called Blackmun into his chambers and asked if he would mind having the case reargued before the full court and redecided the following year. Blackmun agreed. He felt it would give him even more time to work on what would be his most important ruling.

Brennan urged Blackmun to reconsider. The opinion was done and ready. The term was about to end. The nation wanted a ruling. But Blackmun couldn't be moved. Even though he had labored for nearly six months on an opinion, he wasn't yet ready to stand up to the chief. He wrote his colleagues:

> Nearly all of you, other than Lewis Powell and Bill Rehnquist, have been in touch with me about these cases. A number of helpful and valid suggestions have been made.
>
> Although it would prove costly to me personally, in the light of en-ergy and hours expended, I have now concluded, somewhat reluctantly, that reargument in both cases at an early date would perhaps be advis-able. I feel this way because:
>
> 1. I believe, on an issue so sensitive and so emotional as this one, the country deserves the conclusion of a nine-man, not a seven-man court, whatever the ultimate decision may be.
>
> 2. Although I have worked on these cases with some concentration, I am not yet certain about the details. Should we make the Georgia case the primary opinion and recast Texas in its light? Should we refrain

from emasculation of the Georgia statute and instead hold it unconstitutional from the beginning? Should we spell out just what aspects are controllable by the State and to what extent? For example, it has been suggested that upholding Georgia's provision as to a licensed hospital should be held unconstitutional, and the Court should approve performance of an abortion in a "licensed medical facility." These are some of the suggestions that have been made and that prompt me to think about a summer's delay. I therefore conclude, and move, that both cases go over.

In a memo supporting Blackmun's motion to put the cases off for a year, Burger wrote: "I have had a great many problems with these cases from the outset. They are not as simple for me as they appear for others. The states, have, I should think, as much concern in this area as in any within their province; federal power has only that which can be traced to a specific provision of the Constitution."

But on May 31, 1972, Brennan again warned Blackmun against delay. "I see no reason to put these cases over for reargument. I say that since, as I understand it, there are five of us (Bill Douglas, Potter, Thurgood, you and I) in substantial agreement. I question that reargument would change things."

Douglas, who totally lacked the patience, diplomacy, or temperament to persuade or cajole, saw the whole decision slipping away. Blackmun's decision may not have been much, but it was a beginning. Douglas was now more certain than ever that the whole process had been a flimflam to thwart the original four-man majority. He questioned Brennan whether Blackmun had ever really been serious about writing an opinion.

As he had in *El Paso*, Douglas responded with a tactless and potentially self-defeating memo. "The Chief Justice represented the minority view in the conference and forcefully urged his viewpoint on the issues," he wrote. "It was a seven-man court that heard the cases and voted on them. Out of that seven there were four who took the opposed view. Hence, traditionally the senior justice in the majority would make the assignment of the opinion. The cases were, however, assigned by the Chief Justice, an action no Chief Justice in my time would have ever taken. For the tradition is a longstanding one that the senior justice in the majority makes the assignment."

He continued: "When the minority seeks to control the assignment there is a destructive force at work in the Court. When a Chief Justice tries to bend the Court to his will by manipulating assignments, the integrity of the institution is imperiled.

"The abortion cases are symptomatic. This is an election year. Both parties have made abortion an issue. What the parties say or do is none of our business. We sit here not to make the path of any candidate easier or more difficult. We decide questions only on their constitutional merits. To prolong these abortion cases into the next election is a political gesture unworthy of the Court.

"Each of us is sovereign in his own right. Each arrived on his own. Each is beholden to no one. Russia once gave its chief justice two votes; but that was too strong even for the Russians."

Douglas wrote: "I dissent with the deepest regret that we are allowing the institution to be manipulated for political objectives." Then he scratched out "political" and wrote in the word "unworthy."

Brennan was appalled. Confrontation was not his style. He edited a copy of the memo, scratching through large sections. Then he told Douglas: "If anything is made public (and I have serious reservations on that score), I hope the pencilled out portions can be omitted." It was a sign of how far Brennan had come, and how much confidence and balance he represented that even "Wild Bill" Douglas now had come to rely on him. The first excoriating draft, now deposited with Douglas's private papers at the Library of Congress, was marked "For Justice Brennan Only." Only after Brennan had gone through it did Douglas feel confident enough to send copies to Stewart and Marshall.

Even cleaned up, Douglas's memo lit a fire under Chief Justice Burger. Burger claimed that Blackmun's draft opinion of May 18 had not been a decision but merely a memorandum accompanied by his expression for reargument. In any event, Burger had won the battle. The cases would be put over for argument on a full nine-member court, one that would include the two new conservative justices. Just as the conservatives had shot themselves in the foot in *El Paso*, they would do it again with abortion. For if Blackmun's original draft had come down as an opinion of the Court, it would have meant that states did have the power to restrict abortions, they just had to be clear and reasonable about it.

Shortly after the beginning of the 1972–73 term, the abortion cases were reargued before a full nine-member Court. At the first conference after the argument, Burger had the shock of his life. Lewis Powell, an Episcopalian from Virginia, turned out not to have any strong moral opposition to abortion.

To make matters worse from the chief justice's perspective, Stewart, who had spent the summer contemplating his distaste for the chief justice, had adopted, almost in toto, Brennan's sweeping philosophy that the issue was not vagueness but rather the right to privacy derived from *Griswold* v. *Connecticut*. It was a major change in Stewart's thinking because, of the original four who wanted to toss out the Texas law, Stewart had been nearly as unsure as Blackmun.

Still assigned to write the opinion, Blackmun now had a mandate from Stewart and Brennan to write something much stronger. In addition, Powell began to weigh in with his support for a verdict based on the right to privacy. Astutely lobbied by all three justices, Blackmun responded with an opinion that totally abandoned the vagueness argument. Instead he began to pursue Brennan's theory that there was a point in time at which a fetus was entitled to protection.

By January 1973, Blackmun was really picking up steam. Notes and suggestions were flying back and forth between chambers. Brennan's theory that at different stages of the pregnancy a fetus had different rights was written into Blackmun's drafts. It was that concept, spelled out in Brennan's memo two years earlier, that gave birth to the decision that in the first trimester abortions could be had almost on demand; and that in the last trimester the fetus had almost the full rights of a person.

In writing these sections Blackmun for once abandoned his reliance on the overbearing Burger. He ignored protestations from the chief and others that Brennan's trimester theory was a tremendous abuse of judicial authority and was the equivalent of legislating from the bench. Blackmun became increasingly so wrapped up in the *Roe* v. *Wade* decision, he even prepared an unprecedented press release to trumpet the decision. Brennan advised him to hold off on the release, that wasn't the way opinions were announced.

Sure enough when the decision was announced, it sounded remarkably like Brennan's December 1970 memo. It established a right to privacy, as Brennan had urged. Second, Blackmun adopted the language that in the first trimester a state had "no compelling interest" in a fetus. That, too, was just the way Brennan had termed it.

Brennan, naturally, sought neither credit nor opprobrium for the *Roe v. Wade* decision. The Catholic church hierarchy was livid over Brennan's vote in favor of the decision, but the full extent of his involvement was not widely recognized. How ironic it was that the justice who had been appointed at the request of Cardinal Spellman could have played a key role in the issue most dear to the church. But Brennan, as he had promised at his confirmation hearings twenty years earlier, never carried his church's beliefs into the Supreme Court chamber.

At regular Saturday Mass at St. Matthew's Cathedral in Washington, a friend asked Brennan how he could have made such a decision. Naturally Brennan wouldn't discuss the case. But he did reply that when he was confirmed he had taken an oath to the Constitution. And that, he said firmly, was where his professional loyalties remained. He pursed his lips and would say no more.

FIGHTING THE DEATH PENALTY

Even as Bill Brennan worked covertly to steer Harry Blackmun toward an expansive, some would say legislative, end in *Roe* v. *Wade*, he worked tirelessly on numerous other rulings that broadened constitutional interpretation. It almost seemed as if the departure of the chief justice had energized Brennan in a philosophical sense, even while his personal problems, especially Marjorie's illness, weighed heavily on him at home.

Brennan was determined to wage a winning battle against the new conservative tide that the public expected of a Court headed by Warren Burger. Like Aquinas, derided in his century as the "dumb ox," Brennan stubbornly labored on, winning little respect or recognition outside of the Court. Yet, in his universe of former professors and career jurists, Brennan continued to apply the skills he had observed of a very successful city politician back in Newark, his dad. As one justice noted: "When Brennan grabbed you by the lapel and said, 'Now listen fellow,' he was hard to resist."

No one on the Court could ever quite recall having seen an operator like Brennan. Frankfurter had tried, of course. But he was clumsy and ham-handed. It had always been assumed that Warren as a former governor of California was a great in-court politician. But Warren, unfortunately, didn't have the legal mechanics that a career lawyer and judge like Brennan could employ. Warren could find a result and attempt to persuade others that it was fair, but when it came to putting an opinion down on paper, he often had no idea of what to say.

As a junior member of the Warren Court in the late 1950s and early 1960s, Brennan had been the worker bee in a field of giant egos. Now, with Earl Warren retired, he became not just the conciliator and inside operator but the protector of the liberal flame. His clerks, who idolized him for the attention and access he gave them, operated both as intelligence operatives and as point men for the Brennan political agenda. Each clerk familiarized himself with the clerks of the other justices and copied Brennan's habit of wining and dining the opposition. Even elevator operators who might have heard something were cultivated as possible "sources." Their reports back to the boss took the form of what kind of thinking or language might be able to seduce Justice Powell or Blackmun.

When Brennan was asked once if he "lobbied" the other justices, he replied that he didn't have to, his clerks did it for him. Increasingly it was Judge Bazelon who was supplying Brennan's clerks. And while Brennan had taken personal precautions such as selling his stock and calling a moratorium on public statements, he didn't object to those clerks lining the walls of their offices with antiwar and anti-Nixon posters.

Until 1970, Brennan's "liberalism" had taken the form of ensuring an individual's rights against those of the state. It had always been presumed, as Black had taught Brennan, that the citizen's rights against the federal government were protected without question. Not even a justice as "conservative" as Felix Frankfurter had ever questioned that the guarantees against unlawful search or double jeopardy applied to federal prosecutions. The question that had divided the Court so sharply had always been: Does the Bill of Rights apply to the state criminal laws? Black and Brennan had always believed that the Constitution guaranteed all those rights to American citizens and that state legislatures could not abridge them.

But if Black could not find explicit support in the Constitution for a proposition, he would not support it. That led him to his absolute view that all speech, even pornographic speech, was protected. The wall between church and state was impenetrable. Thus there could be no prayer in the schools. But it is a myth that Black was some sort of wild-eyed liberal justice. There was no possibility, for example, that had Black been on the Court in 1973 he would have supported the Brennan-Blackmun ruling on abortion. Contrary to popular notion, Black was the ultimate strict constructionist. By 1970, not even Black could accommodate Brennan's fast-evolving activist jurisprudence.

Brennan had become convinced that the Constitution was a living, changing document. He had concluded that the proper way to interpret the Constitution was to interpolate not what the Founders thought, but what they would have thought if they had lived in the present. It was a view that ran completely counter to that of "original intent," the idea that the key to constitutional interpretation came from studying the lives and thinking of the Founding Fathers.

In 1970, nothing illustrated Brennan's willingness to stretch the Constitution more than his ruling in *Goldberg* v. *Kelly*, a decision that disturbed Black so much that the senior justice was reduced to writing huge X marks in pencil across one of Brennan's drafts, while he called out in distress to his clerks: "Wrong, wrong, wrong."

The case was not complicated. Jack Goldberg was the social services commissioner of New York City. His agency, although it was financed largely with federal funds through the Aid to Families with Dependent Children Act (AFDC), was operated by the state of New York. New York State's policy toward welfare recipients was that when clients failed to show up for meetings with social workers, their benefits could be immediately suspended. There was no requirement that a welfare recipient be afforded a hearing, and no requirement in law that any notice be given. Jack Kelly, the original plaintiff in the case, had been just such a welfare recipient. When his benefits had been arbitrarily halted, Kelly filed suit against the state of New York demanding that he be afforded a hearing.

To Brennan, the issue was simply one of fairness. That was the core question Earl Warren would have always raised at first. Now it was up to Brennan. Once the fairness test was determined, it was only a matter of finding a rationale to support the conclusion. How could the state not give a person a hearing before cutting him off? Brennan's answer was that it couldn't. Now he just had to find some constitutional interpretation to make it so.

In conference, Brennan's heartfelt views not only brought the support of Marshall and Douglas, as would be expected, but lured Harlan and White to his side as well. Brennan became so passionate about this case, so sure that he had found a gross injustice, it became known around the Court simply as "Bill's welfare case." In one fell swoop, Brennan prepared an opinion that he believed would single-handedly remedy the inadequacies of the country's welfare system. With the stroke of a pen, Brennan would elevate welfare from charity to a basic right of citizenship, endowed with all the constitutional protections and due process of law that had previously been awarded to criminal defendants.

When it came time to announce his opinion, Brennan declared:

> From its founding the nation's basic commitment has been to foster the dignity and well-being of all persons within its borders. We have come to recognize that forces not within the control of the poor contribute to their poverty. This perception against the background of our traditions has significantly influenced the development of the contemporary public assistance system. Welfare, by meeting the basic demands of subsistence, can help bring within the reach of the poor the same opportunities that are available to others to participate meaningfully in the life of the community.
>
> At the same time, welfare guards against the societal malaise that may flow from a widespread sense of unjustified frustration and insecurity. Public assistance is not mere charity but a means to "promote the general welfare and secure the blessings of liberty to ourselves and our posterity."

This ruling resulted in the creation of a huge welfare bureaucracy with a thousand hearings a day and all the appointed lawyers and administrative judges that go with such an operation.

But in a rare discussion of his ruling some years later, Brennan clung to his belief that fairness, not the cost to the public, was the central issue. He told a bar association meeting that more than any other opinion, *Goldberg* v. *Kelly* required that nameless, faceless government look into the eyes of the individuals whose lives were being affected by its decisions.

"*Goldberg*," he said, "can be seen as injecting passion into a system

whose abstract rationality has led it astray." In other words, if government was going to operate a welfare system, officials were going to
have to do it fairly and right.

For Black, the Brennan opinion marked the end of his former pupil's
constitutional reason. In his eighties, Black was beginning to sound
more like Frankfurter than the young Hugo. He wrote in dissent:

> Representatives of the original thirteen colonies spent long hot
> months in the summer of 1787 in Philadelphia, Pennsylvania, creating a
> government of limited powers. They divided it into three depart-
> ments—legislative, judicial, and executive. The Judicial Department
> was to have no part whatever in making any laws.
>
> In my judgment there is not one word, phrase or sentence from the
> beginning to the end of the Constitution from which it can be inferred
> that judges were granted any such legislative power.
>
> I regret very much to be compelled to say that the Court today
> makes a drastic and dangerous departure from a Constitution written
> to control and limit the government. . . .
>
> The operation of a welfare state is a new experiment for our nation.
> . . . It should be left to the Congress and the legislatures which the
> people elect to make our laws.

Although Brennan succeeded in making welfare a right of citizenship, he had less success in his other great goal—ending the death
penalty once and for all. Once again it was an area in which Black
would not tread. But even there Brennan managed to significantly
change the manner and care with which the death penalty was administered.

In 1956, the year Brennan was appointed to the Court, 484 executions had been carried out in America. It wasn't until the mid-1960's
that a serious and organized challenge to capital punishment was begun by the NAACP Legal Defense Fund. Those cases challenged the
death penalty on different grounds. It was claimed that it was dispro-
portionately used against blacks and the poor, violating the Fourteenth Amendment guarantee of equal treatment. In the South, for
example, no white person had ever been executed for killing a black.
Many of the juries were all white, since they were taken from voting
rolls where blacks weren't even allowed to register. One curious consti-

tutional problem had to do with the right against self-incrimination. Many defendants in capital cases decided not to take the stand in their own defense. The Fifth Amendment gave them that right. Following the conviction, often on the same day as the conviction, would come the sentence of death. It was argued by many that there should exist a separate penalty phase at which an accused could tell his story and possibly win some sympathy that might mitigate a death sentence.

Then there was the Eighth Amendment argument that the death penalty constituted cruel and unusual punishment. At the Court itself, Justice Goldberg felt most passionately about the death penalty. But by 1965, when he left the Court, only Douglas and Brennan were willing to overturn it on the most sweeping Eighth Amendment grounds.

It wasn't until the 1968 case of *Witherspoon* v. *Illinois* that a substantial death penalty case was even presented to the Court. In that case the Court prohibited states from excluding people from juries on the grounds that they didn't believe in the death penalty. One year later the Court was confronted with a case where a death sentence had been invoked against a person convicted of robbery. Treading narrowly, the Court overturned the particular death sentence in each of these cases but refused to make any general ruling on the constitutionality of capital punishment itself.

In his early days, especially as a state supreme court justice, Brennan had been unsure of the constitutionality of the death penalty. "I have been persuaded that the death penalty is unconstitutional by the arguments of lawyers who made the better case," he said in a speech years later. "This is not to suggest that underneath the robes, I am not, that we are each not, a human being with personal views and moral sensibilities and religious scruples. But it is to say that above all I am a judge." Thus, as his philosophy hardened, he took Douglas's side against the view of Justice Black, who had no doubts that the Constitution sanctioned capital punishment.

Not even during the heyday of the Warren Court, when the liberal bloc was at its most powerful, could a majority be cleanly mustered to strike down the death penalty. In 1969, on a Court that included Warren, Brennan, Douglas, Marshall, and Fortas, they had come close but could never completely agree.

The case that had been chosen as the Court's vehicle for what would have been a landmark decision was *Maxwell* v. *Bishop*. It was a case that concentrated on the self-incrimination issue, whether a separate sentencing jury was required in death penalty cases. It also raised the question of whether a jury, rather than a judge, could have absolute discretion to impose the death penalty. The federal appeals court judge who had heard the case, interestingly enough, was then circuit judge Harry Blackmun of the Eighth U.S. Circuit Court of Appeals.

There had been three principal issues involved in the case. During jury selection, jurors who said they were opposed to the death penalty had been excluded from the panel. In the *Witherspoon* case, noted above, the Court had already ruled that jurors could not be dismissed on those grounds. So on that basis alone, there was no doubt the sentence of death for a twenty-one-year-old Arkansan named William L. Maxwell would be overturned by the Supreme Court.

There were, however, two newer issues that cropped up. One involved the question of whether a person convicted of a capital crime should have a separate hearing before receiving the maximum penalty. A person who had refused to take the witness stand during his trial might well want to testify to mitigating circumstances after the conviction.

The second, newer issue involved what were called "standards." Two men could be convicted of the same crime, yet one would get the death penalty and the other wouldn't. It seemed arbitrary and unfair. In actual practice, as one might imagine, the result was that black defendants most often got gassed or electrocuted, white ones did not. It was the view of some capital punishment opponents, but not all, that states would never be able to agree on specific standards that would mandate the death penalty. Neither would white people in the South want to run the risk that their children might actually be executed. Thus, the theory went, the death penalty itself would die.

In his lower-court ruling, Blackmun had found that conclusive statistical evidence proving racial discrimination in the application of the death penalty was inadmissible in a trial. The statistics were persuasive that blacks had a better chance of being executed than whites. But Judge Blackmun was unmoved by the statistics. "We are not yet ready to condemn and upset the result reached in every case of a Negro rape defendant in the state of Arkansas on the basis of broad theories of social and statistical injustice," Blackmun wrote. "Whatever value that argument may have has an instrument of social concern, whatever suspicion it may arouse with respect to southern interracial rape trials as a group over a long period of time, and whatever it may disclose with respect to other localities, we feel that the statistical argument does nothing to destroy the integrity of Maxwell's trial."

Blackmun called his decision "excruciating for the author of the opinion who is not personally convinced of the rightness of capital punishment and who questions it as an effective deterrent. But the advisability of capital punishment is a policy matter ordinarily to be resolved by the legislature or through executive clemency and not by the judiciary."

Blackmun's ruling fit the classic definition of judicial restraint. He didn't personally believe in capital punishment, but he wouldn't act to stop it.

Since Blackmun's lower-court ruling ran counter to the *Witherspoon* doctrine, if nothing else, a strong majority of the Court that included Stewart and White voted in conference to overturn Blackmun's verdict. In conference the vote was 8 to 1 to overturn the death sentence. Only Justice Black, ironically enough, supported the Blackmun ruling. But among the eight who supported overturning the case, there were not five who could agree on any single rationale that might constitute the voice of the Court. Justice Stewart, for example, merely wanted to overturn on the *Witherspoon* grounds but no other. Only Brennan, Douglas, and Warren wanted to rule that selective application of the death penalty violated the Fourteenth Amendment. Fortas, not as opposed as his predecessor Goldberg, wanted to rule that the states had to have separate sentencing trials. But he didn't want to rule the death penalty unconstitutional. Justice Marshall, who usually took Brennan's side, agreed with Fortas.

The muddle was assigned to Douglas, and that's where the trouble really started. Rather than attempt to accommodate the views of Fortas, Stewart, and Marshall, the justices who might be enticed into a majority ruling, Douglas proceeded to write a passionate screed about the lack of standards by which states distributed death. Seizing on the controversial issue that Blackmun had rejected, Douglas wrote it was simply not constitutional that "one jury may decide that one defendant is not fit to live because he is a black who raped a white woman, while another defendant is fit to live because he is a white who raped a black."

Brennan's clerks had reported back to him that Douglas's opinion had no chance of attracting the concurrence of Stewart and White. Douglas had thought the force of his ruling would win over Fortas and Marshall and thus they would strike down capital punishment by a 5 to 4 majority. But, surprisingly, Marshall and Fortas balked. Marshall feared that Douglas's opinion would give states an opportunity to actually increase the number of executions.

Brennan pleaded with Douglas to soften his opinion by knocking out the standards argument and coming on stronger with the separate trial requirement. "I hope you will sharpen your discussion of the basic proposition that a unitary trial unconstitutionally prejudices the defendant by compelling him to forego his privilege against self-incrimination by taking the stand to make his case on punishment," Brennan told Douglas in an April 1, 1969, memo. As for standards, Brennan suggested it be "omitted entirely." Always the pragmatist, he added: "I feel we're asking more than is necessary at this stage."

Douglas's intemperateness, and his unwillingness in that instance to heed Brennan's warnings, cost the Court an opportunity. Stewart and White backed out of a concurrence with Douglas. By the time Brennan's message finally began to sink through, the opportunity had been lost. Fortas and Warren had left the Court, replaced by Burger and Blackmun.

Instead of a ruling that might have abolished the death penalty once and for all, the Court was reduced to a mere order that a new trial be held and that jurors not be excluded because of their views on capital punishment. It was the ruling on *Witherspoon* grounds that had been Stewart's position. Douglas's stridency cost the Court an opportunity to make history. *Maxwell* might not have been a landmark case, Brennan felt, but it had focused and narrowed the arguments on capital punishment.

A year later, however, on June 28, 1971, another vehicle for overturning the death penalty, *Furman v. Georgia*, appeared before the Court. Before leaving on summer vacation, Brennan directed his law clerks to begin researching the Eighth Amendment issues that the case would present. He also stopped by Douglas's chambers and reminded him that this time around they had to be a little more malleable. This time, Brennan told Douglas, he had to moderate his views. Winning was more important than being right.

The arguments in the *Furman* case took place on January 17, 1972. By the time of the argument, Marshall and Douglas were certain votes to overturn the death penalty. In addition, Brennan collected notes from White and Stewart stating that their minds were open. The memos encouraged Brennan considerably. For the first time he felt a clean majority could be mustered to outlaw the death penalty. As always at the Court, the ultimate ruling would depend not so much on whether the death penalty was moral or not moral but on whether the federal courts could dictate a ban to the legislatures of the states.

For once Douglas decided to listen to Brennan and from the beginning narrowed the focus to issues that could carry a majority. An opinion calling for outright abolition of the death penalty was too strong. Despite his initial optimism, it was clear Stewart would not endorse any decision that severely trod on state's rights. Therefore, Brennan urged Douglas to make sure he gave the states some leeway, but not too much.

In a remarkably modest statement, Justice Douglas relented under Brennan's influence. He continued to believe that the unfair application of the death penalty made it unconstitutional. But he would compromise and agree not to insist on that determination. Brennan's success in restraining Douglas this time brought back the agreement of fence-sitters Stewart and White. The four Nixon appointees, Burger, Powell, Rehnquist, and Blackmun, voted as bloc not to strike down capital punishment. Blackmun's comments symbolized the nature of the conservatives. As he had written in *Maxwell* while on the lower court, he now told Brennan in the Court's conference meeting that if he were a legislator, he would vote against the death penalty. But as a member of the Supreme Court, he declared, he could not. Echoing the complaints of Frankfurter, Blackmun said: "I fear the Court has overstepped. It seeks and has achieved an end." This was just a year before Blackmun sought and achieved the remarkable "end" of his own in *Roe v. Wade*.

With his majority in hand, Brennan then highlighted his own real feelings in a lengthy, remarkable concurrence to the shorter, less emotional Douglas opinion. His opinion would be far too strident to be a majority opinion, but Brennan realized that. The Court would sign on to Douglas's moderate draft, Brennan would then deliver an attack on the death penalty that he hoped would eventually become the standard that judges would follow in striking down capital punishment.

For one who had never even studied constitutional law in college, Brennan had become a true scholar. His separate opinion became a landmark treatise in the history of the death penalty from the beginning of the Republic until the present. But after expounding upon that history, Brennan noted, as he had about the Fourteenth Amendment, that merely studying the intent of the Framers was not enough. "The words of the Clause [on cruel and unusual punishment] are not precise and their scope is not static," he wrote. "We know that the Clause must draw its meaning from the evolving standards of decency that mark the progress of a maturing society.

"At bottom, the Cruel and Unusual Punishments Clause prohibits the infliction of uncivilized and inhuman punishments. The State, even as it punishes, must treat its members with respect for their intrinsic worth as human beings. A punishment is cruel and unusual therefore if it does not comport with human dignity."

And what elements then were relevant?

Certainly pain, Brennan concluded. A death sentence that included excessive pain would obviously violate the Constitution. "More than the presence of pain," he continued, "is comprehended in the judgment that the extreme severity of a punishment makes it degrading to the dignity of human beings. . . . A state may not punish a person for being mentally ill, or a leper. To inflict punishment for having a disease is to treat the individual as a diseased thing rather than as a sick human being.

"In determining whether a punishment comports with human dignity, we are aided by a second principle inherent in the clause—that the State must not arbitrarily inflict a severe punishment. A third principle inherent in the Clause is that a severe punishment must not be unacceptable to contemporary society. The final principle inherent in the Clause is that a severe punishment must not be excessive."

Yet in the history of the Republic, Brennan noted, only three sentences had been found to be excessive: twelve years in chains and hard labor, expatriation, and imprisonment for narcotics addiction.

"The question today," Brennan said, "is whether the deliberate infliction of death is today consistent with the command of the Clause that the state may not inflict punishments that do not comport with human dignity. I will analyze the punishment of death in terms of the principles set out above and the cumulative test to which they lead: It is a denial of human dignity for the State arbitrarily to subject a person to an unusually severe punishment that society had indicated it does not regard as acceptable, and that cannot be shown to serve any penal purpose more effectively than a significantly less drastic punishment. Under these principles and this test, death is today a 'cruel and unusual punishment.' "

He noted the four aspects that made it unconstitutional: the conscious infliction of physical pain absent in all other punishments, the mental torture to the condemned, the loss of any right to an appeal or change in circumstances, and the possibility that occasionally through human fallibility death will be inflicted on an innocent man.

"Yet," Brennan said, "the finality of death precludes relief. In comparison to all other punishments today, then, the deliberate extinguishment of human life by the State is uniquely degrading to human dignity. I would not hesitate to hold on that ground alone that death is today a cruel and unusual punishment, were it not that death is punishment of longstanding usage and acceptance in this country."

After nearly seventy pages, in an odyssey through the civilized world, Brennan found death to be inconsistent with all four principles. "Death," he wrote, "is an unusually severe and degrading punishment; there is a strong probability that it is inflicted arbitrarily; its rejection by contemporary society is virtually total; and there is no reason to believe that it serves any penal purpose more effectively than the less severe punishment of imprisonment. The function of these principles is to determine whether a punishment comports with human dignity. Death, quite simply, does not."

When Douglas had finished reading Brennan's compelling draft, he scrawled hopefully: "I hope total abolition is what we accomplished."

Public reaction was swift and predictable. Conservatives once again took the floor to denounce the Court. But the tenor of the ruling deflected most of the heavy criticism. South Carolina senator Strom Thurmond, for example, referred to the Court's decision as "creating a loophole." Bills were immediately filed to bring the death penalty into conformance with the Court's ruling.

After just six years, the death penalty, under new mandates, was ruled constitutional by a court majority that Brennan did not join.

For the remainder of his years on the bench, Brennan would vote to overturn every sentence of death that came before the Court. Although Brennan was not a great dissenter, in his career he issued 1,517 dissents in death penalty cases, almost all of them with Thurgood Marshall at his side. Of his adamancy on the issue, Brennan explained: "The most vile murder does not release the state from constitutional restraints on the destruction of human dignity."

THE NIXON CASE

THE TRANSITION PERIOD FROM THE Warren Court to the Burger Court marked the last great gasp of judicial activism. Brennan's efforts on abortion and capital punishment ended the phase in which he would push the law to its limits. Personally, the retirement of Earl Warren left a void in Brennan's life that seemed impossible to fill. Brennan had loved the role of being the deputy chief, the leprechaun who could magically turn disagreement into consensus. He loved the fact that he had never lost his anonymity. Brennan was easily the most powerful man in Washington whom no one would ever recognize. He enjoyed all the benefits of power with none of the annoyances.

Critical to his success had been his personality. Inwardly, as could be seen in his nervousness over such things as the Tigar clerkship, Brennan still thought of himself as the mule at the derby. But at the age of sixty-eight, he was outwardly full of bubbly self-confidence and informality. Everyone was "pal." To his clerks, "his boys," he was the beloved "boss." He told his clerks they could pick the colors of his new rug and carpets as long as they chose green. Throughout his life, Brennan was possessed of an unflagging politeness. He produced a torrent of personal notes to friends and acquaintances. An American Civil Liberties lawyer who had met Brennan only briefly once mailed a picture of them together to get signed. He received not only the picture but a letter recalling their meeting in detail, even though it had taken place long before. When a law clerk brought her mother by the office, she was introduced to the justice. Brennan grabbed the mother by the arm and carried her into the office. While the clerk sat nervously outside, the clock ticked. Finally they emerged. The clerk's mother was a scientist and Brennan had pumped her for everything she knew for a speech he was about to give on space law.

His fight with Frankfurter had marked Brennan's only failure of personality. He had been close with Frankfurter's ideological twin, John Marshall Harlan. He had also maintained close friendships with Marshall, Stewart, White, and Powell. And he won the grudging respect of the Court's most difficult member, Douglas. Privately, Brennan felt that Douglas could be a "horse's ass." But that wasn't saying much. Around the Court that was considered more fact than opinion.

Just as his father's death had launched him into an intense period where he felt a keen sense of responsibility to his family, Warren's retirement left Brennan with a sense of obligation to their shared philosophy of fairness and respect for human dignity. Surveying the Court as Burger took charge, Brennan could clearly see that his role would change. With Black gone, it fell on Brennan to deal with Douglas, who was often petulant and childlike. The liberal wing of the Court was reduced to just himself, Marshall, and Douglas. Burger and William Rehnquist comprised the conservative bloc. The battle was now being waged over the center, where Justices Lewis Powell and Potter Stewart had staked their ground.

By 1974, the well-publicized problems of President Richard Nixon effectively served to end the political threat to Brennan's tenure on the Court. Nixon would be so involved in trying to save his own skin, he would have no energy for collecting the scalps of Brennan and Douglas. The Nixon administration's attempts to "get" Douglas, Fortas, and Brennan had hardly told the complete picture. Douglas had been ridiculed in some quarters for suggesting that the White House might actually wiretap justices. But Douglas had not been so crazy after all. Instead the attack on the Court has been revealed to have been another piece of an orchestrated and wide-ranging effort that involved illegal wiretaps, break-ins, politically inspired IRS investigations, and dirty tricks intended to eliminate the president's political enemies.

But the revelations that followed the discovery of the Watergate break-in had put Nixon and his administration on the defensive. By mid-1974, the only thing that stood between Nixon and impeachment was the president's claims of executive privilege with which he could shield from the public the contents of the White House tapes. For a "law-and-order" president, one who had condemned exculpating felons on the basis of legal technicalities, it was an ironic situation. Nixon, like Burger, had always believed the key factor in the justice system should be the bottom line. Was the defendant guilty or not guilty? Neither had ever endorsed the idea that a guilty person should be set free merely because the convicting evidence was tainted.

But when Richard Nixon himself became the defendant, all that changed. Armed with a phalanx of private attorneys, Nixon himself began resorting to legal "technicalities" to save his presidency.

It was quite a change from his election in 1968 when a "liberal" Supreme Court was made into one of his primary reelection issues. Nixon had pledged that if he was elected he would remake the Supreme Court. As fate would have it, Nixon was able to name four new justices in his first term as president. He had tried to name two southern conservative judges, Clement Haynsworth and G. Harrold Carswell. After they were rebuffed by the Democratic Senate, he had turned to Blackmun. Later to fulfill his promise to put a southerner on the Court, Nixon turned to a southern Democrat, Lewis Powell of Richmond. Both Powell and Blackmun turned into rather centrist justices, thus flouting Nixon's intent to dramatically change the nature of the Court.

The beginning of the end for Richard Nixon can be dated to March 1, 1974, the day that seven Nixon aides, including former attorney general John Mitchell, were indicted by a federal grand jury. As part of the evidence needed to prosecute the case, Special prosecutor Leon Jaworski had asked the White House to produce sixty-four tapes of conversations between Nixon and his White House aides. The existence of the tapes had been revealed during the congressional Watergate investigation chaired by Senator Sam Ervin. On April 18, Judge John Sirica directed that the subpoena be delivered to the White House.

But on May 1, Nixon announced that he would fight the subpoena, using the shield of executive privilege. The constitutional separation of powers, Nixon's lawyers argued, did not allow the judiciary to make such demands of the chief executive. Sirica didn't buy the argument and on May 20 again ordered the White House to produce the tapes. Nixon's lawyer, James St. Clair, appealed the ruling to the District of Columbia Circuit Court of Appeals.

The trial of the seven White House aides was expected to take place in September. But a full-fledged appeals-court ruling could have delayed the process until 1975. Already two years of Nixon's term had elapsed. His best hope of hanging on was a legal filibuster. Nixon and his lawyers believed that if they could delay long enough, sentiment for his impeachment might wane. If nothing else, the 1976 election would creep up and an attitude would have developed to let his term limp to an end rather than go through the ordeal of impeachment.

Jaworski, and his top deputy, Philip Lacovara, were determined not to let that happen. Shortly after St. Clair's appeals motion was filed, the special prosecutor asked the Supreme Court to bypass the appeals court and take the case directly. It was a procedure that had been used only six times in the nation's history and not at all in the past twenty-two years. The special prosecutor hung his request on a little-used rule of the federal courts that allows Supreme Court review if a case "is of such imperative public importance as to justify the deviation from normal appellate processes and to require immediate settlement."

At the Court, Jaworski's motion landed with a big thud. In a note to his colleagues, written the day after the motion was received, Burger admonished them not to be "pressured or rushed by the news media or anyone else." On May 31, the eight justices entered the chambers for what would be one of their most historic and closely watched rulings. Justice Rehnquist, because he had worked in the Nixon administration, recused himself from the case. As the justices went around the table in order of seniority, there was little support for Jaworski's motion. Even Douglas was content to let the president stew for as long as possible. He saw no reason to speed up the process. He also argued that the court of appeals would probably sustain Sirica's order. Then the Supreme Court would have to do nothing except deny a further appeal.

Blackmun acknowledged that a delay might take six months. Even though the country was impatient, he argued there was no "irreparable

injury" in letting it drag on. Stewart and White didn't see that Jaworski's motion fit the requirements of the rule; it had failed to state
what harm would come if the normal chain of judicial procedures was
allowed to run its course.

Only Burger seemed convinced that Nixon was actually right, that
there was such a prerogative as executive privilege and that Nixon had
a good case. Burger's basic position, as documented in Woodward and
Armstrong's book, *The Brethren*, was that Watergate was merely a political battle. They quote Burger as saying: "I don't see what they did
wrong." Burger, too, was willing to wait for the appeals court to create
a record on the issue.

Brennan, however, was listening to a different voice. From his
deathbed at Georgetown University Hospital, eighty-three-year-old
Earl Warren would whisper in Brennan's ear that the Court must not
dodge the case. If there was one thing the Warren Court had done, it
was to aggressively confront every issue, just as they had done in Little
Rock. Brennan had entered the conference room with a determination
to succeed that was focused beyond anything his clerks had seen before. His forte was the grasp and the clutch, the whispering in the ear,
the familiarity of his greeting, "Now listen, pal."

Impassioned argument in conference wasn't his trademark. But
more than anything that marked this case, time was of the essence.
For nearly an hour, Brennan held forth on precedents and cases that
would lead the Court to expeditiously take the case and bypass the appeals court. Finally, Brennan pleaded with his colleagues' sense of reason. He declared that two years of Watergate was enough. For the sake
of the country, Brennan pleaded, the Court must guarantee public access to the information that would finally reveal the truth.

It was classic Brennan thinking. From the revelation he had experienced in ruling on the *Tune* case, Brennan had fought a battle to have
all the evidence in a case made public. Prosecutors had long sought to
restrict information to the public and even to the defendant. In this
case, Brennan declared, it was the public that was the jury and it was
the public that was entitled to the material that would make them decide. But there was more. Brennan reminded the brethren of how important it was, for the sake of the Court, that its statement be
unanimous. Brennan spoke of the history of the Court and of its important role in such matters as the 1952 steel strike and the Little

Rock school crisis. The justices simply couldn't follow the Douglas formula and hand the decision over to the lower court. That, Brennan said, was cowardice. He then announced, on the matter of unanimity, that it would be achieved only if the vote was to bypass. Brennan announced that if the vote was not to grant Jaworski's motion, he would write a vigorous dissent.

Douglas was impressed; he announced that he was persuaded and would join Brennan. It fell next to Potter Stewart. The Court had reached a moment of history, he said. He would go with Brennan. Finally Marshall and Powell announced they too had been convinced. The vote was 5 to 3. Douglas was prepared to assign the writing of the opinion to Brennan. But as was his custom, the chief justice tactically changed his vote. He, too, would join Brennan.

But Burger assumed the prerogative of assigning the opinion. Brennan was angry and crestfallen. But there was nothing he could do and it was nothing Burger hadn't done before on numerous other occasions. When Brennan confronted Burger over the matter, the chief justice said that because of the inflamed national passions, the decision should be "restrained."

Brennan later confirmed this version of events in a letter to University of Vermont professor Howard Ball: "Initially, majority sentiment was not for bypass of the Court of Appeals. Two of the justices were definitely against bypass and three others leaned that way. Only two of us [Brennan and Marshall] felt strongly that the nation would think we had let it down."

Once the Court had decided to take the case, it still had to decide whether executive privilege gave Nixon the right to shield his tapes from the special prosecutor. Oral arguments in the case were heard on July 8, 1974. The conference would meet on the following day to reach its decision.

On July 9, 1974, Brennan inconspicuously strolled the cobblestone streets of Georgetown, down Reservoir Road, to the entrance of Georgetown University Hospital. Earl Warren had a week earlier suffered his third and most serious heart attack. Brennan had come to say good-bye. It was a walk that Brennan knew all too well. Marjorie's cancer treatments were usually at Georgetown's Lombardi Cancer Center.

Even in his weakened state, Warren was anxious to know what had happened in conference. Although Chief Justice Warren had been forced to submit his resignation to President Nixon, to his dying day he relished the pickle his longtime adversary found himself in. Brennan assured Warren that the justices were united—Nixon would have to turn over the tapes.

Warren sagged back in contentment. "If you don't do it that way, Bill," he said, "it's the end of the country." Brennan patted the arm of his friend and brother and left the hospital. Two hours later, at 8:10 P.M., Earl Warren was dead.

The opinion didn't turn out exactly as Warren would have wanted. The Court continued in the days after the Warren funeral to coalesce around a single opinion, but it was clear that Burger would have no part in a ruling that diminished the power of the presidency. He was willing to agree with the other justices that the tapes had to be turned over, but he was not willing to deny the existence of a qualified presidential privilege. Instead Burger drew his majority around wording that stated the special prosecutor had made a showing of need for the evidence that overcame the privilege.

As the one who had argued most vociferously for a statement that would once again assert the power of the Court, Brennan was in no mood to quibble. He had achieved the major part of what the "Superchief" had asked him to do: To get the tapes out and to let President Nixon hang by his own words.

Burger had delegated sections of the opinion to the various justices. Memos were flying fast and furious. Burger was a stubborn, proud man. His feelings always had to be soothed. Even a memo to him from Justice Blackmun, commenting on Burger's rendition of the facts in the case, had to be prefaced with a note: "I do this in a spirit of cooperation and not of criticism."

Brennan's role in the final ruling dealt with the central issue of whether the federal courts had the power to review the president's claim of executive privilege. Brennan sent Burger his memo, then tried to cut through all the personal stuff by noting in language only he and Burger could understand: "I freely deed it to you in fee simple absolute." Brennan wrote Burger that a claim of privilege must be balanced against the demands of a fair trial to the seven defendants.

Brennan's conclusion was no surprise: the president may be ordered to turn over the tapes.

But when Burger finished his first draft of the opinion on July 17, he wrote that executive privilege could be invoked when it dealt with a "core function" of the presidency. The problem in this case, Burger argued, was that the Watergate tapes did not relate to a core function.

This was not what Brennan had recommended. As Professor Howard Ball wrote in his book *To Have a Duty*, this implied that executive could be supreme. It was just the type of statement that lawyers for Nixon could seize on if they decided to defy the Court's order. It would give Nixon a whole new area of appeal, to argue that his activities were part of the core function of the White House.

Brennan and Stewart worked together to persuade Burger to modify the language. It was Nixon's argument that only the president could decide the question of privilege. Burger's language seemed to be giving the executive the right merely to describe whether the tapes constituted "core function" or not. Brennan wrote Burger emphasizing that the opinion must state unequivocally that the judicial branch has the power to determine whether something qualifies to be shielded under executive privilege. It could not be a matter left to the president. Mildly disgusted, Brennan left on July 18 for a scheduled vacation at Nantucket. But the break only lasted two days.

Seeing that he was in trouble, Burger called Brennan at Nantucket and asked him to come back and help. Burger told him that the problems and importance of the case were too great to be resolved over the telephone. It must be done "across the table," Burger said. Flattered and surprised by the request, Brennan flew back to Washington.

By Tuesday, July 22, Burger's "core language" sections had been excised from the opinion. All that remained was for the opinion to win the unanimous voice of the Court.

Not since *Cooper v. Aaron*, when the authority of the Court was being openly defied by Governor Faubus, had a case so openly raised the question of Supreme Court power. Just as the Court had no police force to send to Arkansas, there was no militia to arrest the president if Nixon decided to ignore its decree. To strengthen the Court's hand at this eleventh hour, Brennan pleaded with the chief justice to let the Nixon opinion be signed by all, just as his *Cooper v. Aaron* ruling had come down signed by all the justices. Burger was short. "The responsibility for writing the opinion is on my shoulders," he said. Brennan could not convince him.

In less than two weeks, the ordered release of the tapes would drive Nixon from the White House in disgrace. But the unanimous decision of the Court, which Brennan had worked so hard to attain, had averted a constitutional crisis.

TRANSITION

IT WAS THE DEATH OF EARL WARREN that first put the thought of retirement in Bill Brennan's mind. When "Superchief" had been around, Brennan would have never thought of slipping off to Nantucket in the middle of an important case. But under Burger, the whole ambience and spirit of the Court had changed. Brennan missed hearing the sound of Thurgood Marshall strolling into the conference and calling out: "What's shakin', Chiefy baby?" That had never failed to put a warm smile on Brennan's face.

But returning to the Court in October for the 1974–75 term, Brennan felt more acutely than ever his obligation to continue the Warren Court legacy. As much as he wanted to, he couldn't leave now, not with Burger having vowed to undo everything that had been accomplished in nearly twenty hard years of work. Burger was a formidable opponent, with a keen sense of strategy and tactics, but Brennan was just as stubborn. His resolve to stay was heightened by the continuing physical deterioration of William O. Douglas.

The relationship with Bill Douglas had always been a distant, thoroughly complicated affair. Like Frankfurter, Douglas was an arrogant man who saw his judgeship on the Supreme Court as just a launching pad to the world stage. It had been no secret that as late as 1964, Douglas had still entertained the possibility that he could somehow become president of the United States. When Brennan had come on the Court in late 1956, Douglas had already been there for seventeen years. As indicated by his correspondence with Yale professor Fred Rodell, Douglas was initially skeptical about Brennan. The assumption had always been that since Brennan was appointed by Eisenhower, he was suspect. As time went on Brennan alternately delighted and disappointed Douglas. Brennan seemed to want to do the right thing, but Douglas couldn't understand Brennan's willingness to compromise and to horse-trade votes to achieve a result less than total victory. They had never been close. Douglas's personal correspondence contains the names of virtually every other justice with whom he sat on the Court. But not Brennan.

By 1975, Douglas had been on the Court for thirty-six years. Though by Supreme Court actuarial tables he was still a relatively young man of seventy-six, Douglas had turned old and virtually senile. And Brennan was the only justice on the Court that he knew anymore. Increasingly, Douglas in his old age had begun to listen to Brennan. In the death penalty and abortion cases, two areas in which Douglas had been proudly losing for decades, Brennan had shown him how to win.

The end of the Nixon presidency had resulted in a bizarre and painful irony for Bill Douglas. Indeed, politics may have been at heart of why Douglas had initially been in no hurry to push Nixon out of office. As House minority leader, Gerald Ford, the same Gerald Ford who succeeded Nixon as president, had led the attacks on Douglas for years. In 1970, Ford masterminded what became a failed effort in the House of Representatives to impeach Douglas from the Supreme Court. Now, with his health failing and his mind going, Douglas was prepared to bear almost any pain and cause the Court any embarrassment to try to wait out Ford's term, which would end with the inauguration of Jimmy Carter in 1977.

But illness has no sense of time. Douglas had turned paranoid and suspicious. In November 1974, when a team of leaf rakers were hired to do lawn work, Douglas hid inside his house and watched the work. Then when he got a bill for $165, Douglas asked Washington superlawyer Clark Clifford to take action against the rakers. Douglas also got into several tiffs with the Marriott Corporation, one over a $6.92 restaurant bill that he refused to pay. Douglas wrote Marriott, "Your bill of $6.92 for Feb. 15 is quite proper. But the meals on February 19 made Mrs. Douglas and my niece Nancy very ill. They ate your roast beef and were dreadfully sick, all night. Mrs. Douglas will not of course bring suit. But I have not heard from my niece, who lives on the West Coast. My meal, which was beef pie, was very good. But I cannot pay for the poisonous beef served the two ladies."

On New Year's Eve, December 31, 1974, while vacationing in Nassau, Douglas's precarious condition took a severe turn for the worse. A stroke cost him partial use of his left arm and leg. For the next six months Douglas would be in and out of Walter Reed Hospital. But while he was out, he was barely rational. The other eight justices, with even Brennan agreeing, determined that they would rule in no 5 to 4 case in which Douglas was the deciding vote.

Brennan had not gone along easily with that, however. There had never been an occasion where a sick justice had been stripped of his vote before. But that wasn't all Burger wanted Brennan to do. As Woodward and Armstrong first revealed in *The Brethren*, Burger called Brennan into his office and asked that he see Douglas and tell him to resign from the Court. Burger referred to Douglas as one of Brennan's "best friends," a description that was hardly accurate. Douglas had carved out over the years a grudging respect for Brennan, but was it friendship? Brennan refused the assignment and stalked angrily back to his own chambers.

By October of 1975, doctors were pessimistic that Douglas would ever recover. Douglas wrote to a friend in Oregon: "The top therapy man says that my chances for improvement are nil. That is a bleak and dreary outlook. My pain persists as strong as ever. It is the only reason I should ever retire. Cathy, however, is pounding on me to resign. I think she's trying to produce another stroke and unhappily has medical advice as to how to manage it. My son is aligned with her in that cause." By November, Cathy and Bill Douglas junior had won their battle. On November 12, Douglas bit down hard and wrote a letter of resignation to President Ford.

Despite the resignation, Douglas did not immediately leave the Court. It is traditional that retired justices stay at the Marble Palace until death, often in offices on the upper floors. But until Douglas, no retired justice had insisted that he continue to write opinions on cases. Again, Burger asked Brennan to talk to Douglas. This time, Brennan relented. But only, Brennan said, if Douglas would be treated with the dignity and respect due a former member of the Court. Burger told Brennan that whatever they worked out would be fine. Just solve the problem.

Brennan told Douglas that the Court had decided to allow him to keep a law clerk, as well as his old office and a messenger, but that he had to understand, he was no longer a justice. That seemed to satisfy Douglas, who then abandoned working on cases and began writing his memoirs.

Although Thurgood Marshall remained on the Court with Brennan, Douglas and his friends knew that only Brennan had the political and mental skill to block the rising conservative tide. Brennan had truly become the heir of the Black-Douglas tradition.

Nearly seventy years old, Brennan was now the Court's senior justice, and his chair in the Supreme Court chamber moved inward to the immediate left of the chief justice.

Ideologically, Brennan's position changed as well. Gerald Ford's appointment of John Paul Stevens, a federal court judge in Illinois, to replace Douglas strengthened the Court's center. Conservatives had hoped that Ford would name professor Robert Bork to the Court. The darling of those who believed in "original intent," Bork was being recommended by influential Arizona senator Barry Goldwater. But President Ford's attorney general, Edward Levi, was a fellow Chicagoan and an old friend of Stevens. Friendship won out over ideology.

Blackmun, under Brennan's steady coddling, had moved from right to center as well. Potter Stewart remained as enigmatic as ever. Lewis Powell, although conservative, had proven to be an independent thinker rather than the simple follower Burger had once assumed him to be. According to statistics compiled annually by the *Harvard Law Review*, Marshall voted with Brennan in almost 90 percent of all cases. Brennan's next most likely ally was White at 64 percent; then Stevens at 63 percent; then Blackmun at 58 percent.

The conservative wing could solidly claim only two justices, Burger and Rehnquist. On a Court dominated by men like Douglas, Black, Fortas, and Warren, Brennan was himself seen as a centrist. But the center had shifted. Without necessarily changing his views, Brennan

the Court's extreme left. Along with Thurgood Mar-
the only member of the Court totally convinced, for ex-
the death penalty was unconstitutional. His core
—that the Bill of Rights should apply directly to every
American citizen; that those rights could not be abridged by the
states; and that the law should respect the dignity of the condemned
as well as the innocent—were convictions that only Marshall could be
reliably counted on to share.

Surveying the Court in 1975, Brennan knew that he had done all he
could in the area of criminal rights. The abuses that his father had bat-
tled for so many years were now universally unlawful, although still
prevalent. Some of the rulings that seemed so absurd to law-enforce-
ment fanatics like Burger, such as having to advise a person of his
rights, had by 1975 come to be expected as a routine element of fair
play. Yet it was not realistic to push those any further. Burger and
Rehnquist had made no secret of their desire to turn the Warren
Court decisions upside down, but Brennan was confident that while
he could not move ahead, he could hold his ground.

Turning away from his interest in the rights of criminal defendants,
Brennan began concentrating on protecting the rights of blacks, minorities, and women. In no case was his job tougher than in the suit
brought by Allen Bakke, a white would-be medical student, against the
University of California. The issues in *Regents of the University of California* v. *Bakke* defined the debate over affirmative action in the 1970s.
The medical school of the University of California at Davis admitted
100 students each year. A conscious determination was made that 16
of its 100 slots would be specifically reserved for minorities. When
Bakke failed to win admittance to the school, despite having higher
entrance examination scores than most of the sixteen who had places
reserved, he filed suit challenging the college's special admissions program. The lower-court ruling in the Bakke case had struck down the
university's quota system, saying that race could never be taken into
account in admissions. There was an irony in all this, of course. The
very white people who thought Bakke was so discriminated against
were at the same time demanding that schools like Cal Tech reserve
slots for whites, because if test scores were the only criteria, the school
population would be overwhelmingly Asian.

Chief Justice Burger saw the *Bakke* case as an excellent opportunity to put an end to affirmative-action programs, which he believed unconstitutional. At conference it appeared Burger would win the battle when he persuaded four other justices—Rehnquist, Stevens, Stewart, and Powell—to join him. Delighted at finally having bested his tough adversary, Justice Brennan, Burger confidently assigned the opinion in the case to Powell.

In late November 1977, Powell issued a draft of his opinion to his colleagues. In Powell's view, a state had no right to distribute benefits or impose burdens based on skin color. At a conference held to discuss the opinion in December, Powell called the University of California's allotment of a specific number of places "a colossal blunder." Powell conceded that diversity is necessary in a university setting and acknowledged that admissions officers can consider race and ethnic background. But he argued that it could never be proper to set aside a fixed number of places.

When it came his turn to speak, Brennan questioned Powell's statement that race can be a "consideration" in admissions. Powell reiterated that this was what he believed. A "consideration," he said, but no set number of places. No quotas. Brennan then asked if there could ever be a set of circumstances that might justify the University of California's position. Powell promised to think about it.

In an exchange of memos that followed, Powell conceded that Brennan's question had caused him to reconsider one portion of his ruling. He did not, in fact, want to be recorded as believing in the lower court's edict that race could "never" be a factor in university admissions. Until Brennan had asked the question, Powell admitted, he hadn't really focused on all the potential ramifications of the trial court's ruling. "I had not considered the scope of the trial court's injunction," Powell told his colleagues. "If it can be read as enjoining Davis from ever including race or ethnic origin as one element, to be weighed competitively with all other relative elements in making admissions decisions, then I would certainly favor modification of the injunction."

To Burger's considerable alarm, Powell wrote: "In the unlikely but welcome event that a consensus develops for allowing the competitive 'consideration' of race as an element, I think we should affirm as to the Davis program, but reverse as to the scope of the injunction." With that opening, Brennan persuaded his fellow justices to split the *Bakke* ruling into two parts. The specific program of the University of California at Davis was invalid. There was no reason for it, since California had no history of deliberate discrimination that the quota system could repair.

But what of a state, maybe an Alabama or Mississippi, that did have a history of discrimination? Brennan asked. Wouldn't a plan to set aside slots be reasonable in that case? It was a subject with which Powell was very familiar. He had been president of the Richmond, Virginia, school board during desegregation. He admitted that Brennan might be right. Backed into a corner by Brennan's persistence, Powell agreed to join a second half of the opinion that would say exactly that. Brennan then convinced the usually conservative pair of White and Blackmun to go along. Marshall's vote was automatic.

Brennan had moved the Court's final determination to the exact philosophical opposite of what Burger had originally intended when he assigned the case to Powell. In writing a separate opinion for the *Bakke* case, Brennan took it upon himself to let the world know that the "central meaning" of the case was his, not Powell's. In the separate opinion Brennan explained that Powell's majority ruling "should not mask the central meaning" of the decision. Brennan wrote: "Government may take race into account when it acts not to demean or insult any racial group, but to remedy disadvantages cast on minorities by past racial prejudice."

Powell told Brennan that his "central meaning" did not reflect the opinion of the Court or the discussion at conference. Powell complained that he had never said anything about "government"; he had been talking specifically and only about a state university. But in a memo to Brennan, Powell resignedly said he would not make an issue of Brennan's reinterpretation of his ruling. "I have not objected to your characterization of what the Court holds," Powell wrote Brennan. "As I have thought you could put whatever gloss on the several opinions you think proper."

The bizarre result was the same that had been achieved in numerous other cases that would come to the Court. Brennan's minority view became the part of the ruling that explained publicly what it had meant and it was Brennan's spin on quotas rather than Powell's that became accepted by lower-court judges as the law of the land. Instead of *Bakke* being a case that struck down quotas, it became a case that

endorsed and approved of government and educational insti
ing race as a factor in admissions programs.

As NYU professor Bernard Schwartz conceded: "If not fo
indeed, it is probable that the Burger Court would have ruleu an raciai
preferences unconstitutional. He saw the opportunity to change the
Powell unqualified vote against the Davis special admissions program
to one that reversed the lower court's refusal to allow race to be considered."

A year later in a case protesting affirmative-action quotas at the private Kaiser Steel Corporation, *Local 28, Sheet Metal Workers* v. *Equal
Employment Opportunity Commission*, Brennan commandeered a majority and decided to write the decision himself. Any uncertainty
about what he had done in *Bakke* would be removed. The Civil Rights
Bill of 1964, a law Bill Brennan had surreptitiously helped enact by
convincing his colleagues not to decide the constitutional issues in a
series of sit-in cases, had specifically stated that race could not be a
factor in hiring. But times had changed. The idealistic notion held by
Earl Warren that a colorless society could emerge simply if barriers to
black advancement were removed proved to be too hopeful. It wasn't
enough to remove the barriers, Brennan had now come to believe. As
he had stated in *Bakke*, those who had suffered a history of discrimination needed help. Affirmative action was their boost. Oddly, it was the
conservatives trying to block affirmative action who now looked to the
colorblind 1964 Civil Rights Bill to support their position.

Thus, just one year after Brennan's opinion in *Bakke* had given the
okay for racial admissions plans in government and publicly supported
universities, Brennan now extended them to the workplace. "We con-
cede that the white plaintiff's argument, based on a literal interpretation of the Act which makes it unlawful to discriminate because of
race, is not without force," he said, referring to the Civil Rights Act.

He noted: "But it would be ironic indeed if a law triggered by a Nation's concern over centuries of racial injustice and intended to improve the lot of those who had been excluded from the American
dream for so long, constituted the first legislative prohibition of all voluntary private race-conscious efforts to abolish traditional patterns of
racial segregation and hierarchy."

For the short remaining years of the Carter administration, employers actually worried about hiring blacks. Owners of newspapers would look out over all-white newsrooms and wonder: "Where can I find a black reporter?" Television stations began looking for black anchormen. Factory owners became concerned about the percentage of blacks, because buoyed by Brennan's rulings, the Equal Employment Opportunity Commission had become a force with some clout behind it. For a brief moment in time, opportunity knocked for minorities as never before. Bill Brennan had made it happen.

Brennan's rearguard action in cases like *Bakke* had preserved the forward movement in race relations. But it could not halt the inevitable personal toll that the years were taking. In 1978, even while Marjorie continued what would be a thirteen-year struggle against cancer, Brennan himself developed cancer of the throat. His own treatments were painful and debilitating. The following year Brennan suffered a mild stroke, which made it impossible for him to write. It was a crushing blow, given how hard he had worked at keeping his health. In later years he had abandoned his morning walks but switched to a stationary bicycle. Marjorie often joked that Bill rode to Newark and back every morning.

But his illness was nothing like what Marjorie had gone though. Characteristically, Brennan felt guilty when his own cancer went into remission and Marjorie's condition worsened. To his clerks he seemed perpetually depressed. Conversations in chambers would suddenly be interrupted by a call from home. Brennan would wheel around in his chair and his bass voice would drop another octave. People sitting a few feet away couldn't hear what he was saying, but they knew to whom he was talking and they could see the pained, empathetic expression on his face. *The Washington Post* described him as despondent, frail, and still constantly thinking about retirement.

In late November 1982, Marjorie suffered her most serious relapse. She was admitted to Georgetown University Hospital, but there was little that could be done. Two weeks later, on December 1, 1982, with Bill Brennan at his dying sweetheart's bedside, her battle ended. They had been married for fifty-four years. For the seventy-six-year-old justice, Marjorie's death came as almost a relief. She had been ill for so long. No woman had suffered more. No wife had taken her suffering with more dignity and courage. For his part, no husband had ever been more devoted.

In his depression and self-imposed exile from social functions during his wife's illness, Brennan had spent the years in study. If he was never the scholar that Freund and Frankfurter would have liked, he had become in the easy chair of his home, a scholar. But with Marjorie buried in a plot at Arlington Cemetery, just yards from the grave of Oliver Wendell Holmes, it was time to begin a new life. Three months after her death, Bill asked his longtime secretary, seventy-year-old Mary Fowler, if she would marry him, just as Hugo Black had married his secretary, Elizabeth, after the death of his first wife, Josephine. The Court community was in a state of shock. Brennan's relationship with Mary had always seemed most proper. Few who knew Brennan could even remotely conceive of them as a married couple, but that's the way it would be. Mary agreed, and in March 1983, the couple was married by Brennan's best friend, Judge David Bazelon. Brennan sheepishly notified the brethren by memo of the wedding: "Mary Fowler and I were married yesterday and we have gone to Bermuda." With that, Mary resigned from the Court. They then departed for the honeymoon trip, careful to return before the end of the Court's two-week recess.

On their return, the Brennans moved into a $210,000 condominium across the river in Virginia. Ironically, it would turn out, the apartment was owned by Washington, D.C., developer Charles Smith, whose real estate partnerships Brennan had withdrawn from seventeen years earlier. Later, after Brennan left the Court, Smith gave Brennan the condo, forgiving $120,000 of their $170,400 mortgage. In a note on the transaction to the Judicial Ethics Office, Brennan swore that "at no time since I have lived at the condominium did Mr. Smith or any of his companies have any matters before the Court or that were affected by Court decisions. The gifts reflected only the affection and generosity of a dear friend."

The marriage marked the end of Brennan's blue period. Almost immediately, his friends saw a changed, revivified man, anxious once again to do battle.

RENAISSANCE
AND RETIREMENT

HE HAD BEEN AN ACTOR ON A MAJOR world stage for nearly thirty years. But true to his mother's wishes, true to Marjorie's wishes, he had stayed out of the playbill, often amazingly so. It would only be in the last six years of his thirty-four-year career as a justice that William J. Brennan, Jr., would finally move front and center. Part of it was his own new attitude of rebirth, fueled by his marriage to the energetic Mary Fowler. But a good bit was reactive. The Reagan Justice Department, first headed by Attorney General William French Smith and later by Edwin Meese III, would turn Brennan into a target of the right wing. It was Meese, more than anybody else, who contributed in Brennan's last years to a sudden public recognition of his contribution to the country.

Shortly after being named attorney general in 1985, Meese embraced a theme that then law professor Robert Bork had fathered some fifteen years earlier in a speech at Indiana University. Bork's idea was that the proper function of the Court was to rule by examining the "original intent" of the Founders. As Brennan had made clear in his death penalty opinion, in his mind nothing could be more ludicrous. It was doubtful that the Founders themselves could have agreed on what every clause in the Constitution meant after the filter of two hundred years of history and practice. Furthermore, neither Meese nor Bork had any clue about what the original Founders would have thought of the Fourteenth Amendment, the crucial linchpin of Brennan's activist jurisprudence.

Nonetheless, echoing many of the same complaints that had accompanied the Warren-Brennan Court rulings of the 1960s, Meese told the American Bar Association in 1985 that the Court had erred in applying the Bill of Rights to the states. "There is danger," he declared, "in seeing the Constitution as an empty vessel into which each generation may pour its passion and prejudice. . . . In recent decades many have come to view the Constitution as a charter for judicial activism on behalf of several constituencies. Those who hold this view often lacked demonstrable textual or historical support for their conclusions."

Meese claimed that people like Brennan had grounded their rulings in social theories, moral philosophies, personal notions of human dignity, or to " 'penumbras' somehow emanating ghostlike from various provisions—identified and not identified—in the Bill of Rights.

"This isn't bad constitutional law," Meese declared. "It isn't constitutional law at all."

After more than thirty years, his obscurity protected by the secret silent traditions of the Court and its decision-making methods, Brennan suddenly emerged at ground zero in clear sight of a right-wing attack squad. There was no Bill Douglas or Abe Fortas to run interference this time. An administration attack on Thurgood Marshall might be construed as racist, bad politics. Brennan, for the first time, stood in the middle of an open field. It was hardly as vicious an attack as those that had come against Warren in the 1960s or Douglas in the 1970s. But at the age of seventy-nine, Brennan decided the time had come to go public.

On October 12, 1985, he took the podium in the lecture hall of Georgetown University Law School, just a few blocks down the hill from the Marble Palace. About to celebrate his thirtieth year on the Court, Brennan had decided it was time to start explaining himself. He said: "There are those who find legitimacy in fidelity to what they call the intention of the Framers. In its most doctrinaire incarnation, this view demands that justices discern exactly what the Framers thought about the question under consideration and simply follow that intention in resolving the case before them.

"But in truth it is little more than arrogance cloaked as humility. It is arrogant to pretend that from our vantage we can gauge accurately the intent of the Framers on application of principle to specific, contemporary questions. All too often, sources of potential enlightenment such as records of the ratification debates provide sparse or ambiguous evidence of the original intention. Typically all that can be gleaned is that the Framers themselves did not agree about the application or meaning of particular constitutional provisions, and hid their differences in cloaks of generality."

Waxing poetic, Brennan called the two hundred years of American history "a prism refracting all we perceive." He accused Meese of turning a blind eye to social progress and eschewing adaptation of overarching principles to changes of social circumstance.

Brennan told the Georgetown audience that majority rule could turn to tyranny. He said that while the majoritarian process has appeal, "ultimately it will not do."

In a strangely candid assessment of the American form of government, Brennan said: "Unabashed enshrinement of majority rule would permit the imposition of a social caste system or wholesale confiscation of property so long as a majority of the authorized legislative body, fairly elected, approved. Our Constitution could not abide such a situation. It is the very purpose of the Constitution—and particularly the Bill of Rights—to declare certain values transcendent, beyond the reach of temporary political majorities.

"We current justices read the Constitution the only way we can: as twentieth-century Americans. We look to the history of the time of framing and to the intervening history of interpretation. But the ultimate question must be, What do the words mean in our time?"

He concluded: "For the genius of the Constitution rests not in any static meaning it might have had in a world that is dead and gone but in the adaptability of its great principles to cope with current problems and current needs. Our Constitution was not intended to preserve a preexisting society but to make a new one."

For his new enemies in the Justice Department, Brennan's decision to move out of the protected corridors of the Supreme Court Building, and into what might legitimately be called the political debate that Meese had begun, was just what the attorney general wanted. It was the extrajudicial activities of Justices Fortas and Douglas that had caused them trouble. The Reagan Justice Department was going to make things as difficult for Brennan as Nixon's attorney general, John Mitchell, had for Brennan's colleagues.

After Brennan had repeated the same basic themes on August 8, 1986, at an American Bar Association speech, Meese's deputy, William Bradford Reynolds, the assistant attorney general for the civil rights division, plotted a counterattack. He had been invited to give a lecture at the University of Missouri, and Reynolds made Brennan a public and named target.

Said Reynolds: "There is currently afoot a disturbing jurisprudential emphasis that is aimed at wrenching the Constitution free from its great historical and philosophical moorings in the name of a much distorted notion of equality.

"It is this emerging aconstitutional, or even anticonstitutional jurisprudence—moved largely by a seemingly unrelenting commitment to a radically egalitarian society—that I view as posing a great danger to the cause of individual rights and liberties under a written Constitution."

Noting the Meese speeches on original intent, Reynolds argued that Meese's comments had sparked a spirited and robust public debate.

Almost a year ago, in a speech at Georgetown University, Justice Brennan entered the debate, offering his view of constitutional interpretation generally and of original intent jurisprudence in particular. This year before the American Bar Association meetings in New York, Justice Brennan touched again upon those issues. A look at these two speeches reveals clearly the degree to which the justice's liberal orthodoxy has shaped his doctrine.

Justice Brennan's fundamental point made unabashedly and apparently without qualifications is that the Constitution is essentially a dead letter, a document that has probably outlived its usefulness except as a fond memory to celebrate every so often. Justice Brennan proceeds to sketch a picture of the Constitution so bereft of intrinsic meaning as to be nothing more than an empty vessel into which judges pour new wine.

The Constitution as Justice Brennan understands it, is a document of "great" and "overarching" principles and "majestic generalities and ennobling pronouncements that are both luminous and obscure." He prefers to regard it as nothing less than the embodiment of the "aspiration to social justice, brotherhood, and human dignity that brought this nation together." In a word it represents for him "a sublime oration on the dignity of man" and "a sparkling vision of the human dignity of every individual."

It is not this mystical and shimmering vision of the Constitution that so offends, however, it is Justice Brennan's abiding belief in what he regards as the sanctity of judicial power, that he allows to range unchecked, across an ever-increasing moral landscape that is defined and can be conveniently redefined by resort to his particular brand of judicial interpretation.

Rather than viewing the Constitution as creating a plan of government supported by such sturdy historical principles as federalism and separation of powers, Justice Brennan would have us understand it as the embodiment of "substantive value choices."

Reynolds ridiculed Justice Brennan's belief that the Fourteenth Amendment is the prime tool by which judges can reshape society, repeatedly referring derisively to Justice Brennan's "radically egalitarian jurisprudence."

The Justice Department's intent in taking so bold and direct aim at a sitting justice of the Supreme Court was twofold—to galvanize public outrage and put Brennan on the defensive, while at the same time creating a climate for the appointment to the Court for the conservative hero of the moment, Robert Bork, whose nomination had just been made by President Reagan.

But Reynolds failed on both counts. It neither galvanized opinion against Brennan nor diverted the public from the main battle at hand, which was the confirmation battle of Judge Bork, whose own opinions on original intent dated back to his 1970 speech in San Diego. Despite the best efforts of the Justice Department, Bork was defeated by the Senate. In his place, President Reagan named a less controversial judge, Anthony Kennedy, who very shortly would find himself as enthralled with Brennan's expansive interpretations of the Constitution as Blackmun had been in 1972.

As scholars began to review Brennan's now lengthy tenure on the Court, he began, at last, to get some scholarly recognition for his years of backstage directing. In 1984, John J. Gibbons, then a judge on the federal bench, wrote an appreciation of Brennan's twenty-eight years on the bench. He called Brennan: "More humane than Holmes, broader in outlook than Brandeis, more practical and flexible than Black, a finer scholar than Warren, more eloquent than Hughes, more painstaking than any of them. He appears in other words as the most outstanding justice in our century."

On Brennan's eightieth birthday, he was presented with a surprise party by the entire Supreme Court family. Invited by his beloved clerks to the conference room for what Brennan assumed would be a modest affair, he was greeted by two hundred court employees, including his eight colleagues. A four-foot cake was topped by a marzipan model of the Court building. The thirty-three Supreme Court clerks, even those employed by the other justices, wore T-shirts emblazoned with the words: "In Re the 80th Birthday of Justice Brennan." On the back of the shirt was an order overturning *Gregg* v. *Georgia*, the case that had restored the death penalty over Brennan's objections and best effort.

"I never thought turning eighty could be this much fun," Brennan said through tears. In a birthday interview on the occasion, Brennan vowed that he would not retire from the Court. "As long as the Good Lord lets me stay here you can expect to see me sitting right where I am now," he told the *Los Angeles Times*.

But the love was not shared by all. In May 1986, just a month after his eightieth birthday, Brennan was in Los Angeles to deliver an outdoor lecture at Loyola Marymount University. A fundamentalist Baptist minister, upset by Brennan's vote in *Roe* v. *Wade*, hired an airplane that bore a streamer: "Pray for Death: Baby-killer Brennan." Since the streamer was pointing down not up, the preacher, Robert Hymers, after landing, convened a prayer meeting with his congregation to repeat the prayer, so "He" could hear it. Superiors in Hymers's denomination condemned the banner, saying it was wrong to hire the airplane, that he should have expressed his thought in a quieter fashion.

Brennan's subterranean role in writing *Roe* v. *Wade* was no help against critics. Catholics, who had been cool to Brennan for years, turned downright hostile. On several occasions Brennan had to cancel invitations to speak at Catholic colleges for fear of demonstrations.

One Catholic college, Seton Hall University in Brennan's hometown of Newark, canceled an invitation because of possible protests.

But on the Court, Brennan had lost none of his influence or staying power. On June 17, 1986, a messenger from the chief justice's office walked into Brennan's chambers and handed him a note. Brennan read the letter as he walked to the conference room. Chief Justice Burger was leaving the Court. When Burger had come to the Court, it was widely assumed he would lead the "counterrevolution" that would undo the Warren Court. But it had never happened. The Warren Court had not ended with the resignation or death of Earl Warren, it had simply gone underground in the person of Bill Brennan. For twelve years he thwarted Burger, whom Brennan could not even bring himself to call "chief." "There was only one chief," Brennan would say.

Burger's replacement, Justice Rehnquist, might have proven to be a much more formidable adversary. Rehnquist, if such a thing was possible, was far to the right of Justice Burger. Brennan had cultivated Blackmun and Stevens, and as always could still count on the vote of Justice Marshall. But Rehnquist had even less interest in accommodation than did Burger. Even though Potter Stewart and Warren Burger had been replaced by two new justices even more committed to turning back the clock, Sandra Day O'Connor and Antonin Scalia, Brennan's influence was actually enhanced. Unlike Burger, who often voted with the majority so he could assign an opinion to himself or the "least convinced" member of the majority, thus insuring weak rulings, Rehnquist would make no such personal concessions. For the next five years, Brennan's influence by controlling the assignment of opinions when he was in the majority would grow even stronger.

His new position as vocal counterpoint to Rehnquist was not without its hazards. With Rehnquist as chief, and Ed Meese as attorney general, it had become more and more impossible for Brennan to avoid public controversy. His opposition to capital punishment gnawed at him. The justice who had reveled in accommodation now became as stubborn and adamant on the issue as Douglas had ever been. In case after case he wrote lonely dissents, blasting capital punishment as a deprivation of human dignity.

One clerk recalled seeing the justice return to chambers near tears after losing a death penalty argument in conference. Another told the story of a clerk working on a last-minute appeal in 1988. The clerk, Joshua Rosenkranz, wrote a spirited brief, then in a moment of self-doubt read it to the judge with the comment: "It may cross the line." Replied Brennan: "Josh, when it comes to state-sponsored death, there is no line."

By 1988, Brennan's health was unmistakably beginning to fail. In August of 1987, he had flown to the Mayo Clinic to undergo tests for prostate cancer. The following year he was hospitalized at Bethesda Naval Hospital in Maryland for pneumonia. Shortly after the diagnosis, he had his gall bladder removed. But for all the surgery, Brennan rarely missed a day in Court. He scheduled his entry into the hospital for pneumonia to coincide with the Court's four-week Christmas recess. As always, Brennan brooked no sympathy from anyone. But when a clerk's mother went into the hospital, she later found an official order on her desk, signed by Brennan, ordering her mom back to good health.

Despite all the newfound notoriety that came with age and the attacks from the right, an April 1990 poll in the *National Law Journal* indicated that only 41 percent of the American people could even name one justice. The most well known was Justice Sandra Day O'Connor, the only woman on the Court. Eight percent knew the chief justice or Justice Marshall, as the only black member of the court. Only three percent of the American people, according to the poll, recognized the name William J. Brennan, Jr. And many of those were antiabortion protesters who had continued to make Brennan's life miserable. He had to give up an honorary degree from Spalding University in Louisville after protests. Columnist George Will didn't do much for Brennan's public persona, attacking Brennan's opinions as "working on the frontiers of absurdity."

At the age of eighty, he had done it all. And yet, more would come. It was a case at the end of Brennan's career, and one which by comparison with his landmark rulings two decades earlier seemed almost comical, that suddenly awakened the liberal community to the contributions Brennan had made to the cause.

On August 22, 1984, at the Republican National Convention in Dallas, an undercover police officer named Terry Stover had infiltrated an anti-Republican party demonstration. The leaders of the demonstration were a hairy nostalgia seeker from the sixties, Gregory Lee

Johnson, and a woman, Denise Williams. The line of protest snaked
past the schoolbook depository from which Lee Harvey Oswald fired
on President Kennedy and stopped at an office tower. There Johnson
and Williams led their group of several dozen in a "die-in." The protesters would count down from ten and then fall to the ground, moan-
ing and yelling. This demonstrated that evil corporations were killing
people in such hotspots as South Africa, Nicaragua, and Central
America in general.

Following the die-in, the marchers headed over to the Republic
Bank Building. There, the group seized and ripped deposit slips, pulled
up potted plants, and dumped dirt on the ground. They weren't done
yet though. Next was the locked-up Diamond Shamrock Building,
where Johnson's group, social activists that they were, overturned more
plants and spray-painted the floor.

Eventually this cadre of committed peaceniks arrived at the Mer-
cantile National Bank Building. One of the protesters took down the
American flag in front of the bank and handed it to Johnson. With
the flag wadded up and stuck into his shirt, Johnson led the group to
the Dallas Power & Light Company, where Johnson distilled his political philosophy down to a few words even his group could understand.
"Fuck the Republicans," he cried. "Fuck You, America."

At city hall, Johnson pulled the flag from inside his shirt, held Old
Glory aloft, and began trying to set it on fire with a cigarette lighter.
The feat, however, strained his capacities. So one member of his mob
handed Johnson a container of lighter fluid. Johnson poured the fluid
on the flag and set it afire.

This was apparently too much for Roland Tucker, another Dallas
police officer doing undercover work. It was okay to spray-paint buildings, turn over plants, destroy property, and steal a flag; but burning
the thing was going too far. He radioed a report of the episode to pa-
trol cars. About thirty minutes later a contingent of Dallas police arrived to arrest Johnson for violating a Texas statute making it unlawful
to desecrate the American flag.

After a Dallas jury trial, Johnson was sentenced to a year in prison
and fined $2,000. Not for stealing the flag but for desecrating it. The
Texas Court of Criminal Appeals, that state's equivalent of the
Supreme Court, overturned the conviction, concluding that a person
can't be sent to prison for exercising the right of political dissent. The

state of Texas appealed the constitutional issue to the U.S. Supreme Court, confident that Reagan's new conservative majority would uphold their antidesecration statute.

There seemed little doubt as *Texas v. Johnson* wended its way toward the U.S. Supreme Court that the Texas flag-burning ban would be reinstated. There were few issues more dear to the heart of Chief Justice Rehnquist. In previous cases in which the flag had been an issue, Rehnquist had waxed poetic about the flag, especially the one at the Iwo Jima Memorial in Arlington. The flag was so precious, Rehnquist had written, that true feelings for it "cannot be fully expressed in the two dimensions of a lawyer's brief or a judge's opinion. The government may prohibit even those who have purchased the physical object [not even a stolen one] from impairing its physical integrity. For what they have purchased is not merely cloth, dyed red, white, and blue, but also the one visible manifestation of two hundred years of nationhood."

By the time the flag case came to the Supreme Court, Rehnquist's strong and emotional view was likely to be shared by a Court that now was deeply imbued with his philosophy. He had been joined by Justice Antonin Scalia, as well as Anthony Kennedy. Along with Sandra Day O'Connor and the usually conservative Byron White, they seemed sure to support the right of a state to pass such a law.

Brennan, naturally, had no such inclination. He could remember stories from the back-home porches of Vailsburg of Irish patriots being arrested for burning the Union Jack. At a time when Americans were praising the courageous students of Tiananmen Square, Brennan wondered to his clerks how Americans would feel about Chinese protesters sentenced to a year in prison for burning the Chinese flag.

Gregory Johnson was a creep, all right. But why couldn't the state of Texas just have arrested him for vandalism or petty theft? Brennan told his clerks he couldn't see someone sentenced to a year in prison for making a political statement. Burning the flag offended people. That was exactly why Johnson had burned it. It was the whole point.

Following the oral argument in the case, Brennan immediately began trying to fashion his thinking in a way that might attract Justice Scalia to his side. Scalia had taken the lead in the Court's oral argument, which wasn't unusual for him. He often annoyed his colleagues by asking too many questions. But Scalia had shown in past rulings a belief that if a First Amendment guarantee was going to be taken away by the state, there had to be a strong, compelling state or national interest in doing so (like endangering a theater crowd by yelling "Fire.") Yet Gregory Johnson's actions had hardly threatened the government.

At the conference following the argument, Brennan was surprised to find that Scalia had decided Gregory Johnson could not be imprisoned for expressing his opinions about the flag. Even more shocking was that Scalia had brought Justice Anthony Kennedy along with him. Brennan reached for his two automatic votes of support, Thurgood Marshall and Harry Blackmun, and he had his 5 to 4 majority.

Those who believed in original intent could only see that the First Amendment applied to speech. Johnson had not engaged in speech, he had committed an act. But Brennan's opinion was about to stretch the usual definition of speech. He wrote:

> If there is a bedrock principle underlying the First Amendment, it is that the government may not prohibit the expression of an idea simply because society finds the idea offensive or disagreeable.
>
> We have not recognized an exception to this principle even where our flag has been involved. . . . Nothing in our precedents suggests that a State may foster its own view of the flag by prohibiting expressive conduct relating to it. Government may not prohibit expression merely because it disagrees with its message.
>
> If we were to hold that a State may forbid flag burning wherever it is likely to endanger the flag's symbolic role—as where a person ceremoniously burns a dirty flag—we would be saying that when it comes to impairing the flag's physical integrity, the flag may be used as a symbol only in one direction. We would be permitting a State to prescribe what shall be orthodox by saying that one may burn the flag to convey one's attitude toward it and its referents only if one does not endanger the flag's representation of nationhood and national unity.
>
> It is not the state's ends, but its means to which we object. We reject the suggestion that the government lacks any state interest whatsoever in regulating the manner in which the flag may be displayed. Congress, for example, enacted regulations describing the proper treatment of the flag, and we cast no doubt on the legitimacy of its interest in making such recommendations. To say that the government has an interest in encouraging proper treatment of the flag, however, is not to say that it

may criminally punish a person for burning a flag as a means of political protest.

We are fortified in today's conclusion by our conviction that forbidding criminal punishment for conduct such as Johnson's will not endanger the special role played by our flag or the feeling it inspires.

It was Brennan's reasoning that impressed Justice Kennedy, who up until the last instant wavered precariously on the fence. For the Reagan appointee from California, it was the most difficult ruling he had ever made as a judge. "I write not to qualify the words Justice Brennan chooses so well," Kennedy wrote, "for he says with power all that is necessary to explain our ruling. I join his opinion without reservation, but with a keen sense that this case, like others before us from time to time, exacts its personal toll.

"For we are presented with a clear and simple statute to be judged against a pure command of the Constitution. The outcome can be laid at no door but ours.

"The hard fact is that sometimes we make decisions we do not like. We make them because they are right, right in the sense that the law and the Constitution, as we see them, compel the result. And so great is our commitment to the process that, except in the rare case, we do not pause to express distaste for the result, perhaps for fear of undermining a valued principle that dictates the decision. This is one of those rare cases."

Reminded by Rehnquist that his ruling would dismay veterans groups, Kennedy apologized. "Though symbols are often what we ourselves make of them, the flag is constant in expressing beliefs Americans share, beliefs in law and peace and that freedom which sustains the human spirit. The case here forces recognition of the costs to which those beliefs commit us. It is poignant but fundamental that the flag protects those who hold it in contempt."

From a man like Anthony Kennedy, it was a remarkable decision. As emotional as Rehnquist was about the flag, he could not hold the vote of his two conservative brethren. That Brennan could write an opinion accommodating himself and Marshall, as well as Scalia and Kennedy, was the ultimate tribute to his ability to create majorities. It would also be Brennan's most publicly controversial ruling. While far from his most important, it couldn't compare to the landmark Warren Court rulings of the 1960s, the flag-burning case marked the first time that many Americans became aware of his existence. In his own state of New Jersey, residents of Hudson County, where Brennan's judicial career had started, began a petition drive to stop a proposed statue of the man who approved of flag burning.

On the last day of the 1989–90 term of the Court, June 27, 1990, Brennan released what would become his final ruling as a justice. Some eighteen years after the departure of Earl Warren, and a good three years into the tenure of Chief Justice William Rehnquist, Brennan would save one of his most remarkable rulings for last.

In the legislative and executive branches, the concept of affirmative action had fairly well run its course. The emphasis at the Republican Justice Department was on ending reverse discrimination; that is, making sure that affirmative-action plans didn't injure white applicants.

But at the Federal Communications Commission, a policy lingered to encourage black ownership of radio stations. Radio station ownership, although heavily influenced by black listeners and black artists, was overwhelmingly in the hands of white investors. The FCC's figures showed that by 1986 minority businessmen owned just 2.1 percent of the 11,000 radio and television stations in the United States. Even that number was deceiving because the black-owned stations were largely of small power and in geographically limited markets.

During the four short years of the Carter administration, from 1976 to 1980, the FCC had worked hard to eliminate discrimination in the radio and television industry. It was among the first federal agencies to crack down on employment discrimination. Although the agency did not always give preference to minority bidders when stations' licenses went up for sale, it actively sought black participation through seminars and conferences.

Despite its best efforts, the FCC failed miserably. Finally, it decided to reverse the decades-old policy of not considering race, and issued a new regulation identifying race as a major factor in new license proceedings.

In 1983, the FCC was put in the position of selecting one of three applicants to operate a new television station in Orlando, Florida. An administrative judge then gave the award to a company called Metro Broadcasting, a company which had 19.8 percent minority ownership. But when the decision was revisited by an FCC review panel, the award was shifted to Rainbow Broadcasting, a company with 90 percent Hispanic ownership. In 1986, the full FCC ratified the award to Rainbow.

With the Reagan Court in full bloom, Rainbow's chances for keeping its station were deemed small. Affirmative-action programs, like that of the FCC, had barely hung on, mainly through Brennan's machinations in the *Bakke* case. But this was eleven years later. Surely a Supreme Court dominated by the four Reagan appointees would strike down the FCC requirements as unconstitutional. But the officials who had believed that underestimated the influence and power of a shrunken eighty-five-year-old man.

In the flag-burning case, it had been Kennedy whom Brennan had pulled into his majority. This time it was White and Stevens. Affirmative action was something in which Brennan had become a deep and passionate believer. He couldn't bear the thought of turning back the clock on racial progress. Poor White, seeing Brennan's passion, agreed to vote with him. Rehnquist looked solemnly around the conference table and saw the familiar specter of defeat. He could hardly believe his eyes.

"The interest in enhancing broadcast diversity is at the very least an important government objective and is therefore a sufficient basis for the commission's minority ownership policies. Just as a diverse student body contributing to a robust exchange of ideas is a constitutionally permissible goal on which a race conscious university admissions program may be predicated, the diversity of views and information on the airwaves serves important First Amendment values," Brennan declared.

"The benefits of such diversity are not limited to the members of the minority groups who gain access to the broadcasting industry by virtue of the ownership policies; rather the benefits redound to all members of the viewing and listening audience," he said.

To attract the key vote of a conservative like White, Brennan was perfectly amenable to including in his opinion some words about the intent of Congress. Often, Brennan would ignore such things. But he needed White, so this time he threw in some language about how Congress had passed legislation during the Carter administration requiring that the commission maintain minority ownership policies. "We would be remiss if we ignored the long history of congressional support for those policies," Brennan said. To get White's vote, that was all it took. In a way, it was Brennan's most remarkable majority.

Stepping off the bench, Brennan retreated to the robing room and shook hands with the brethren. Each would soon be going his or her own way for the summer. None had higher expectations for a relaxing three months than Brennan. Mary had helped him book a summer's cruise in the North Sea, with stops in several Scandinavian countries.

But as he prepared to board a plane at Newark International Airport, Brennan fell. He continued with the cruise but suffered dizziness and memory loss. On his return three weeks later, doctors told him that he had suffered a minor stroke. Although his memory faltered, one thing he could recall was the undignified and embarrassing exit of his colleague Justice Douglas. Brennan confided to his wife, Mary, that this was one example he didn't want to follow.

On July 20, 1990, Brennan sent a letter to the White House and re- tired from his seat on the Court. "The strenuous demands of Court work and its related duties required or expected of a justice appear at this time to be incompatible with my advancing age and medical con- dition. I, therefore, retire effective immediately as an associate justice of the Supreme Court of the United States." It was relayed by fax ma- chine to President Bush, who at the time was on his way to Wyoming on Air Force One.

In an accompanying statement, Brennan expressed his hope that the edifice of opinions he had constructed would stand: "It is my hope that the Court during my years of service has built a legacy of inter- preting the Constitution and federal laws to make them responsive to the needs of people whom they were intended to benefit and protect. This legacy can and will withstand the test of time."

Only a day before, few in the public had known who he was. Sud- denly there was a sense of great loss. Wrote Anna Quindlen in *The New York Times*: "I am taking the resignation of Justice Brennan per- sonally. His work is full of empathy and that is an uncommon thing not only in a judge but in our society. One of the best friends an indi- vidual ever had has left the arena and we will all miss him, whether we know it or not." The pattern was repeated in editorials and columns

around the country. In a way, it was as if Brennan had just been dis-
covered.

It had been a mind-numbing career. All he had done was single-
handedly rewrite the nation's criminal laws, declare how we treat
pornography and obscenity, require the redistricting and political
equalization of every county in America, restrict and slow the death
penalty to a crawl, uphold and expand affirmative action and equal
opportunity. Should any one man have been that powerful? Will any
man be that powerful again?

The trick was that Brennan had done it all so quietly. His father had
changed Newark in thirteen stormy years. The son had quietly
changed the country without anyone really knowing who he was.

The last part was the way his mother would have wanted it. But his
thanks in the end went not to Agnes but to his dad. How was it possible? he was once asked. "All I am," Brennan said in one candid moment shortly after his retirement, "I am because of my father."

With that, Brennan turned over his chambers to Justice David
Souter of New Hampshire, who, like Brennan, came on the Court
with something of an obscure past. As is traditional with living ex-jus-
tices, Brennan moved upstairs to an auxiliary office in the Supreme
Court building. The stroke had seriously impaired Brennan's memory.
In public appearances, it often became difficult for him to finish a sentence or a thought. His wife, Mary Fowler, would sit in the front row
and prompt him. The experience would turn Brennan's face red with
frustration. But at other times, especially when he was talking privately with friends, he could seem like the old lapel-pulling playmaker
of the Court. Souter, in particular, has made a point of seeking out his
predecessor on the Court. In addition, Brennan is frequently seen slipping into the dining room with Justice Sandra Day O'Connor on his
arm. Both had been appointed to the Court as supposed conservatives
but over time have moved increasingly to the moderate side of the
Court now led by Justice Blackmun, who followed the same path.

There is no way to say for sure, of course. Deliberations of the
Supreme Court are the most secret discussions in Washington. But
few doubt that Justice Brennan is still working hard to change minds
and votes—and, as usual, succeeding.

It had taken nearly a lifetime for William Joseph Brennan, Jr., to become a folk hero. His credo had been to provide human dignity to every man, woman, and child on the planet. After his retirement, Brennan received word that a young couple had named their new daughter Brennan in his honor. He immediately wrote them a congratulatory note: "I hope you will devote yourself to expanding the civil rights of all people. This is the fervent wish of your namesake."

SOURCE NOTES
AND BIBLIOGRAPHY

THE PRIMARY SOURCING FOR THIS book came from the papers of Justices Brennan, Black, Douglas, Frankfurter, Harlan, Burton, and Warren. All of those collections, except Harlan's, are available from the Library of Congress Manuscript Room. Harlan's papers are stored at the Mudd Manuscript Library at Princeton University. The staffs of both libraries were enormously helpful and patient with me. The greatest amount of material came from the papers of Justice Douglas, with whom Brennan exchanged many notes about his thoughts and opinions. Douglas also kept the best records of what happened at the confidential conferences of the nine justices.

Among previously published material, I relied heavily on Professor Bernard Schwartz's exhaustive histories of the modern Supreme Court, *Super Chief* and *The Ascent of Pragmatism*. The story of William Brennan, Sr.'s political rise was made possible through the cooperation of the Newark Public Library, which provided extensive newspaper clips from *The Newark Evening News* in the 1920s. To complete the section on Brennan's Harvard years, I contacted every surviving member of his class of 1931. Additional help on Brennan's troubled relationship with Harvard was given by former Harvard Law School dean Erwin Griswold. Likewise, his years as a private attorney were reconstructed through numerous interviews with Newark lawyers who practiced with and against him in Newark, including former members of his firm, Pitney, Hardin, Ward & Brennan. I am particularly indebted to Morris Schnitzer, editor of the *Harvard Law Review* in 1931 and a Newark lawyer.

Other accounts of Brennan's New Jersey years can be found in the *Passaic County Law Reporter*. However, those accounts, written by Brennan's friends, suffer from the "hometown" syndrome and badly exaggerate his educational background and experience. In particular, Brennan is repeatedly referred to as being at the top of his class and president of the Harvard Legal Aid Society. He was neither. Excellent articles on Brennan's fellow justice Nathan Jacobs can be found in the *Rutgers Law Review*, 1974.

Self-descriptions of his years in the the army can be found in Brennan's testimony to the Senate War Investigating Committee, which held hearings on his activities in 1946 and 1947.

The story of his appointment to the court relies on interviews with then attorney general Herbert Brownell, now a partner at Lord, Day & Lord, and Brownell's successor, William Rogers, a partner at Rogers & Wells. In an interview in his office in New York, Brownell contradicted one of the most widely disseminated beliefs about Brennan's appointment—that Arthur Vanderbilt recommended Brennan to Eisenhower. Brownell confirmed accounts by Brennan's friends in Newark that Vanderbilt in fact was not informed until after the appointment was made. Brownell said he himself made the call.

Another sharp area of controversy was over what role Bernard Shanley played in the Brennan nomination. It is accepted almost as conventional wisdom that Shanley intervened on Brennan's behalf. Shanley died in 1990. For those who are skeptical of my account, I refer them to *New Jersey Reports* for the year 1977. There it is reported, in the transcript of a portrait unveiling in his home state, at an occasion when it would have been entirely appropriate to take credit for Brennan's career, that Shanley confirmed that he had virtually nothing to do with Brennan's appointment. Shanley himself observed: "If I had had anything to do with it, I certainly would be very proud of the fact." This is consistent with Brownell's and Rogers's accounts as well.

Additional help on Brennan's relationship with Eisenhower was provided by the Eisenhower Library in Abilene, Kansas.

Brennan's Court years are based on the papers of the justices, as well as interviews with clerks who served under Brennan, particularly in the early years. The Paul Freund letter ridiculing Brennan's appointment is contained in the Felix Frankfurter papers at the Library of Congress. In 1991, I mailed a copy of the letter to Freund and requested his comments on the Brennan appointment. Freund, in failing health, responded that he had no recollection of writing the note. He died in late 1992. The accounts of the Landau and Tigar episodes, which are referred to in Bob Woodward and Scott Armstrong's book *The Brethren*, are verified through Brennan's correspondence on the incidents found in the Earl Warren papers at the Library of Congress Manuscript Room. In my descriptions of oral arguments, conferences and other information about cases, I relied on *U.S. Law Week*, Supreme Court edition, which reported on oral arguments at the Court. I also consulted the annual Supreme Court issues of the *Harvard Law Review*. Neither Justice Brennan nor his family cooperated with the preparation of this book.

Books

Ball, Howard. *We Have a Duty*. Greenwood Press, 1987.

Black, Elizabeth and Hugo. *Mr. Justice and Mrs. Black*. Random House, 1986.

Caplan, Lincoln. *The Tenth Justice: The Solicitor General and the Rule of Law*. Alfred A. Knopf, 1987.

Charns, Alexander. *Cloak and Gavel: FBI Wiretaps, Bugs, Informers, and the Supreme Court*. University of Illinois Press, 1992.

Congressional Quarterly. Guide to the U.S. Supreme Court. Congressional Quarterly Inc., 1979.

Cooney, John. *The American Pope*. Times Books, 1984.

de Grazia, Edward. *Girls Lean Back Everywhere: The Law of Obscenity and the Assault on Genius*. Random House, 1992.

Douglas, William O. *The Autobiography of William Douglas: Go East Young Man*. Random House, 1974.

———. *The Autobiography of William Douglas: The Court Years*. Random House, 1980.

Eisler, Kim I. *Shark Tank: Greed, Politics, and the Collapse of Finley, Kumble*. St. Martin's Press, 1990.

Frank, John P. *The Warren Court*. Macmillan, 1964.

Fried, Charles. *Order and Law: Arguing the Reagan Revolution—A Firsthand Account.* Simon & Schuster, 1991.

Goldstein, Joseph. *The Intelligible Constitution.* Oxford University Press, 1992.

Hall, Kermit. *The Oxford Companion to the Supreme Court of the United States.* Oxford University Press, 1992.

Kalman, Laura. *Abe Fortas: A Biography.* Yale University Press, 1990.

Kennedy, Caroline. *In Our Defense: The Bill of Rights in Action.* William Morrow, 1991.

Lewis, Anthony. *Make No Law. The Sullivan Case and the First Amendment.* Random House, 1991.

Martin, John Bartlow. *Adlai Stevenson and the World.* Doubleday, 1977.

Murphy, Bruce Allen. *Fortas: The Rise and Ruin of a Supreme Court Justice.* William Morrow, 1988.

Novick, Sheldon. *The Life of Oliver Wendell Holmes.* Laurel, 1989.

O'Brien, David M. *Storm Center: The Supreme Court in American Politics.* Norton, 1986.

Rehnquist, William. *The Supreme Court: How It Was. How It Is.* William Morrow, 1987.

Savage, David. *Turning Point: The Making of the Rehnquist Supreme Court.* John Wiley, 1992.

Schwartz, Bernard. *Super Chief: Earl Warren and His Supreme Court.* New York University Press, 1983.

———. *The Unpublished Opinions of the Warren Court.* Oxford University Press, 1985.

———. *Swann's Way: The School Busing Case and the Supreme Court.* Oxford University Press, 1986.

———. *The Ascent of Pragmatism: The Burger Court in Action.* Addison-Wesley, 1990.

Simon, James F. *In His Own Image: The Supreme Court in Richard Nixon's America.* David McKay, 1973.

———. *Independent Journey: The Life of William O. Douglas.* Harper & Row, 1980.

———. *The Antagonists.* Simon & Schuster, 1989.

Smith, Richard Norton. *Thomas E. Dewey and His Times.* A Touchstone Book, Simon & Schuster, 1982.

Sutherland, Arthur. *The Law at Harvard.* Belknap Press of Harvard University, 1967.

Thomas, Evan. *The Man to See: Edward Bennett Williams.* Simon & Schuster, 1991.

Urofsky, Melvin I. *The Douglas Letters.* Adler & Adler, 1987.

———. *A Conflict of Rights: The Supreme Court and Affirmative Action.* Scribner's, 1991.

Warren, Earl. *The Memoirs of Chief Justice Earl Warren*. Doubleday, 1977.

Woodward, Bob, and Scott Armstrong. *The Brethren: Inside the Supreme Court*. Simon & Schuster, 1979.

Articles

Barbash, Fred. "Judge Bazelon's Network: The Salon of the Ultimate Liberal." *The Washington Post*, March 1, 1981.

Bazelon, David. "A Tribute to Justice William J. Brennan." *Harvard Civil Liberties Review*, 1980.

Bernstein, J. L. "Ordeal in Washington." *The Passaic County Bar Association Reporter*, Spring 1984.

Bickel, Alexander M. "The Decade of School Desegregation: Progress and Prospects." *Columbia Law Review*, February 1964.

Bork, Robert H. "Neutral Principles and Some First Amendment Problems." *Indiana Law Journal*, Fall 1971.

Brennan, William J. "Formulae for the Settlement of Labor Disputes." *New Jersey Law Journal*, May 9, 1946.

———. "After Eight Years: New Jersey Judicial Reform." *American Bar Association Journal*, June 1957.

———. "Chief Judge Bazelon's Contributions to the Law." *Georgetown Law Journal*, October 1974.

———. "State Constitutions and the Protection of Individual Rights." *Harvard Law Review*, January 1977.

———. "Remarks at 75th Anniversary of Rutgers Law School." *Rutgers Law Review*, Summer 1984.

———. "Constitutional Adjudication and the Death Penalty: A View from the Court." *Harvard Law Review*, 1986.

Ely, John Hart. "The Wages of Crying Wolf: A Comment on *Roe* v. *Wade*." *Yale Law Journal*, 1973.

Farber, Daniel A. "The Supreme Court and the Rule of Law: *Cooper* v. *Aaron* Revisited." *University of Illinois Law Review*, 1982.

Fiss, Owen. "A Life Lived Twice." *Yale Law Journal*, March 1991.

Fortune magazine. "Brennan on Bigness." July 1957.

Greenhouse, Linda. "New Look at Obscure Ruling, 20 Years Later (*Goldberg* v. *Kelly*)." *The New York Times*, May 11, 1990.

Heck, Edward. "The Socialization of a Freshman Justice: The Early Years of Justice Brennan." *Pacific Law Journal*, 1979.

Hentoff, Nat. "The Constitutionalist." *The New Yorker*, March 12, 1990.

Hutchinson, Dennis J. "The Black-Jackson Feud." *The Supreme Court Review*, 1988.

Kalven, Harry, Jr. "Uninhibited, Robust, and Wide Open—A Note on Free Speech and the Warren Court." *Michigan Law Review*, December 1968.

King, Wayne. "In Re Brennan Birthday." *The New York Times*, April 25, 1986.

Kopkind, Andrew. "Brennan v. Tigar." *The New Republic*, August 27, 1966.

Los Angeles Times. Interview with Brennan by Philip Hager. April 19, 1986.

Maledon, William J. "Justice William Brennan, a Personal Tribute." *Arizona State Law Journal*, Winter 1990.

Mauro, Tony. "With Remarkable Swiftness, an Era Ends." *Legal Times*, August 6, 1990.

Michelman, Frank. "Super Liberal: Romance, Community, and Tradition in William J. Brennan, Jr.'s Constitutional Thought." *Virginia Law Review*. October 1991.

Middleton, Michael. "Securing Justice: A Response to William Bradford Reynolds." *Missouri Law Review*, 1987.

Mountain, Worrall. "When We Were Young." *Passaic County Law Reporter*, 1976.

O'Murchu, Sean O. "Lone Justice." *Irish America*, June 1990.

Pirsig, Maynard. "Justice Arthur T. Vanderbilt in Retrospect." *Rutgers Law Review*, Spring 1958.

Reynolds, William Bradford. "Securing Equal Liberty in an Egalitarian Age." *Missouri Law Review*, 1957.

Rodell, Fred. "Crux of the Court Hullabaloo." *The New York Times Magazine*, May 29, 1960.

Rosencranz, E. Joshua. "Tributes from Former Law Clerks." *Nova Law Journal*, Winter 1991.

Schnitzer, Morris. "Justice Nathan Jacobs—Architect of New Jersey's Court Structure and Judicial Exponent of Civil Procedure." *Rutgers Law Review*, 1974.

Seitz, Virginia. "Recollections of Justice Brennan. Presentation of Virginia A. Seitz Esq." *Judicature*, February, March 1991.

Stone, Geoffrey. "Justice Brennan and the Freedom of Speech: a First Amendment Odyssey." *University of Pennsylvania Law Review*, May 1991.

Tepker, Harry F. "Justice Brennan, Judge Bork, and a Jurisprudence of Original Values." *Oklahoma Law Review*, Winter 1991.

Totenberg, Nina. "Beneath the Marble, Beneath the Robes." *The New York Times Magazine*, March 16, 1975.

Tribe, Lawrence. "Justice William J. Brennan, Jr.: Architect of the Bill of Rights." *American Bar Association Journal*, February 1991.

Will, George. "Why Liberals Look Silly." *The Washington Post*, April 29, 1987.

ACKNOWLEDGMENTS

About the only thing that can be said of William Brennan without starting an argument is that he was a truly beloved justice, adored by his clerks and those of rival justices. He was a man of unfailing politeness and consideration. In the years I have covered law for a variety of publications, it was never unusual to dial Brennan's chambers and have the justice himself answer the phone. Occasionally reporters were so surprised to hear the rough voice of the boss, when they were actually seeking one his clerks, that Brennan was sent to fetch a clerk. He never seemed to mind.

This work does not attempt to be a definitive statement on Justice Brennan's judicial career. Many of the areas in which his rulings were important, labor law, zoning matters, and tax law, are not the subject of this book. Brennan's judicial writings are so vast that it would be impossible to deal with the ramifications of all of them in a liftable volume. I have tried to concentrate on the areas and decisions of greatest public interest: abortion, the death penalty, political reform, and affirmative action. Rather than a final statement, this book stands as an important first step in a process of consideration that will doubtless go on for decades.

I am indebted to my agent, Jane Dystel; my original editor, Paul Aron; and especially my final editor, Gary Luke, and his assistant, Megan Paris Rundlet.

Most of all I owe the completion of this project to my wife, Judy Sarasohn Eisler. During the course of this book she wrote a book of her own, continued to work at her newspaper, and gave birth to our daughter, Sara Sophie Eisler. It seemed like she never missed a beat. Much like the justice who is the subject of this book, Judy combines a pit bull–like tenacity with a heart the size of the Capitol Building. There is no one like her.

INDEX